CENSUS OF INDIA 1931

Census of India 1871-1951, 9 Sets In 384 Bindings (9788121258876) Rs. 700000

Census of India 1931, 28 Vols. In 52 Bindings (9788121271233) Rs. 102000

1. India - Report (9788121276153) Rs. 2820 (Vol. I, Pt. 1)
2. India - Imperial Tables (9788121276139) Rs. 3210 (Vol. I, Pt. 2)
3. India - Ethnographical and Administration Report (9788121276115) Rs. 2900 (Vol. I, Pt. 3 & 5)
4. The Andaman And Nicobar Islands - Report, Tables (9788121276078) Rs. 720 (Vol. II, Pt. 1, Pt. 2)
5. Assam - Report (9788121276054) Rs. 1340 (Vol. III, Pt. 1)
6. Assam - Tables and Administrative Report (9788121276030) Rs. 1830 (Vol. III, Pt. 2 & 3)
7. Baluchistan - Report, Imeprial and Provincial Tables and Administrative Report (9788121276016) Rs. 2320 (Vol. IV, Pt. 1 & 2 & 3)
8. Bengal & Sikkim - Report (9788121275972) Rs. 2860 (Vol. V, Pt. 1)
9. Bengal & Sikkim - Tables (9788121275958) Rs. 1660 (Vol. V, Pt. 2)
10. Calcutta (9788121275910) Rs. 960 (Vol. VI, Pt. 1 & 2)
11. Bengal, Sikkim And Calcutta - Administrative Report (9788121275934) Rs. 580 (Vol. V & VI, Pt. 3)
12. Bihar And Orissa - Report (9788121275897) Rs. 1780 (Vol. VII, Pt. 1)
13. Bihar And Orissa - Tables and Administrative Report (9788121275873) Rs. 1190 (Vol. VII, Pt. 2 & 3)
14. Bombay Presidency - General Report (9788121275835) Rs. 3620 (Vol. VIII, Pt. 1)
15. Bombay - Statistical tables (9788121275811) Rs. 3060 (Vol. VIII, Pt. 2)
16. Bombay Presidency Aden - report and tables and Administrative report (9788121275798) Rs. 520 (Vol. VIII, Pt. 3 & 4)
17. Cities of the Bombay Presidency Report & Statistical tables (9788121275750) Rs. 2020 (Vol. IX, Pt. 1 & 2)
18. The Western India States Agency, In Two Parts - The Report & The Statistical Tables (9788121275736) Rs. 2560 (Vol. X, Pt. 1 & 2)
19. Burma - Report (9788121275712) Rs. 1860 (Vol. XI, Pt. 1)
20. Burma - Tables and Administrative Report (9788121275699) Rs. 1690 (Vol. XI, Pt. 2 & 3)
21. Central Provinces & Berar - Report (9788121275651) Rs. 2340 (Vol. XII, Pt. 1)
22. Central Provinces & Berar - Tables and Administrative Report (9788121275637) Rs. 3120 (Vol. XII, Pt. 2 & 3)
23. Coorg - Report And Tables and Madras - Report (9788121275613) Rs. 2680 (Vol. XIV, Pt. 1)
24. Madras - Imperial And Provincial Tables and The Administration Report (9788121275576) Rs. 1950 (Vol. XIV, Pt. 2 & 4)
25. North - West Frontier Province - Report & Tables (9788121275538) Rs. 2300 (Vol. XV, Pt. 1 & 2)
26. Delhi - Report & Tables (9788121275514) Rs. 1180 (Vol. XVI, Pt. 1 & 2)
27. Punjab - Report (9788121275491) Rs. 2070 (Vol. XVII, Pt. 1)
28. Punjab - Tables (9788121275477) Rs. 1690 (Vol. XVII, Pt. 2)
29. United Provinces of Agra And Oudh - Report (9788121275453) Rs. 3380 (Vol. XVIII, Pt. 1)
30. United Provinces of Agra And Oudh - Imperial And Provincial Tables and Administrative (9788121275439) Rs. 3600 (Vol. XVIII, Pt. 2 & 3)
31. Baroda - Report (9788121275415) Rs. 2800 (Vol. XIX, Pt. 1)
32. Baroda - Tables (9788121275392) Rs. 730 (Vol. XIX, Pt. 2)
33. Baroda - Administrative (9788121275378) Rs. 780 (Vol. XIX, Pt. 3)
34. Central India Agency - Report (9788121275354) Rs. 1690 (Vol. XX, Pt. 1)
35. Central India Agency - Tables and Administrative Volume (9788121275330) Rs. 2260 (Vol. XX, Pt. 2 & 3)
36. Cochin - Report & Tables (9788121275293) Rs. 2460 (Vol. XXI, Pt. 1 & 2 - A & B.)
37. Gwalior - Report (9788121275279) Rs. 1470 (Vol. XXII, Pt. 1)
38. Gwalior - Tables (9788121275255) Rs. 980 (Vol. XXII, Pt. 2)
39. H. E. H. The Nizam's Dominions (Hyderabad State) - Report (9788121275231) Rs. 1540 (Vol. XXIII, Pt. 1)
40. H. E. H. The Nizam's Dominions (Hyderabad State) - Tables (9788121275217) Rs. 1510 (Vol. XXIII, Pt. 2)
41. Jammu & Kashmir State - Report (9788121275194) Rs. 2060 (Vol. XXIV, Pt. 1)
42. Jammu & Kashmir State - Imperial & State Tables (9788121275170) Rs. 1940 (Vol. XXIV, Pt. 2 & 3)
43. Mysore - Report (9788121275156) Rs. 1950 (Vol. XXV, Pt. 1)
44. Mysore - Tables (9788121275132) Rs. 1380 (Vol. XXV, Pt. 2)
45. Ajmer-Merwara - Report And Tables (9788121275118) Rs. 780 (Vol. XXVI)
46. Rajputana Agency And Ajmer-Merwara - Report and Tables and Administrative (9788121275095) Rs. 2380 (Vol. XXVII, Pt. 1 & 2)
47. Travancore - Report (9788121276092) Rs. 2960 (Vol. XXVIII, Pt. 1)
48. Travancore - Tables & Administrative (9788121275996) Rs. 1360 (Vol. XXVIII, Pt. 2 & 4)
49. Jaipur State- Report (9788121275859) Rs. 1280 (Pt. 1)
50. Jaipur State- Tables (9788121275774) Rs. 2030 (Pt. 2)
51. Mayurbhanj state- Report (9788121275675) Rs. 3180 (Pt. 1)
52. Mayurbhanj state- Tables (9788121275552) Rs. 3070 (Pt. 2)

Owing to the antiquity and rarity of this book, certain pages are regrettably absent, and readability is compromised due to the blurring of the original text. If you possess any insights regarding the availability of these missing sections, kindly inform us. Your assistance is crucial in ensuring the completion of this significant work for the benefit of future generations.

CENSUS OF INDIA, 1931

BOOK - 33: VOLUME - XIX

BARODA

PART III - ADMINISTRATIVE

SATYA V. MUKERJEA

GYAN

Published by

Gyan Publishing House
5, Ansari Road
Daryaganj, New Delhi-110002
Phone: 011-47034999, 9811692060
E-mail: books@gyanbooks.com

Distribution Network
gyanbooks.com
India, USA, Canada, UK, Australia

ISBN: 978-81-212-7123-3 (Set) 28 Vols. In 52 Bindings

ISBN: 978-81-212-7537-8 (PB) Vol. XIX, Pt. III

First Published, 1932

2nd Impression 2024

Printed at: Gyan Press, Delhi.

CENSUS OF INDIA 1931

Census of India, 1931

VOLUME XIX

BARODA

PART III—ADMINISTRATIVE VOLUME

By
SATYA VRATA MUKERJEA
B. A., (Oxon.) F. S. S. (London)
CENSUS COMMISSIONER
BARODA STATE

1932
PRINTED AT
THE BARODA STATE PRESS
BARODA

TABLE OF CONTENTS

APPENDICES

ADMINISTRATIVE VOLUME

CHAPTER I

GENERAL

1. **Introductory.**—This Report is concerned with a detailed description of the various stages of census operations in the State. In the main essentials, except in one material particular, the details of census taking on this occasion followed the instructions of the Census Commissioner for India; and except in that respect, the Census of 1931 differs but little from those of previous years. This Report, therefore, will follow generally the method of arrangement of chapters, and of presentation of material as was used in the last Administrative Volume; the exception referred to above was in respect of the method of the actual taking of the Census. Instead of the Standard Schedule, we decided to adopt the system of enumeration of the people in books of cards with a view to obviate the necessity of having any intermediate process of slip-copying at all. This change with its very important reactions on the accuracy of the record, economy in establishments and expedition in work will be described at its proper place in detail.

2. **Starting of Census Operations.**—The Government of the State, as usual, was asked to co-operate with the Government of India in the taking of the seventh decennial Census, and 26th February 1931 was fixed as the date of the Census. The Karma Sachiv submitted to Government several names including mine for appointment as Head of the Census Department of the State. In view of the successful work at the last Census of 1921, for which I had the good fortune of being complimented not only by the then Census Commissioner for India, but also by the Government of the State, His Highness the Maharaja Saheb was pleased to reappoint me as Head of the Census Operations (*vide* H. O. Huzur Central Office No. 78/18 dated the 24th March 1930). I was then acting as Sar Suba (Revenue Commissioner of the State). I went on short leave and joined my new duties on the 12th June, 1930.

3. **Office Establishment - Appointment of Assistants.**— In the order of my appointment, I was asked to recommend the name of the Assistant, as well as my Personal Assistant. I thereupon put up my proposals indicating what preliminary steps should be taken at once and further I asked for the assistance of Mr. Maganlal N. Thakkar, B. A., LL. B., as my assistant. Mr. Maganlal had done very successful work for me as Assistant Census Superintendent in 1921. Mr. Jhaverbhai T. Patel, who was my Head Clerk in 1921, was also chosen by me as my Personal Assistant. My proposals were sanctioned by Government (*vide* C. O. Huzur Central Office No. 77/15 dated the 13th March 1930).

4. Office opened: Establishment sanctioned.—Mr. Maganlal, who was then the Munsif of Karjan opened the office on the 1st May 1930. The marginally noted establishment was sanctioned finally for the Central Census Office by C. O. (Census Department) No. 2/1 dated the 12th May 1930 and No. 9/6 dated the 25th. June 1930. I was empowered without reference to rules re: age, domicile, examinations, etc. to appoint any body I selected to those posts and offer them any pay up to the amount sanctioned against each post. The Personal Assistant Mr. Jhaverbhai did not join till the 1st December 1930. At first Mr. Dhanjibhai Shah, B. Com., was appointed as Head Clerk on the 18th August 1930 on Rs. 60, but he proving not very suitable, Mr. Shantaram N. Oke B.Com., was appointed first on Rs. 65 on probation. He joined on the 12th November 1930 and was given the full pay of the post on having done work to my satisfaction from the 12th January, 1931.

Office establishment				
Serial Number	Name	Strength	Pay per month	Total amount sanctioned per month
1	Assistant ...	1	300+50 Allowance	350
2	Personal Assistant	1	150+30 Allowance	180
3	Head Clerk ...	1	75	75
4	Shirastedar ...	1	60	60
5	Accountant ...	1	40	40
6	English Typist...	1	40	40
7	Vernacular Typist	1	40	40
8	Record Clerk ...	1	30	30
9	Jamadar ...	1	18	18
10–17	Sepoys	8	15	120
18–19	Faras	2	14	28
20	Faras	1	13	13
21–22	Cycle Swars ...	2	15	30
	Total ...	22		Rs. 1,024

5. Change of designation of Head of Census Department.—Early on taking charge, it struck me that the name "Superintendent of Census Operations" was not suitable in view of the autonomous nature of our State census organisation and the terms of independent co-operation that were offered in this regard to the Government of India. Also in other important Indian States like Hyderabad, Gwalior, Travancore, Kashmir, etc., the name "Census Commissioner" was used for the chief Census Officer of the State. These circumstances were pointed out to the Government, and the C. O. (Census Department) No. 10/7 dated 1st July 1930 was passed changing the designation of the State Census Officer to "Census Commissioner", and the Government of India, as well as all other census organisations were duly notified. Since that date, the words "Census Commissioner" and "Assistant Census Commissioner" have come into general use in official correspondence, both with the State offices as well as with Government of India and other governments.

6. The Census Act of 1930.—A special Census Act was enacted for the first time in 1921. For the Census of 1931, the Government of the State went further in its co-operation, and as if in anticipation of Federation, adopted the whole of Census Act of India (No. X of 1929) with slight modifications to suit local conditions. This Act came into force from 1st August 1930. In view of the urgency and importance of the census operations, the Government specially empowered the State Census Commissioner to make all rules and circulars under the Act (*vide* Dewan Order No. 7/1 passed on this Office letter No. 12 dated the 11th August 1930 and this Department Circular No. 3/87 dated the 16th August 1930.

7. Census Code–Part I and Circulars thereunder.—By virtue of the powers above given, the Census Code was prepared and promulgated. A Power Statement defining the powers of the Census Commissioner, and other Census Officers was prepared and got approved by Government (as per Dewan Office letter No. 17/2 dated the 31st July 1930). This Statement was published as Appendix I of the Census Procedure Code, Part I of which was published in English and concerned all the preliminary operations from the start upto (and including) the final census–taking on the 26th February 1931.

8. List of important Circulars and Office Orders issued before the Census.—The following important circulars and office orders were issued in Gujarati and in English to elucidate and amplify the instructions given in the Code :–

1. Circular No. 2 dated the 2nd May 1930 re: the preparation of the General Village Register.
2. Circular No. 3 dated the 21st May 1930 re: the formation of blocks and circles, with a provisional list of towns.
3. Summary of Charge Superintendent's duties dated the 13th June 1930.
4. Rules regarding the Census of Railway areas dated the 10th July 1930.
5. Special instructions to the City Municipality of Baroda regarding tenement census dated the 1st August 1930.
6. Vat-hukum No. 2/86 re: the numbering of houses, classification of homesteads and the census of livestock, dated the 1st July 1930; and special circular re: classification of homesteads (सुचना नं. २ dated the 24th November 1930).
7. Circular No. 1/87 dated the 12th August 1930, appointing certain Range Forest Officers as Assistant Charge Superintendents.
8. Circular No. 2/87 dated the 15th August 1930 re: the peoples' responsibilities regarding the Census.
9. Circular No. 3/87 dated the 16th August authorising the Census Commissioner to promulgate rules under the Census Act.
10. Circular No. 10/87 dated the 18th September 1930 appointing Census Committees and detailing their functions.
11. Circular No. 11/87 dated the 13th October 1930 directing Charge Superintendents to submit fortnightly reports of progress.
12. Circulars No. 5/87 and 12/87 issued respectively by the Chief Medical Officer and the Educational Commissioner directing their departments to offer all co-operation in respect of Sex Enquiry.
13. Confidential *yadi* dated the 18th October 1930 and circular no. 15/87 dated the 12th January 1931 and special letters containing instructions re: Sex Enquiry dated the 23rd December 1930 and 1st January 1931.
14. Special Instructions to Census Committees with questionnaires re: caste changes, divorce, etc. dated the 18th September 1930 and the 23rd December 1930.

9. The Military and Railway Census Organisation.—Apart from the Census Central Office, the Census Department directly controlled the following Military and Railway organisations :—

I. *Military and Railway Areas*—not under the State jurisdiction.

1. The Cantonment Civil Area: Chief Executive Officer being the ex–officio Census Officer.
2. The Cantonment Military Area: The Officer Commanding acting through his adjutant as Census Officer.
3. The Baroda Marshalling Yard : Mr. Miller as the Station Master, Marshalling Yard, acting as Charge Superintendent ex–officio.
4. The Baroda Passenger Railway Station : the Station Master being the ex–officio Charge Superintendent.

5–6. The Railway Stations of Mehsana and Kalol constituted each into a separate charge under the Station Masters as Charge Superintendents.

II. *Railway Areas*-under the State jurisdiction.

7–8. Goya Gate Colony and Dabhoi Railway stations, under Messrs. Iyer and Salder respectively as Charge Superintendents.

10. Arrangements for Censusing of above areas.—Since 1921, the organisation of Census even in areas not within the jurisdiction of the State, but falling within the Census area of the State has been given to the State Census Department, and the work was organised and completed in these places with the fullest co-operation of the Railway and Military authorities concerned. Not only did they co-operate in the taking of the ordinary census, but also they readily agreed to undertake most of the special enquiries which were carried on alongside. The Cantonment even undertook to take up the work of Sex Enquiry, which the B.B. and C.I. Railway administration, however, declined to do.

11. Railway Areas.—As a consequence of the network of railways in the State, the organisation of the Railway Census has always been a difficult and delicate matter. The State Census has to deal with 209 stations distributed as noted in the margin and controlled by six different organisations. Besides, the State Railway system, over whose census this department had full control as it had over the other administrative divisions of the State, there were five foreign Railway administrations: (1) B.B. and C.I. Broad Gauge, (ii) B.B. and C.I. Metre Gauge, (iii) Gondal Railway, (iv) Jamnagar Dwarka Railway and (v) Bhavnagar State Railway,—with which this Department had to carry on correspondence delimiting jurisdiction, numbering houses, appointing supervisors and enumerators and so on. But I am happy to be able to put on record that the work was well done and that there were few complaints. A Station Master in the G.B.S. Railway was impertinent to an Assistant Charge Superintendent in the City and had to be severely dealt with, but there were no other incidents to record.

Name of Division	No. of Railway stations and Rly. areas including special Rly. charges
City ...	6
Amreli ...	11
Baroda (Ex. City) ...	98
Mehsana ...	62
Navsari ...	24
Okhamandal	8
Total...	209

12. Arrangements for Training the Staff in special areas.—In the above areas, every step was taken for making the presence of the State Census organisation felt. To each of the eight Military and Railway Charges, personal visits were paid more than once by myself and the Assistant Census Commissioner and special care was taken to train the enumerating staff. The cost of supplying them with leaflets, circulars, copies of the Census Code and enumeration books was borne by the State. At each stage of the operations, their work was inspected and tested. Special appendices dealing with the censusing of railway and military areas were prepared and promulgated (Appendices II and III of the Census Procedure Code, Part I).

13. The District Census Organisation.—Under the Census Act of 1930 Sec. 3, the Suba of each District, the Suba (now called the Naib Suba) of Okhamandal and the Sudharai Kamdar (Municipal Commissioner) of the City of Baroda were appointed Census Officers in their respective jurisdictions. By virtue of Sec. 37 of the Census Code, the following officers were deemed to have been appointed ex-officio census officers of the grade mentioned against their names :—

1.	Naib Suba	Sub-divisional Census Officer.
2.	Vahivatdar or Mahalkari	Charge Superintendent.
3.	Chairman of every Municipality	Charge Superintendent for the respective municipality but under the general supervision of the mahal or peta-mahal Charge Superintendent.
4.	Naib Fouzdar or Tajvijdar	Supervisor for the villages in the mahal, *thanas* or *mohallas* in the towns.
5.	Talati	Enumerator for his *saja* (group of villages).

The above arrangement which followed the precedent of previous years was adhered to, and strengthened, to cope with the later and more elaborate stages of enumeration. There was one difficulty at the outset. The *thana* organisation of the Police is now abolished: so is the *tajvijdar's* circle system in the Revenue organisation of the State. The villages in the mahal had therefore, to be apportioned anew among the *tajvijdars* and *Naib fouzdars* and the apportionment worked fairly well up to the preliminary enumeration stage, when the above staff had to be supplemented from other departments. In the forest areas, the Range Forest Officers were requistioned as Assistant Charge Superintendents. In large towns, certain selected head masters were drafted as Assistant Charge Superintendents; and for supervisors and enumerators, the whole body of teachers and mahal establishments was utilised for the work of enumeration. (*vide* Appendix C.)

14. The Census organisation in the City and Towns.—In the Baroda City, the Municipal Commissioner appointed Honorary Charge Superintendents with Assistant Charge Superintendents and a paid establishment as noted in the margin, which lasted right up to the Census day. The paid staff did the work of house numbering, as well as the Tenement Census. In other municipal areas, the local municipal establishments sufficed together with some help from mahal offices to work up the business of house numbering, etc., upto the time of preliminary enumeration. The Census Act provided that the cost of house numbering, of light on the Census

Name of post	No.	Total amount sanctioned per month in rupees
Census Assistant	1	65
„ Shirastedar	1	41
„ Supervisor	1	16 (allowance)
„ Clerks	17	340
„ Peons	8	120
Total...	28	582

night and other incidental charges was to be defrayed (i) by the Municipality where such existed, and otherwise (ii) from the *mal vero* grant of the village, and (iii) where even the *mal vero* failed, from the village punchayat fund or from the local board. The *mal vero*, it may be explained, is the amount fixed by the State for the expenses in each village to meet the conveniences of travelling officers and others using the village *chora*. The amount is sanctioned in the name of the village patel, who receives it along with his own honorarium.

15. Special Enquiries.—The following special enquiries were conducted by this Department along with the ordinary taking of the Census :—

I. Undertaken about the time of house-numbering.

(i) Census of Livestock;

(ii) Classification of homesteads according to standards of house rooms;

(iii) Classification of tenements in the City of Baroda with a tenement census of the City.

II. Undertaken along with the preliminary enumeration.

(iv) The Size of the Normal Household.

III. Undertaken along with the general census.

(v) The Census of the Educated Unemployed;

(vi) An estimate of the political immigrants to this State from British Gujarat on account of the Civil Disobedience Movement.

IV. Continued after the Census.

(vii) An enquiry into the Size and Sex Constitution of Families;

(viii) The work of Census Committees conducting detailed enquiries into

(a) general social changes;

(b) marriage customs with special reference to the prevalence of divorce in castes;

(c) the strength of industrial establishments; and

(d) a food survey amongst the principal castes in the State.

A brief description of the methods employed in respect of these enquiries, the agency employed, the measure of success achieved, and the processes used for tabulating results will be given when each stage of the Census Operations, along with which these enquiries were successively taken up is dealt with in the later sections of this Report.

16. Miscellaneous items.—Before we close this general chapter, it will be useful to summarise here a few miscellaneous items of interest for future guidance :—

(i) Accommodation of the Census office.—Soon after I took charge, the problem of housing the Census Office engaged my attention. I was at first accommodated in the Huzur Central Office and my central office was given a room at a remote part of the old Kothi building, some distance away from me. This was an inconvenience, and as soon as this was pointed out, the Government very kindly allowed me the use of the commodious Saroj bungalow near the Motibag Palace, to which place the Census office was removed on the 7th July 1930. (Vide Dewan Order No. 11/9 dated the 30th June 1930).

(ii) Permission to go outside State territory on Government work.—In previous Censuses, the Census Commissioner used to be given a general permission to go outside the State for government work. He was, however, bound not to enter into stipulations adverse to state interests without the previous permission of the Government of the State. This permission was renewed on the present occasion by Dewan Order No. 11/4 dated the 15th July 1930, passed on the Census Department Tippan No. 9 dated the 8th July 1930.

(iii) Powers of the Census Commissioner.—For this Census it was deemed necessary to draw up a definite table of powers for the Census Commissioner. The previous power statement was based on the Rules of 1901, and the Census Superintendent of 1921 had only the powers of a Suba, except where higher powers were specially given. On this occasion, the Census Commissioner was given the full powers of the Sar Suba, and in certain specified matters, he was given even higher powers.

(iv) Provision of cycle swars and police guard.—In view of the large staff engaged for the Abstraction office, and the costly furniture and other reasons, it was usual in previous Censuses, (and indeed it was so laid down in the Rules of 1901), for the State Military department to supply two swars for the use of the Census Office. This was the practice since 1901, but in this Census the Military Department pleaded shortness of men. The Government was approached (under Tippan No. 5 dated the 29th May 1930) with a request to sanction two cycle swars in the Census Budget and the proposal was sanctioned by the Council (*vide* C. O. Census No. 7/6 dated the 16th June 1930). Later when the office was moved to the Saroj bungalow, after the dead-stock — chairs, tables and pigeon-holes for the Abstraction office was bought, it was thought advisable to approach Government either to direct the Police Department to supply a Police Guard free of cost, or to sanction an additional protective establishment of two sepoys and one Havildar. The latter alternative was sanctioned under Government order (C. O. Census No. 7/4 dated the 21st February 1931) and the additional cost of Rs. 68/-per month was charged to the Census budget.

(v) Insurance of the Census office against fire.—The Census Commissioner for India having suggested in his letter No. 1- Misc., dated the 7th April 1931, the advisibility of getting the Census Central and Abstraction offices insured, arrangements were made to insure the Saroj Bungalow with the Census deadstock and records against fire for Rs. 15,000 with the Vulcan Fire Insurance Company for a period of three months.

CHAPTER II

THE TAKING OF THE CENSUS

A. Preliminary Arrangements

17. Village Register.—The first requisite in the taking of a Census is the preparation of a correct and complete list of villages. Each Mahal should prepare an accurate *dehzada* of inhabited and uninhabited villages and of hamlets within a village. Without such a list no division into charges, circles and blocks can be made with any degree of measurable accuracy.

18. The Register: How prepared.—In 1921, the practice was adopted of preparing the Census *dehzada* exactly on the same basis as the Revenue *dehzada.* The village taken as the census unit corresponded exactly with the revenue village or *moję (mauza)* and the entire area comprised within the revenue unit was taken for census purposes. Thus the preparation of the Register was considerably simplified. The difficulty lay however, in finding out, and explaining the variations from previous censuses. In 1931, the same practice was followed. In several respects the Census *dehzada* is distinguished from *Mulki dehzada.* In the first place, the hamlets or residential areas under each village are shown; new hamlets are added wherever such have come into existence, and old depopulated hamlets are excluded from the list of inhabited areas. In the second place, the Census list does not contain those villages in which the Gaekwar's sovereignty or jurisdiction is co-shared or where the owner of the village is a payer of tribute or *ankdo,* but under a different political jurisdiction. Thus the co-shared villages of the Dangs, the village of Chandod where the owner is the Rana of Mandwa and the Gaekwar exercises civil and criminal jurisdiction, and certain villages in Kheralu, Patan, etc., where this State does not exercise administrative jurisdiction are examples of villages not figuring in the Census *dehzada* at all. Thirdly, as to the residential areas within the forest tracts, not administered by the Revenue Department, a different principle had to be adopted. There were scattered places where population was found in the different ranges, to which the Conservator of Forests was moved by academic objections to hesitate to give the name of village. But they were residential areas right enough, although they lacked the fixity of revenue villages, and I decided to treat them as census villages. Fourthly, in Dhari mahal, we had to deal with the problem of temporary halting places of Rabaris (goat-herds) which are called *nes* (नेस). Many such temporary abodes of this tribe were found in existence. These were not entered as *peta paras* (hamlets), except a few which were permanently inhabited. They were joined on to the parent village and only such temporary abodes which were distant from the villages proper were formed into separate blocks. All these difficulties were overcome and a final list of villages for the whole State was prepared by about the end of August, 1930. This list was further verified and corrected from the final list of blocks and circles (Form No. 7) which was received in the Central Office on the 15th November, 1930.

19. **The Form of the Village Register.**—This form was the same as in 1921, with the innovation that the villages were arranged according to *thanas*, and not alphabetically as in 1921. The instructions were to prepare the Register according to the geographical position of the village and after comparing with *Dehzada* (Revenue) Register to send three copies of it on to the Suba. The Suba was to scrutinize the Register, make such changes as he deemed necessary, retain one copy in his record, return one to the Mahal and send the third to the Central Census Office by the 30th June 1930 at the latest. In the *remarks* column, the area of the mahal in square miles was to be entered.

20. **Advantages as well as Disadvantages of the Innovation.**—The above form of the Register was decided on particularly with a view to keep correspondence with the blocks and circles register (provisional as well as final) where the alphabetical lettering is given to circles by *thanas*. There are one or two disadvantages however in this method, which must be noticed. In the first place the *thana* system of lettering of circles is inconvenient. In the next place, the Census *dehzada* Volume (Village Tables) has the alphabetical arrangement like the Revenue *dehzada*, and it has to be prepared from this Register and therefore there is danger, from the difference in principle of arrangement, of mistake in posting of names and figures. But on the whole as the preparation of blocks and circles is a highly important matter, it is far more to the purpose that they be prepared accurately. There is no reason, however, why the lettering should not follow a uniform plan. We advert to this point later on in para 25 *infra*.

21. **Area of the State and of the City of Baroda.**—Early steps were taken to ascertain and verify the area of the mahals and of the City of Baroda. Under this Office Order No. 2/86 dated the 30th June 1930, mahal officers were also directed to submit statements of the area of village sites as well as of huts and hamlets on *sim* lands and the total area of each village (residential area and fields combined). In respect of area, it was found that the Survey Department figures were not up-to-date, and whole blocks of villages e.g. the villages belonging to the Thakore of Lal Mandwa, were hitherto omitted from the total area of the State. The area of the City occasioned also great difficulty. The P. W. Department, the City Municipality, the Mahal records, as well as the Survey Department, each vied with the other by setting up independent estimates which bore no relation to one another. Ultimately all these were reconciled, a correct map of the City was prepared, the area of each ward was carefully estimated, the Railway areas and the portion occupied by the State military lines, the population of which had been always included in the City Census, were added in, and a final estimate was arrived at, which all the different authorities agreed to accept as correct. It is trusted that future censuses of the State will show less of the vagaries of the statistician in this respect than before.

22. **Census Maps.**—While the preparation of the village register was in progress, tracings of taluka maps were obtained from the Vahivatdars, with the areas of the police *thanas* and revenue circles indicated by inked lines of different colours. They were very useful in revising the provisional circles and charges formed on the commencement of the operations (Article 44 Baroda Census Code,

1931). It was also ordered that Vahivatdars should have an additional copy of the tracing, prepared for their own use and should mark against each village its serial number in the Register and the number of houses it was estimated to contain. Subsequently when final circles were formed, the boundary of each circle was ordered to be indicated by a broad red line and the letter of the circle noted in red ink within the area thus enclosed. Each charge superintendent and supervisor was subsequently ordered to have a copy of the portion of the map relating to his charge or circle.

23. **Census Divisions.**—Having obtained a complete list of villages, the next step was to form census divisions. As in previous censuses there were three classes of Census officers: Charge Superintendent, Supervisor and Enumerator. As explained already, up till the completion of the work of house-numbering, the whole Census work for the village was left to the *talati* as enumerator, the work for the *thana* was left to the *naib fouzdar*, or where he was not available to a *tajvijdar* as supervisor and the work for the whole taluka (except the municipal area) was left to the Vahivatdar, as Charge Superintendent who had also to look to the work in the municipal areas in the mahal.

Blocks.—The person who actually filled in the enumeration books was the enumerator and the area assigned to him was his block. The size of the block depended on the number of houses, which an enumerator could reasonably be expected to visit between 7 and 12 P.M. on the Census night. It was laid down that the number should not exceed 100 and that ordinarily it should range from 60 to 75. In exceptional cases, this number of 100 was allowed to be exceeded. This scale is a little higher than what prevails elsewhere, but experience in the past censuses has proved that having regard to the close proximity in which houses are situated in most of the State towns and villages and the fact that most of the enumerators are government servants, it was deemed quite possible for one person to visit about 100 houses within the time allowed. Next after the enumerator, came the supervisor whose duty it was to supply his enumerators with forms, to train them, to check the entries in their books and collect their enumeration books and check the totals prepared by them after the Census had been taken. From ten to fifteen enumerators' blocks were grouped to form the Supervisor's Circle. Over the Supervisors was the Charge Superintendent. He was the Head of the Census Operations in his Charge. The blocks and circles were formed by the *naib fouzdars* (thana police officers) or *tajvijdars* under the supervision and guidance of the taluka Vahivatdars. The *naib fouzdars* or the *tajvijdars* went to each village within the limits of the *thana* assigned to them and with the help of the patel and the talati, divided it into the necessary number of blocks. Their instructions were to include about 60 to 100 houses whether occupied or unoccupied into one block; and in forming blocks, to keep intact the recognised sub-divisions of a village, such as *falias*, *khanchas*, *khadkis*, *wadas*, etc. As a general rule, the determination of blocks was to be commenced from the outside of the village and continued till the whole village was demarcated into successive blocks. If two small villages adjoined and there was only one enumerator available for both, still they were to be numbered as distinct blocks. Dependent hamlets of a village (*paras*, etc.) were not to be formed into separate blocks unless this was necessary on account of their size or distance from the parent village. A village containing one hundred houses or less was not generally to be divided into more blocks than one. A whole village and a portion of another village or portions of two independent villages were not to be included in one block. Jails, Hospitals, etc. were to form separate blocks, if the number of persons residing therein was so large as to make it convenient to do so.

Circles.—After the demarcation of the blocks, they are to be grouped into circles. A Circle was ordinarily to contain ten blocks, but there was no objection to its including more or less, having regard to the circumstances of different localities. The maximum number of blocks that a circle may contain was, however, limited to 15. The circles were to be of such a size that the Supervisors can exercise effective supervision over all the enumerators and check the whole of the preliminary enumeration. As *naib fouzdars* or *tajvijdars* were entrusted with the whole of census work till house-numbering, they had to group all the blocks into circles, in all villages included within *thana* limits. The grouping was carried out with the aid of the census map, so as to make the circles as compact as possible. A circle consisted of one or more complete villages. No village was to be partly in one circle and partly in another. In case of towns, parts of different wards were not to be included in the same circle.

Charges.—The Charge was generally identical with the Taluka, but all places which had municipalities were treated as separate charges, and the City of Baroda was divided into five charges corresponding to the five wards of the City. Jungle charges were five viz. Songadh, Vajpur, Sadadvel (in Songadh Taluka), Vyara and Vakal (in Mangrol Taluka) under the supervision of the Range Forest Officers concerned as Assistant Charge Superintendents. But these Range Forest Officers were to work under the orders and the general supervision of their respective Vahivatdars who as taluka Charge Superintendents, were primarily responsible for the proper census arrangement within their jurisdiction.

24. Provisional charge register form No. 4.—The next step was the preparation of the Circle list or the Register of Census divisions. The form prescribed in Census Procedure Code Part I Chapter III para 46 was adopted. Each circle was to be commenced on a fresh page. The serial number of each village was entered in the order in which it appeared in the Village Register. On receiving the register from their supervisors, Charge Superintendents carefully revised it and ordered such additions and alterations as appeared necessary. The circles in each *thana* were numbered in Gujarati alphabets as follows :—

अ, इ, उ, ए ओ, क, ख, ग, घ, च, छ, ज, झ, ट, ठ, ड, ण, त, थ, द, ध, न, प, फ, ब, भ, म, य, र, ल, व, श, ष, स, ह, ळ, क्ष, ज्ञ. की, कु, के, को, खी, खु, खे, खो, etc.,
and these letters were repeated with the next *thana* and so on.

25. Correction of defects : improvements suggested.—As soon as the Charge Register was prepared, an abstract of it was sent to the Central Census office where it was scrutinised and defects noticed were corrected. Where discrepancies were found between this list and the village register, these were revised and corrected. The abstract of circle list was, however, mainly used as a guide for giving orders to the press for printing forms. In respect of this Charge Register Abstract, the form as shewn in the Code-Chapter III para 49 was adopted. In the course of our inspections, it was noticed that this arrangement of lettering of circles by *thanas* was inconvenient; sometimes the name of *thanas* was inadvertently omitted; at other times the provision about keeping the lettering of circles within towns distinct from circles in rural areas in a mahal was forgotten. On the whole for the next census, I would suggest that it would be a simpler plan to have continuous lettering beginning with the towns first and then the rural areas and the whole lettering co-ordinated on a uniform plan by the mahal officer himself. The difficulty where circles are too numerous for the letters of the alphabet can be obviated by having numbers below letters where all letters are exhausted.

B. Preparations for numbering of houses

26. Local Census Organisation.—In para 13, we have indicated the nucleus of the ex-officio census organisation. These were augmented at the time of the preliminary count of the people. The principle adopted was that all government servants were bound to assist in the work of census taking whenever called on to do so (vide § 51–53 of the Census Code). The wide extension of primary education made it possible for the Census Department to utilise the full resources of the teaching staff, all of whom were expected to be utilised for the work of enumeration. For the most part, government servants were readily available for the purpose. But these appointments were not made till December, 1930. Till then, the main brunt of the work was borne by the revenue and police establishments, and the municipal staff in towns. There were 50 towns fixed for the State including the City of Baroda and the Cantonment. Of these, 45 were municipal areas. Generally, the municipal clerks, the sanitary inspection staff and the collection establishments were drafted for these preliminary operations. The City Corporation employed at its own cost an establishment of 20 clerks and 8 menials on a monthly pay of Rs. 582 for working the tenement census as well as numbering of houses. In the rural areas, in the 2,920 villages of the State, 853 talatis were entirely responsible for these operations until the enumerating staff was formally appointed in December. Some idea of the magnitude of their task, which they bore with cheerful loyalty without any hope of remuneration, can be had from the fact that they numbered altogether 602,196 houses in the rural areas. Thus the average of houses numbered by each talati comes to 706. They were responsible also for their classification. They also took a census of the livestock and they helped the mahal office in the preparation of the village register, the provisional register of blocks and circles and the final Charge Register. Over these talatis were the *ex–officio* supervisors, who were the *naib fouzdars* and *tajvijdars* and their number was 133. The police element was not found very intelligent. Some of their number were very negligent and had to be sharply dealt with.

27. Census Calendar.—For a work of the magnitude of the Census a proper time-table for the various stages is necessary, and a calendar was prepared following the practice of previous censuses. This calendar is printed as Appendix A of this Report. Very stringent steps were taken to ensure that the calendar was properly and punctually worked up to by all the mahals. Certain severe steps had to be taken against one or two vahivatdars, and a few others were warned. The bulk were however very punctual and dutiful. The severity of the measures taken was a guarantee that the different stages of the census were to be successfully accomplished.

28. Preliminary Training.—The training of census officers was at once taken in hand. From July to September, general preliminary training in census work was given to groups of Naib Subas and Vahivatdars, municipal staff, *naib fouzdars*, *tajvijdars* and talatis. The State was divided between my Assistant and myself. I took up Baroda, Mehsana and Navsari *prants* touring 28 days visiting 11 talukas before house numbering began in October. Mr. Maganlal toured 6 days and travelled in 5 Talukas during this period. A detailed analysis of our tours is sub–joined as Appendix B of this Report. We held census conferences everywhere we went, explaining the normal routine of the Census, besides telling them about the new features of our work, the special enquiries undertaken and the responsibilities of census officials. In these preliminary conferences, officers of the rank of Charge Superintendents were specially taken into confidence and given detailed instructions. In this preliminary period, I took advantage of the general permission accorded to me by Government (*vide* para 16 *supra*) to travel anywhere out of the State on duty, to go to Bombay and Poona, where I had most helpful conferences with the Bombay City Census Officer, Dr. Nerurkar, Mr. Dalal, the Municipal Commissioner, and Mr. Dracup, the Provincial Superintendent of Census.

C. *Numbering of houses and their classification*

29. **House Numbering.**—Thus the ground was prepared for the next important stage in the taking of the census — namely the numbering of houses. The definition of a "house" was the same as adopted in the State Census since 1911.

30. **Definition of House in the Census of 1891.**—The definition of a 'house' fixed for the enumerators in the Censuses of 1881 and 1891 was "the space within the external and party walls of each building or tenement having a separate and independent communication with a road, either common to the public or to all inhabitants of the building of which the tenement forms a part." Under this definition a *mala* or chawl was considered as only one house though inhabited by many distinct families; and a bungalow with its out-houses was also classed as one house. The Census Commissioner to whom this definition was communicated in the Census of 1891, intimated that it had been ruled that servants' quarters in a compound, distinct from the bungalow, should receive separate numbers. He also recommended that the various tenements in chawls should be sub-numbered, so that the danger of omission of obscure tenants of a small room or two in the main building could be avoided. After personal discussion with the Census Commissioner for India, when he visited Baroda in 1901, it was decided to add a clause in the instructions to the enumerators warning them to see that the inmates of no subordinate tenements of a house escaped enumeration.

31. **Definition in the Census of 1901.**—The definition of a 'house' adopted in the Census of 1901 was "the dwelling place of one or more families, having a separate entrance, whether the entrance be from a public road, compound, corridor, balcony, gallery, or otherwise." Sir Herbert Risley had formulated his own definition of a 'house' which was communicated to this State but as it practically meant the same thing as the definition previously promulgated here, we were allowed to retain our own definition.

32. **Defects of the definitions adopted in the past censuses.**—The definition of a 'house' adopted in the Census of 1901 led to the rooms of a chawl, and the rooms in the compound of a bungalow, which were in 1891 only sub-numbered, to be numbered separately. But it left the building to be called one house, although inhabited by more than one family. It enabled us to know the total number of houses of varying size from a hut to a big mansion in the State and the mean number of persons living in a house. But it gave us no information about the number of families dwelling in them. It gave the structural but not the social information, which latter would alone enable one to ascertain the mean size of the family, which varied with the comparative prosperity of the locality, the prevalence of scarcity or disease, the effect of migration taking off the young men, and with the comparative fertility of particular races or religious groups.

33. **Bengal Definition of a 'House' as residence of a commensal family suitable to Gujarat.**—From this point of view the definition of a 'house' adopted in Bengal in 1891, as also in 1901, appeared to be very satisfactory; and

from the published reports, seemed to have worked well. It solved the difficulty of bringing structural and social units into conformity. A 'house' was defined as consisting of "the buildings, one or many, inhabited by one family; that is by a number of persons living and eating together in one mess with their resident dependents, such as mother, widowed sisters, younger brothers, etc., and their servants who reside in the house." In other words, a 'house' was defined as the dwelling place of a family. This definition is admirably suited to Gujarat. where by the common understanding of the people, it conveys the idea of a place, where people living together either in a whole house or in a part of it have one common *chulah* (hearth). It is a custom in most of the Hindu castes to make a present (lahni लहाणी) of utensils, etc., on festive occasions to the members of the caste. A *lota* or a *thali* is given to each *ghar* in the caste and for this purpose those who have one *chulah*, that is, who mess together, are taken to mean one *ghar*.

34. Definition adopted in the present census.—For the above reasons, a house was defined in the Census of 1911 as the dwelling place of a commensal family. The proposal was approved by the then Census Commissioner for India, as well as by the Government of His Highness the Maharaja and a census house was accordingly defined in 1911 as under :—

"A house is defined for census purposes as consisting of the buildings, one or many, inhabited by one family, that is, by a number of persons living and eating together, of food cooked on one *chulah* (hearth) or in one mess, with their resident dependents such as mother, widowed sisters, younger brothers, etc., and their servants who reside in the house. In other words, the unit is the commensal family and not the homestead or enclosure." (Article 27, Chapter I, Baroda Census Procedure Code 1911).

The same definition has been retained in the Census of 1921 and also in the present one.

35. Exceptions to the standard definition.—The above definition was well understood by the people and gave rise to no difficulty. One or two special provisions were made. In the first place, one room tenements where more than one family resided, were not divided but given only one number. Such cases were not numerous. Again, in respect of bungalows of higher class persons – European, Anglo–Indian and other persons of status – the residence of the master and his family was numbered separately from his servants' quarters. Police and military lines, jails, dispensaries, lunatic asylums, etc., were formed into separate blocks where necessary and each house, apartment or ward within their precincts was to be treated as a house and separately numbered. A third departure from the above definition was observable in all municipal areas, particularly in the City of Baroda, where in spite of instructions to the contrary, as above seen, in the case of a family residing in more than one building, as many numbers as there were structures were given. The municipalities in doing this were apparently following a design of their own. They wished to utilise the census as an opportunity for revising their register of tenements for purposes of house–tax or other fiscal reasons. In the City of Baroda, this departure from instructions was however, formally allowed by the Department, as the census of tenements was also taken along with the numbering of houses, and the structural definition had to be combined with the social.

36. The Numbering of Houses.—The numbering of houses was timed to begin after the *diwali* on the 23rd October, everywhere in the State, and to finish by the 15th November 1930. Between these dates, the supervisor initiated the work in each block of his circle. The materials generally used and found most suitable were yellow ochre (*geru*) and white–wash. Where huts were made of wattled bamboos, a small space was plastered with mud and the number painted on the plaster. Huts made of interwoven leaves could not be so dealt with, however, and in their case, the numbers were painted on bits of wood or tin, tiles, bricks, earthen pots, etc., and these articles were given to the residents of these huts with a strict injunction that they be carefully preserved till the next *holi* and produced whenever required by the *Sarkar*. These instructions were scrupulously observed and no complaints were received from the census staff on this score.

37. **Permanent House–number Plates.**—It was pointed out to all municipalities and vishisht panchayats that it was most useful in their own interests to have permanent house numbers. Some of the more enterprising of these bodies took advantage of this counsel. In 1921, fifteen municipalities including the Corporation of the City had permanent house–number plates. On the present occasion, 14 of these bodies agreed to continue this practice but it was remarkable that Navsari Municipality stood out for the primitive way of house–numbering. Patan and Amreli were at first inclined to follow Navsari's lead but they were later persuaded to adopt the more modern and neater method. In addition, sixteen other municipalities including Dwarka, Gandevi, Dharmaj, Sinor and Kadi refused to accept the Department's advice, but altogether 27 municipalities adopted permanent house numbers. Their names are shown in the margin.

Serial No.	Name of Municipality	Serial No.	Name of Municipality
1	Baroda City	15	Sidhpur
2	Petlad	16	Unjha
3	Sojitra	17	Patan
4	Dabhoi	18	Chanasma
5	Padra	19	Dhinoj
6	Savli	20	Bilimora
7	Karjan	21	Kathor
8	Vaghodia	22	Variav
9	Bhadran	23	Vyara
10	Makarpura	24	Mahuva
11	Dahgam	25	Amreli
12	Vijapur	26	Damnagar
13	Mehsana	27	Beyt
14	Visnagar		

38. **Arrangement of Numbers.**—The numbers ran in a continuous series from block to block, each block beginning a series. Enumerators were to begin from the right hand end, facing the house, and then going to the left and keeping to it continuously. The circle was indicated by the Gujarati letter chosen for it, the blocks were serially numbered per circle and the number for each was shown as the numerator. Again, when a block was begun, the first number was enclosed in a triangle e. g., (triangle: અ ૧/૧); where the block was finished, the sign used was a square e. g. (square: અ ૧/૬૦); and where a circle was completed, a circle sign was used e. g. (circle: અ ૧/૬ ૦/૦). In addition to the ordinary dwelling houses, care was taken to affix numbers to *dharamshalas*, temples, encampments, *ghats*, shops and other places where people were likely to sleep on the night of the census.

39. Suggestion for improvement in the above arrangement.—Our practice differs from the standard in British India and that obtaining in certain other States. In Bombay Presidency, the numbers are continuous for the whole town or village. This is inconvenient as continuous numbering is liable to mistakes. While I was visiting Bhavnagar and Junagadh States, I noticed that they had a very sensible arrangement; as the number of the house was the most significant, it was painted in bold letters with the letter of circle and number of block painted in smaller size one above the other, *before the house number* e. g. our અ૧/૧૦ would be shewn there as અ/૧ ૧૦ : which in my view is a decided improvement on our present practice. I make a note of this point here, so that in future censuses, this suggestion may be borne in mind.

40. Cost of House-numbering.—In the past censuses till 1901, the cost of house–numbering was defrayed from the general expenses sanctioned for the census operations. In 1901, Rs. 2,402–7–10 were distributed in small amounts to all the Charge Superintendents with instructions that they should keep a regular account and submit bills for sanction to the Census Superintendent. This caused a great deal of writing work and delayed adjustments of the accounts till they were audited and finally passed. In 1911 proposals were submitted to Government to change the procedure and order instead that the cost of house–numbering and contingent charges in connection with the actual census should be met in villages from the *mal vero* and local funds, and in municipal towns from municipal funds. This proposal was accepted and the cost of house–numbering which was trifling was met from such local funds in 1911. In 1921, and on the present occasion also, the same procedure was observed (vide para 14 above). The cost of house–numbering, etc. was thus defrayed.

41. Inspection of House–numbering.—While the numbering of houses was taken in hand, and right on till the beginning of preliminary enumeration I travelled continuously. This was my second census tour in the State. As will appear from Appendix B, in this period I toured for 57 days, travelled in 13 talukas, visited 16 towns and 48 villages. I inspected approximately 6,281 house numbers. The Assistant Census Commissioner was similarly travelling. He toured 34 days, travelled in 14 talukas and visited 17 towns and 6 villages. He also inspected 4,900 house numbers. Under the Code (Sec. 32) the scale of inspection work for touring officers is laid down. A Naib Suba was expected to inspect 10 per cent of house numbers in each circle, a Charge Superintendent 25per cent of house numbers in each village; and a supervisor, the whole work of all the blocks in his circle. This scale may seem too severe, and some of the Naib Subas failed to come up to the standard. A few charge superintendents were conscientious, and constant progress. reports that they were expected to submit every fortnight kept them up to the mark. The supervisors were more negligent. These could be properly controlled only by the charge superintendents of whom few had the courage to use the powers allowed in the code to exact work from naib fozdars. But on the whole the actual work of house numbering was well done. In a few places, such as Sinor, Kheralu and Vijapur, it was noticed that the proper method of numbering was not observed; a few houses were omitted elsewhere and the omissions were found and corrected. A whole line of houses belonging to the guards *karkhana* in the City was found omitted. Some huts in the fields were similarly left out. But everywhere the tendency observed was to over–number houses, rather than otherwise. This was designedly encouraged in municipal areas by the municipal authorities themselves, so much so that in their zeal, the house numbering staff in the city did not omit even fowl houses in the bungalows of high officials in their count.

42. Total number of Houses Numbered.—Altogether the total number of houses numbered in the State was 815,381, showing an increase of 10.4 per cent since 1921. The occupied houses increased by 9.7 per cent during the same period; and as the rate of increase in population is nearly 15 per cent, it cannot be said that the tendency to over-number houses which I noticed even in 1921 is on the increase. Owing to the social definition adopted, the increase in families has led to increase in "houses". But there has not been much real increase in houses in the State.

Area	No. of houses numbered	
	1931	1921
STATE ...	815,381	738,498
City and towns	213,185	187,679
Rural Areas ...	602,196	550,819

43. Corrected Return of Houses.—On the completion of house numbering, the supervisor was required to send a corrected return of the number of houses and blocks in his circle to his charge superintendent who was then to prepare a final Charge Register (Form No. 7 *vide* Sec. 27 of Circular No. 2/86 of 1st July 1930). One copy was to be sent through the *prant* to this Office; a revised return was prepared for the whole State from which we could have an idea of the forms required for the taking of the census. In Statement No. IV is given a detailed list per taluka of blocks with number of houses and circles per taluka. We thus arrived at a total of 1,206 circles and 12,074 blocks to which were to be added 10 circles and 64 blocks for railway, military and other special areas, which were independent charges, thus making a total of 1,216 circles and 12,138 blocks in the whole State. A summary of the 12,074 blocks by number of houses contained in them is given below:—

Serial No.	Size of block	Total blocks
1	Blocks of less than 10 houses	340
2	" " 10 and more but below 20 houses	575
3	" " 20 and more but below 30 houses	869
4	" " 30 and more but below 40 houses	1,784
5	" " 40 and more but below 50 houses	2,812
6	" " 50 and more but below 60 houses	2,570
7	" " 60 and more but below 70 houses	1,660
8	" " 70 and more but below 80 houses	892
9	" " 80 and more but below 90 houses	411
10	" " 90 and more but below 100 houses	132
11	" " 100 and more but below 110 houses	20
12	" " 110 and more but below 120 houses	9
	Total....	12,074

The above total includes 20 uninhabited blocks, *dharmashalas*, shops, factory dwellings, etc., which were found tenantless, when house numbering was going on.

44. Preparation of House or Block Lists.—While the houses were being numbered, the enumerator also prepared a list of houses per block, showing the circle letter per *thana*, the number of block on the top and the name of mahal and village or town. The form as relating to the ordinary census (Form No. 6) was simple enough, but it had a second part (Form No. 6 A) on which the classification of the house-room in occupation of each family, and the census of the livestock was recorded. Form No. 6 had six columns as under :—

5

<table>
<tr><td colspan="2">Name of Mahal
Name of Village or Ward
Name of Thana</td><td colspan="3">1. A house means the residence of a commensal family.
2. Column 5 should be filled in after the preliminary enumeration which will take place from 15th January 1931.</td><td>Alphabetical symbol for the Circle
Number of Block</td></tr>
<tr><td>Sub-division i. e. hamlet, quarter, street, etc.</td><td>Serial No. of house</td><td>Description—dwelling house, shop, sarai etc.</td><td>Name of head of family</td><td>Total No. of persons per family</td><td>Remarks</td></tr>
<tr><td>1</td><td>2</td><td>3</td><td>4</td><td>5</td><td>6</td></tr>
</table>

Form No. 6 will be explained later.

The above form was fairly correctly filled in. Only the number of persons in the family was to be left blank; and the list did not indicate exactly whether a house was uninhabited or not. Column 3 did not give this indication either; although sometimes the enumerators utilised this column as also the *remarks* column to show whether a house was inhabited at the time this list was filled in. The form of this list was modified in 1921, when the two new enquiries re: classification of house-room and census of livestock were instituted as part of the census; and the modified form was continued for this census also. But the fact that column 5 was not to be filled in till the preliminary enumeration, became a great inconvenience. In Baroda City, we saw this and as part of the tenement census, we required that there should be a count of persons in each family while the houses were being numbered. This gave us an accurate idea of the number of forms required for the City where there was very little wastage. In the rest of the State, estimates were largely exceeded in some places and in others, there was considerable wastage. I should suggest therefore, that in the next census, this column should be filled in at the time of house-numbering itself.

D. *Appointment and Training of Census Staff*

45. Appointment of Census Staff.—In December, the full complement of the census staff was to be got ready and appointed. Form No. 7 above referred to does contain a column for showing the name of supervisor as well as enumerator for the area concerned (columns 5 and 9) but these are usually left blank, because at the time when the form is prepared, which is before the 15th November, the census staff is not appointed at all. For the purpose of the formal appointment another form is used: viz. the old form No. 22 prescribed according to Sec. 440 of the old Census Rules of 1901. These rules are technically not in existence now, but some of the forms prescribed therein, which are not specifically incorporated in the new Code or circulars, are utilised also; and the appointment form is one of these :—

Serial number	Name of taluka	Village, Town or City	Circle letter	Number of block	Name of enumerator	His permanent department and designation	His present pay	His present address	Name of supervisor	His premnent department and designation	His present pay	His present address	Remarks
1	2	3	4	5	6	7	8	9	10	11	12	13	14

The appointments are recommended on this form and I request that it be formally incorporated in the next Census Code.

The above appointments were made by the Suba for each *prant* and the City census officer for the city and by the Census Commissioner for other areas. Generally the appointments made by the *prant* were confirmed by this office, but occasionally they had to be revised, as in one mahal, where the Vahivatdar with more zeal than discretion recommended three women as enumerators and the Suba had sanctioned without any scrutiny, these appointments had to be cancelled.

46. Number of Appointments made.—All the departments in the City were required to submit names of their establishments to the City Census Officer, as also local officers in all mahals were required to submit such lists to the Charge Superintendents concerned. Some offices as usual pleaded pressure of work, but most of these pleas were tactfully but firmly turned down. The Karma Sachiv very kindly assisted the Department by circulating a strongly worded order that all departments should desist from encouraging their clerks in these attempts to avoid census work (*vide* Huzur Central Office letter No. Census 32/1 dated 6th January 1931). As a result there were few cases of inter-departmental friction, and almost everywhere the offices co-operated with cordiality. The Education and Revenue departments were however the main agency employed. Non-officials were not enlisted to any large extent, as it was not possible to give them personal training and the department had no power to punish them if they shirked their duty. In this census, the number employed as enumerators and the high degree of accuracy attained showed that it is possible without the least trouble to entrust more than one block to one enumerator. In Harij taluka, where schools are few, and clerks are not many, some enumerators were given as many as 6 blocks apiece. In Statement No. I, the details of the agency employed are given by administrative divisions. Altogether 106 charge superintendents (including 10 assistant charge superintendents), 1,255 supervisors (including assistant supervisors) and 9,409 enumerators were employed, giving an average of numbered houses, per charge superintendent, 7,692, per supervisor, 649; and per enumerator, 86. I should suggest even a greater economy of personnel in towns and such like closely populated areas, giving an average of 150 houses per enumerator. This will free a large number of persons to look after scattered rural areas.

47. Kind of Agency Employed.—Statement No. IV at the end of this Chapter shows the distribution of this agency according as they are public servants or non-officials. In the case of public servants they are further sub-divided according to the departments to which they belong. A summary for the whole State is sub-joined below:—

Census Staff	Total	Public servants					Non-officials
		Revenue tajvijdar, clerk etc.	Talati	Police	Educational	Other department	
Supervisors ...	1,255	197	...	71	483	442	62
Enumerators ...	9,409	...	958	...	5,485	1,721	1,245

Of the 96 charge superintendents, 40 were Vahivatdars or Mahalkaris, one was the Okha Port officer and 47 were municipal chairmen or vice-presidents (non-officials). Included thereunder also were 2 British military officers in charge of the Cantonment civil and military areas respectively, 4 B. B. and C. I. Railway employees and 2, G. B. S. Railway servants.

48. Training of the Census Staff.—

(*i*) *Intensive touring.*—For this enormous army of census workers, elaborate steps had to be taken, even more intensively than in any previous census, for training in the *minutiae* of enumeration. In the first place the general preliminary training which was given to charge superintendents, supervisors, talatis and others had to be intensified and extended to the general census staff as well. The railway and military areas had to be tackled. The special enquiries which were optional to them were carefully explained and their sympathy and co-operation secured. Instruction classes of teachers and clerks were held—conferences of higher officials were frequently convened—actual enumeration books were got filled; leaders of castes and communities had to be met and their sympathies won over for the census. Altogether I travelled before the census date, 119 days and visited 53 towns and 79 villages, examined 6,251 house numbers in 151 blocks, scrutinised 952 census, and 75 sex enquiry, books and held 41 meetings and listened to 15 deputations (*vide* Tour Analysis Appendix B). My Assistant travelled 67 days, visiting 35 towns and 10 villages, held 29 meetings, examined 4,900 house numbers and enumeration books.

(*ii*) *Manuals and instructions leaflets.*—In addition to the above method of intensive touring for purposes of inspection and touring, the department published broadcast numerous leaflets and instruction books of which the following are the chief :—

Name of leaflet or booklet	In English or Gujarati	Number of copies issued
List of birth-place districts and provinces ...	Gujarati	4,000
List of languages	Gujarati	4,000
List of castes and sub-castes	Gujarati	4,000
List of religious sects	Gujarati	4,000
List of occupations	Gujarati	4,000
Instructions to Enumerators	Gujarati English	6,000 500
Instructions to Supervisors	Gujarati English	2,000 200
Instructions to Charge Superintendents ...	Gujarati	400

The above table does not include either the Census Code Part I which was issued in English or numerous elucidatory circulars and orders, a list of the chief of which has been given already.

E. Special areas

49. **Non-synchronous Areas**.—There were a few tracts where the general rule of a final census on the night of the 26th February could not be observed; this was the case with hilly and forest areas where the huts were scattered, and a night census exposed the census staff to danger from wild beasts. These were the so-called non-synchronous areas where the final count was taken during the day on the 26th February and it was finished by sunset. Care was taken by the local authorities to prevent the migration of people between these areas and the more settled parts. But usually after sunset, all commerce between these acts and other portions ceases, and it is not unfair to assume therefore that the accuracy of a day census in these areas is about as good as the general census. The marginal table gives the area of these non-synchronous tracts and their population.

Name of area	Area of tract in sq. miles	No. of villages	Population
Songadh Taluka(rural area)	580·52	217	43,525
Vyara Taluka (rural area)	315·23	150	63,834
Anaval (Mahuva) Tappa	35·43	11	8,715
Vankal and Umarpada tappa (Mangrol)	195·60	74	17,439
Amroli tappa (Tilakwada Petamahal)	27·44	30	7,305
Total	1,154·22	482	140,819

50. **Ports**.—The only port of importance dealt with by the Census was the new and growing port of Okha. In previous censuses we had no port problem to deal with; so I on this occasion, had to make a special visit to Port Bedi, Port of Bhavnagar and Junagadh to study their arrangements at first hand. A special appendix detailing the arrangements for the special census of the Port was prepared—the Port area was delimited from the civil area of Port Okha, and the Port Officer of Okha was appointed charge superintendent under the general orders of the Okha Prant Census Officer. Other smaller ports were placed under the civil charge superintendents in charge of the mahals concerned. The agents of the steamer companies usually touching at Dwarka (Rupen) and Okha ports were addressed and the Port Officer arranged all details about the enumeration of the country crafts, etc. A register of boats and boat-houses was prepared and the customs and harbour staff were thoroughly trained in census work.

51. **Census of Railways**.—Arrangements for the taking of the census of the permanent Railway population, passengers and the trains in motion on Railways passing through the State were in the hands of this department, in this census as in 1921; and all the arrangements for taking a census of the railway areas and passengers, etc., were made by us; the authorities of the different railway administrations helping with the supply of supervisors and enumerators. A railway area ordinarily meant the space between the two distant semaphores. In para 11 above, the names of the five railway administrations who co-operated with us are given, as also details regarding the special railway charges.

52. Details re: Railway Census Arrangements.—The following is a brief description of the different stages in the census operations in railway areas :—

(A) The preliminary arrangements for the census of railways :

1. A list of all stations in the State limits was prepared, after making enquiries of Mahal Officers, State Engineering department and the railway authorities. As the railway authorities had no proper data as to the limits of any State or Zilla, they committed mistakes in the list, which were got corrected.

2. The area between the two distant semaphores was in charge of the railway authorities for census purposes. Gangmen's quarters and gatemen's huts etc., outside the semaphores were censused by the State authorities within the respective towns or villages.

3. Big Junction Stations such as Baroda, Goya Gate, and Dabhoi, Mehsana and Kalol were made into separate charges.

4. All other stations (except flag stations which had no local population) were each made into a circle and the Station Master was appointed ex-officio supervisor for it.

5. Besides the special railway charges very few railway stations had more than 50 houses; these were Kosamba, Miyagam and Navsari. At these stations a suitable number of blocks was organised.

(B) House-numbering in railway areas :

1. Generally permanent railway buildings are all numbered by the Engineering department of the Railway. Those numbers were continued for census purposes and were entered in the house lists.

2. If some such number had more than one family residing therein a separate sub-number (such as T. 6/A, B or C) was given.

3. House-numbering in railway areas was done from the 1st of November to the 15th November 1930. In some places such as Dabhoi, Mehsana, the Baroda Marshalling Yard, Miyagam, etc., the Assistant Census Commissioner and myself started the numbering of houses ourselves; at various other stations, station masters had to be helped in the work of house-numbering by the village *talati* or *tajvijdar.*

4. *Cutcha* huts in the Railway areas were given consecutive numbers after the permanent buildings were dealt with.

5. The State railway areas were more within the definite control of this department and almost all large stations within our jurisdiction were visited, the staff was trained, and care was taken that the work was done properly.

(C) Final count in railway areas :

Preliminary enumeration was completed 15 days before the final census and the final count of the resident population was done as in the whole State between 7 P. M. and midnight of the census day.

(D) Station and platform enumerations :

1. Those stations which had no trains stopping during night gave no trouble in the matter.
2. At those stations where the trains stop during night, the passengers for trains were numbered by the Railway enumerator if not already enumerated by the Baroda State enumerator of the place and a pass was given to each. Similarly persons alighting from trains were numbered before they got out of station and were furnished with passes. Arrangements were made at every such station for a platform enumerator.
3. At Baroda Station, the rush of passengers was very heavy and my office staff and my assistants had to write out schedules for passengers to expedite their departure. I personally superintended the work of platform enumeration on the night of the 26th.

For Station enumeration or platform enumeration, a separate block was constituted and the books were kept separate from the books of the local population. This ensured against their being missed.

(E) Train enumeration :

There was train enumeration only at one place viz., Vyara and it was taken on the 27th February at about 6 A. M. in the morning.

(F) Provisional Totals :

The railway authorities were asked to wire their provisional totals direct to the Civil Census Charge Superintendent, except those stations which were formed into separate charges, the totals of which were to be sent to this office by wire. The railway authorities put in bills for these for payment; but as there was no precedent for this, the bills were returned for withdrawal and the Government of India also ordered that the cost incurred by Railways for telegrams and postage was to be borne by then (*vide* C. C. letter No. 47 Enmn dated 12th June 1931).

53. Census of Baroda Cantonment.—The census of the Baroda Cantonment was taken by the Chief Executive Officer. Such instructions and suggestions as were given were carried out in a friendly and cordial spirit and there was not the least difficulty at any stage of the work. My Assistant and Head Clerk personally instructed the enumerators and supervisors; and actually painted numbers on many houses in the civil area as also in the mlitary lines. While the preliminary enumeration was begun, my assistant instructed the enumerators in the actual work.

F. Special Census — Enquiries along with House Numbering

54. Cattle Census.—At the house-numbering stage, there were as indicated in para 15 above, three special enquiries made, of which the census of live-stock was the most important. This census was first taken along with the general census operations in 1921, and it was decided to continue the arrangements on this occasion also. Except in the census years, an annual estimate of live-stock together with ploughs and carts is made per village by the talati and details are compiled for the annual report of the Revenue department. On this occasion, as in 1921, the house list form was enlarged to make room for this enquiry as well as for the classification of homesteads. Form 6 A was the supplementary portion of Form 6 which concerned the census proper. This supplementary Form contained columns for different kinds of cattle, other animals such as horses, goats, camels, etc., ploughs and carts per each inhabited house, whose number was repeated in this form. After the house-numbering was over, this Form A was detached from the house lists and despatched to the Census Office. Most mahals forgot to total up the figures for blocks and mahals, and the registers had to be returned for further scrutiny. Any violent departures from the figures of 1921 were to be explained. The mahal officers were required to scrutinise these lists and the census department staff was also continuously on the move to test the accuracy of these figures. Revised figures were received about the middle of December and State Table No. IX was compiled with the help of a clerk from the Director of Agriculture's office.

55. The Classification of Homesteads.—In 1921, following the Economic Enquiry in a Bengal district by the late Mr. Jacks, I. C. S., an enquiry was conducted into the kind of houses in the Raj, divided according to the standards of camfort or house room. This enquiry was continued in this census also. Form No. 6 was used again, and the preliminary columns of Form 6 A were devised to show the results. A room was defined as a living room, which included the *parsal* (front room) and the *mal* (first floor room or loft) but not the *osri* (verandah) or *rasoda* (kitchen). From the calculation of families, all children below ten were excluded, as all persons above that age were deemed according to accepted standards of decency to require separate accommodation. As the classification was based on the proportion of living rooms to the number of adult persons in a family residing therein, it follows that all uninhabited houses were to be excluded. An exception was made however in respect of four-roomed bungalows with compounds which were placed in the first class, whether they were then inhabited or not. All tenements, where there was only provision for one living room for a resident family of three adults were placed in the third class i. e. *below comfort*. All residences where there were at least six living rooms for a family of three adults (or two rooms per adult) were to be placed in the first class, i. e. *above comfort* along with the bungalows above referred to. All other residences would go into the second class i. e. *in comfort*. The above instructions were simple enough, they were printed prominently on the top of the Form itself, and yet in no part of the census operations were more mistakes met with than in this work of classification. Many mahal registers had to be returned for revision; revised and further detailed instructions had to be sent. My assistant and myself personally got some of the work revised as in Savli, Sinor, Waghodia, Patan, Navsari, etc. Some Vahivatdars foolishly included uninhabited houses in the classification and missed the whole point of the enquiry altogether. But the work was thoroughly revised.

56. The Tenement Census in the City.—In addition to the above work of classification, a special tenement census with a provisional count of the residents was taken along with the number of houses and the preparation of the house lists. It was decided to collect the following particulars about houses in the City :—

(i) the nature of the structure (whether *pucca* or *kutcha*),

(ii) the number of floors in the structure,

(iii) whether the structure is used as (a) residence, (b) office, (c) shop with the kind of articles sold, (d) store house, (e) stable, or (f) for any other purpose,

(iv) whether the structure is owned by the persons tenanting it, or hired by them, and

(v) the number of families living in the structure, with the total number of persons in possession, and the number of rooms or floors in their occupation.

The following form which was devised after my visit to Bombay was used for this purpose :—

BARODA CITY MUNICIPALITY

ENTRY OF BUILDINGS AND FAMILIES RESIDING THEREIN

Census No. of 1921	Serial No. of the building	Name of the owner	Building Kutcha or Pucca		Number of floors in the Building	Serial No. of the house (family)	Name of chief man of the family	In possession of each family	
			Kutcha	Pucca				Rooms	Floors
1	2	3	4	5	6	7	8	9	10

Kind of use					If shop: sort of articles sold	Whether the house (building, floor or room) is used by the owner	Whether the owner is		Occupied or Vacant		Remarks
Residence	Shop	Ware-house	Stable	Other			Government	Private	Occupied	Vacant	
11	12	13	14	15	16	17	18	19	20	21	22

G. *Printing and Supply of Forms*

57. The New Enumeration Book:—While the training of the census staff was going on, the central office was getting feverishly busy with the work of printing and supply of forms. The chief form was the Enumeration Book in respect of which the only material innovation which we undertook to introduce and carry out was the devising of a form by which we could do away with the necessity of slip-copying altogether after the final census was taken. Quite early it struck me after taking charge, that it was possible for a compact and organised census unit like Baroda to do away with the delaying and wasteful intermediate process of slip copying. In 1921, the Sex enquiry was carried out by means of books of perforated slips which were sent out to the mahals and got back therefrom duly filled in, cut up into slips and then sorted in the usual way for tabulating results. No particular difficulty was experienced and the slips were received intact and no material was lost in the process of sorting. The system required of course constant supervision and very rigorous control over the mahal agency. But on the other hand it meant a large saving in the cost of establishment which, considering the high cost of the Baroda Census, was a vital consideration. In the subsequent paragraphs it will be detailed how the new system was introduced and what special steps were taken to see that the enumeration books were returned from the mahals, in the same condition as they had been sent.

58. The Paramount System: Why it was Rejected.—Early in the course of my investigations for some method to do away with the necessity of slip-copying, the Paramount System of coding and open-punching was pointed out to me as the most efficient method of dealing with the problem. The system involves the printing in England of books of cards—each card containing the standard items of enquiry in the centre with the outside margin containing holes—each hole containing a number on which the information contained on the card is to be coded. After this very laborious process is gone through the cards are sorted by a needle and the process of sorting was found thenceforward to be exceedingly rapid. A sample card as prepared to suit our local requirements and with the object of reducing coding to a minimum is given in the margin.

SPECIMEN CARD DEVISED

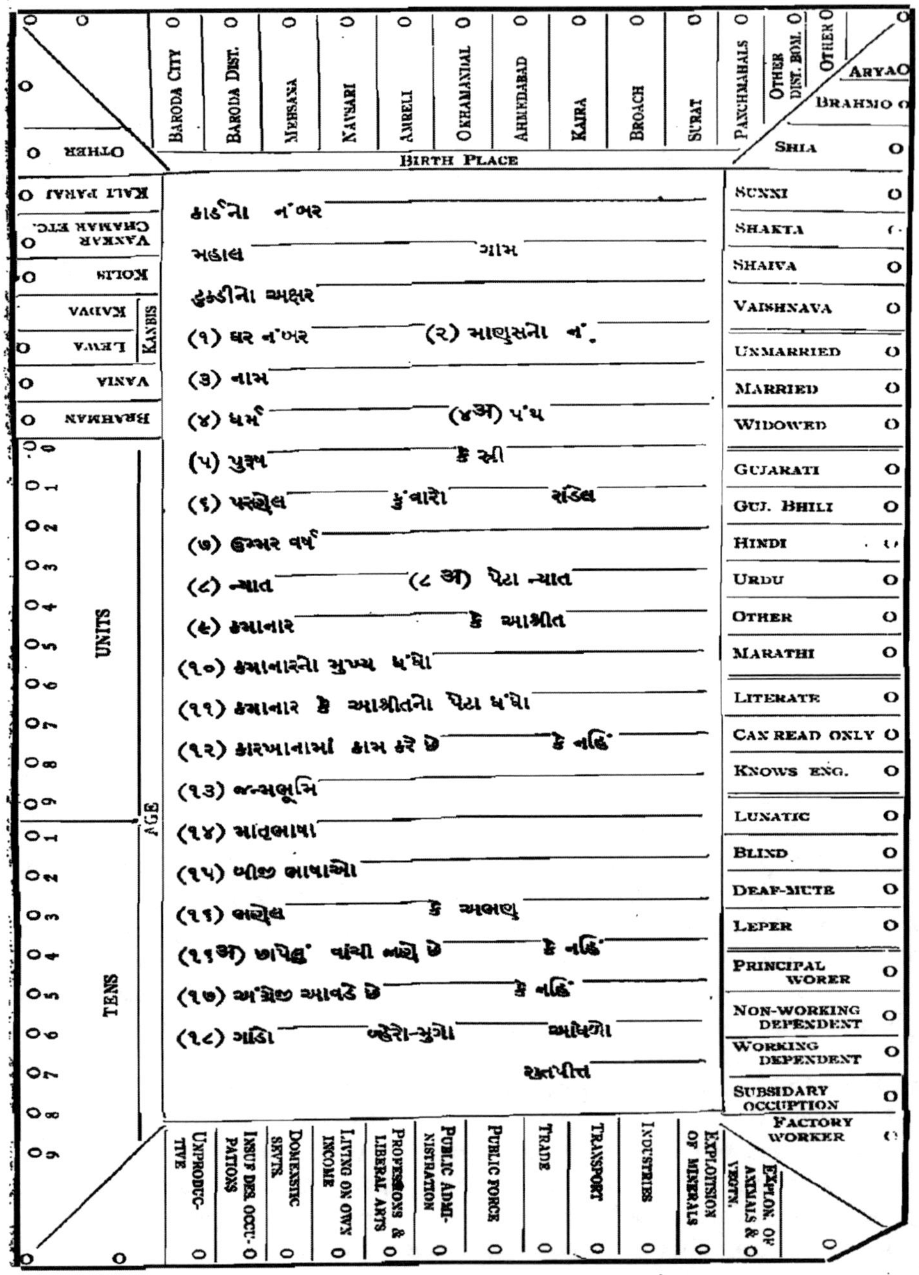

The Census Commissioner for India in his letter of 25th July 1930, recommended this system to us, leaving us to our option to adopt it, while he approved of our plan to dispense with slip-copying altogether. We gave to this experiment very anxious consideration but found that, interesting as it was, it did not economise either in time or money. For a population of 2·5 millions, it required at least 25 *coders* to finish the work of coding in over four months. Then there was the time necessary for undressing the enumeration books and cutting out the perforated cards—which would take also many laborious days; it was only after all these preliminary processes that sorting could be begun by the mechanical process; as to sorting, it must be observed that quite extravagent claims were made on its behalf by the local agent of the Copeland Chatterson, Co. who were the authors of the system. In my letter to the Census Commissioner for India (No. 144 dated the 29th July 1930) I pointed out that if this system was adopted, there would be no advantage in point of time as against the old process of slip copying. "We finish our slip copying in less than 2 months and our final results are out by that time. It is true that the later stage of sorting with a hand ticket and a needle will require much less time than crude sorting by hand. But even then, this appreciable saving in time is more than made up for by the time taken in coding." As the Census Commissioner himself pointed out in his letter No. 35 Enmn. dated 25th July 1930, "the question seems to resolve itself into the cost of cards and cost of coding and whether in view of these two items the system can be worked more cheaply or as cheaply as the present system." In my reply aforesaid, I pointed out that the cost of coding and printing of 2·5 million cards (according to the local agents' figures) would come to Rs. 17,500, the cost of covers and instruction pages being extra. We estimated a net saving of Rs. 13,058 by the adoption of enumeration slip books, with sorting by hand. By adopting the copeland process all this saving in money would be wiped off and there would besides be no saving in time. We finally decided therefore on the direct recording of details on to slips with subsequent sorting by hand. The Census Commissioner agreed to this arrangement in his letter of 25th July above referred to and remarked "I think the idea which you propose to bring into practice is a good one, and I shall be very much interested to know the result of carrying it out and should be very grateful for a comparative estimate of its cost as compared with that of the old system with a view to possible experiments of the same kind in British India. I do not see that the objection, which you suggest, that the slip books may be lost refers to any danger greater than that which the enumeration books undergo under the present system."

59. The Enumeration Slip Book.—The Enumeration Book was to consist of cards—three to a page—each being 7¼″ by 3½″ in size; thus a ream of paper of the size of 22″ by 29″ would produce 11,520 cards. The following is the exact reproduction of the card, for male and female persons respectively:—

1

CARD FOR MALES

1 Serial No.______of person
2 Mahal______Village______
3 Circle____Block No.____House No.____
4 Name______
5 Religion (with sect)______
6 Married____Unmarried____or Widowed____
7 Age (in years only)______
8 Caste, tribe or race (with sub-caste)
9 Whether earner—working dependent—or total dependent—
10 Principal occupation of earner______
11 Subsidiary occupation of earner; or occupation of working dependent
12 Industry in which employed (if any)
13 Birth District______
14 Mother Tongue______
15 Other languages ordinarily used
16 Whether literate or not______If literate whether in Hindi______or Urdu______
16 (a) If not literate, whether able to read only____
17 Whether literate in English or not
18 Whether insane______totally blind______ deaf-mute______or leper______

1

CARD FOR FEMALE

1 Serial No______of person
2 Mahal______Village______
3 Circle____Block No.____House No.____
4 Name______
5 Religion (with sect)______
6 Married____Unmarried____or Widowed____
7 Age (in years only)______
8 Caste, tribe or race (with sub-caste)
9 Whether earner—working dependent—or total dependent
10 Principal occupation of earner______
11 Subsidiary occupation of earner, or occupation of working dependent
12 Industry in which employed (if any)
13 Birth District______
14 Mother Tongue______
15 Other languages ordinarily used
16 Whether literate or not______If literate whether in Hindi______or Urdu______
16 (a) If not literate, whether able to read only
[illegible]

As the card shows there was no difficulty about sex—information regarding males being required to be entered on to white cards, and that in respect of females on to buff-coloured ones. The books of cards were printed in following sizes :—

Serial No.	Sizes of Books	No. of slips printed	
		In English	In Gujarati
	I. ORIGINALLY PRINTED		
1	Books containing 6 male and 6 female cards	...	...
2	" " 12 " and 12 " " ...	...	4,800
3	" " 24 " and 24 " " ...	6,480	14,400
4	" " 48 " and 45 " " ...	...	279,000
5	" " 72 " and 69 " " ...	...	282,000
6	" " 96 " and 90 " " ...	...	372,000
7	" " 120 " and 114 " " ...	...	585,000
8	" " 120 " and 120 " " ...	18,000	...
9	" " 144 " and 138 " " ...	...	846,000
			2,383,200
	II. SUPPLEMENTARY		
1	" " 6 " and 6 " " ...	...	60,000
2	" " 12 " and 12 " " ...	...	139,200
3	" " 24 " and 24 " " ...	...	33,600
4	" " 48 " and 45 " " ...	...	186,000
5	" " 12 male cards only	...	84,000
6	" " 12 female cards "	...	84,000
7	" " 6 male cards only	...	18,000
8	" " 6 female " "	...	18,000
			622,800
	Total	24,480	3,006,000

The above is the total no. of slips printed, but only 2,983,179 slips were issued to the different divisions. Of these, only 2,548,790 were used. This figure differs from the actual population of 2,443,007 persons returned on the Census day, and tne difference of 105,783 represents wholly the movement of population between the first count and the final enumeration. These rejected slips must also be reckoned in, in order to arrive at a true estimate of wastage in the matter of enumeration books of slips.

Divided according to districts as shown in the margin, we see the largest proportion of wastage in slips occurring in Okhamandal and the least in Baroda City. One reason for this was that in the City, the total number of persons residing in each house having already been entered in the house lists at the time of house numbering, our estimates of slips required were not greatly in excess of the truth. In Okhamandal, Dwarka and Beyt being pilgrim places, an influx of pilgrims was always expected, and the demands of local officers for slips had to be considerably in excess of actual requirements. In Baroda and Navsari, the factor of *hijratis* (political immigrants from British districts who had taken temporary shelter within this State on account of the civil disobedience movement) had to be taken into account. Very exaggerated notions were entertained by the public and even by local officers, who ought to have known better,of the volume of these immigrants. Something like a total of over a lac of immigrants were supposed to have come over. As it is, the total number now found was 26,755. The Naib Suba of Petlad wrote in an alarmist fashion of rumours of wholesale immigration on Census day, for which reason he asked that a large number of slips should be sent to the Vahivatdars of his mahals for being kept in reserve. Similar fears were expressed by local officials in Navsari too. In consequence, large numbers of supplementary books of slips were printed off at a rush and sent to the mahals which had to deal with this kind of immigration. Again in certain other places, our estimates of slips required from the corrected return of houses were somewhat in excess of the truth, because these estimates were generally based on totals of inhabited houses numbered, and not on the actual number of inhabitants. In Amreli, the enumerating staff was not very efficiently organised or trained. In consequence, a large number of slips were rejected and the work had to be revised and recopied in some places.

Number of slips supplied and used			
Name of Division	Total No. of slips supplied	Total No. used (i. e. actual population as well as slips cancelled at final count)	Proportion of wastage
Baroda City	129,316	116,530	10·9
Amreli Division	215,172	183,537	17·2
Baroda „	877,239	743,658	17·9
Mehsana „	1,243,500	1051,194	18·3
Navsari „	477,534	421,978	13·1
Okhamandal	40,419	31,893	26·7
Total ...	2,983,179	2548,790	17·1

60. **Difficulties in respect of Paper for the Slips.**—The above remark in para 58 of the Census Commissioner, about the cost of cards leads us to the consideration of the most important difficulty with which we had to deal, namely the procuring of paper of sufficient thickness for our purpose. We took very early steps to get an adequate supply of paper for our cards as soon as we decided on the adoption of the new system. On the 29th July 1930, the Census Department placed an order with the State Government Printing Press to supply super-royal unglazed paper of 22″ x 29″ size necessary for printing about 2·5 million slips. Quotations were therefore asked for by the Press; those quoted by the Bombay Stationery Mart being the lowest, the order was placed with that firm for 210 reams of 22″ x 29″ paper of 72 lbs. at Rs. 0–3–9 per lb; the stock was to be supplied within 8 to 10 weeks of the date of receipt of the order (i. e. from 7th August 1930). Subsequently as it was decided to have different coloured slips for females, on the 5th September 1930, the Press was required to

supply 100 reams out of the 210 ordered either in buff or green colour. The Bombay firm agreed to do this. An additional supply of 10 white and 10 buff coloured reams was also ordered out on the 27th September 1930. By about the middle of October, the paper had not arrived, and the department getting anxious sent urgent reminders. By about the first week of November it became apparent that the contract could not be fulfilled; and as any further delay was fatal, the Government Press was instructed on the 15th November to cancel the contract and get the required amount of paper of the same, or of similar size and weight, from other Bombay firms against the contractor. The Manager of the Press and the Assistant Census Commissioner were specially sent to Bombay for the purchase of the stock. On the 19th November the Bombay Stationery Mart definitely informed us of their inability to fulfil the contract. The following kinds of paper were bought eventually from the different firms :—

(i) *White Paper.*—

(a) from Bombay Stationery Mart:
60 reams (60 lbs.) } Size
28 reams (54 lbs.) } 22″×29″

(b) from Allibhai Akbaralli } Size
51 reams (54 lbs..) } 22″×29″

(ii) *Kraft Paper.*—

(a) from Asok Brothers:—
67 reams (80 lbs.) which is equivallent to 134 reams of 22″×29″ size. } Size 44″×29″

The white paper was utilised for unemployment slip books and the kraft paper was also used, for covers of 47,000 enumeration books including supplementary books and 500 English books.

61. Distribution of Enumeration Books.—The paper as soon as received was rushed through the Press, and within an incredibly short time, enumeration books were ready for distribution to the talukas. Baroda City and Mahal being the nearest were dealt with first; the clerks from the rest of the mahals were specially called and given charge of books. Bhimkatta and Beyt being single towns, books concerning them were sent by post. How the distribution within the mahal was to be made was carefully explained to each mahal; and between the 15th and 23rd December 1930, the distribution was completed throughout the state:—

15-12-1930	16-12-1930	17-12-1930	18-12-1930	19-12-1930	20-12-1930
1 Karjan	7 Petlad	11 Mahuva	19 Vijapur	25 Kheralu	31 Amreli
2 Padra	8 Sinor	12 Palsana	20 Dehgam	26 Visnagar	32 Dhari
3 Vaghodia	9 Savli	13 Mangrol	21 Atarsumba	27 Harij	33 Damnagar
4 Bhadran	10 Tilakwada	14 Vyara	22 Kadi	28 Chanasma	34 Khambba
5 Sankheda		15 Gandevi	23 Mehsana	29 Sidhpur	
6 Dabhoi		16 Navsari	24 Kalol	30 Patan	23-12-1930
		17 Kamrej			35 Dwarka
		18 Songadh			36 Kodinar
					37 Ratanpur

62. Precautions re: Despatch and Return of Enumeration Books.—As the enumeration books were the only material available for subsequent tabulation and compilation of results, unusual precautions were taken so that not one slip was lost. They were as follows :—

(a) Every slip had a printed number which was serial for each sex in each book and every enumeration book both of the original and of the supplementary series, had a serial number.

(b) A very elaborate Distribution Register was kept in the Central Office of which a sample extract for Baroda City is given here for guidance :—

Name of Mahal	6+6* Serial No. or books	Total No. of books	12+12* Serial No. of books	Total No. of books	24+24* Serial No. of books	Total No. of books	48+45* Serial No. of books	Total No. of books.
1	2	3	4	5	6	7	8	9
Baroda City	...	...	12,604 to 12,613	10	12,001 to 12,014	14	1 to 46	46
	...	...	...	...	12,029	1	2,351 to 2,360	10
	...	...	...	...	...	...	2,799 to 2,821	23

Name of Mahal	72+69* Serial No. of books.	Total No. of books.	96+90* Serial No. of books.	Total No. of books.	120+114* Serial No. of books.	Total No. of books.	144+138* Serial No. of books.	Total No. of books.
1	10	11	12	13	14	15	16	17
Baroda City	3,001 to 3,099	99	5,001 to 5,126	26	7,001 to 7,132	132	9,001 to 9,109	109
	4,985 to 4,986	2	...	...	...	...	...	...
	...	...	...	...	...	...	...	...

6+6, 12+12 etc. denote the number of male and female slips in each book.

In the above form of 17 columns, against each class of book, the number of books supplied was shown; thus 10 books containing each 12 slips for males and 12 for females were given; and the serial numbers printed on the books were shown also in the Register, so that a missing book and even a missing slip could at once be traced and responsibility for the loss could at once be affixed.

(c) In addition to the above, a distribution register for each charge by circles was devised under which books containing a particular number of slips were supplied for blocks of corresponding sizes. The following was the standard laid down :—

Size of Block	No. of slips required	
	Male	Female
1 For blocks with less than 5 inhabited houses	12	12
2 For blocks having upto 10 inhabited houses	24	24
3 For blocks having 10 to 30 inhabited houses	48	45
4 For blocks having 30 to 40 inhabited houses	72	69
5 For blocks having 40 to 50 inhabited houses	96	90
6 For blocks having 50 to 60 inhabited houses	120	114
7 For blocks having 60 inhabited houses and upwards ...	144	138

(d) On the above basis, each mahal had to prepare a circle distribution register of which the following is a sample:—

Name of Circle letter	Serial number of block containing inhabited houses							
	1 to 4	5 to 9	10 to 29	30 to 39	40 to 49	50 to 59	60 houses and upwards	Total
	...	...	(2)	(1)	(4)	(7)	(5)	5
			(3)		(9)		(6)	3
					(10)		(8)	2
Total No. of Blocks in Circle	...	...	2	1	3	1	3	10

In addition, the mahal kept a register showing per each block the serial numbers of enumeration books supplied.

(e) When the books were sent to a Mahal, each bundle had a covering letter containing detailed instructions as to how the distribution per block was to be made and also in that letter, a list was made of the number and kind of books sent as could be provisionally estimated from the size of blocks contained in the Circle Summary (Form No. 7) which the mahals had already spplied. A sample list is shown as follows :—

Serial No.	No. of slips contained in books sent			Total No. of books	From what serial number to what serial number of books sent	
	Male slips	Female slips	Total		With instruction covers	Without instruction covers
1	2	3	4	5	6	7
1	6	6	12	5	13,071–5	...
2	12	12	24	10	12,990–12,999	...
3	24	24	48	15	15,410–15,419	6,105–6,109
4	48	45	93	35	10,347–10,382	...
5	72	69	141	27	3,490–3,517	...
etc.						

(f) At the end of this covering letter was a receipt, which the mahal Charge Superintendent had to sign and send back indicating that he had received charge of the exact number of books and slips as sent. He had similarly to take a receipt from each enumerator for the number of books and slips which had been consigned to him. For this purpose a book of receipts with counterfoils was given to each mahal of the following form:-

श्री.	श्री.
टीप:–गणत्री करनारने गणत्री बुक आप्या पछी आ नमुना प्रमाणे पहोंच लेवी; अने एवी एकंदर तमाम पहोंचो जथा टुकडीना अनुक्रमवार गोठवी चार्ज सुपरिन्टेन्डन्टे बांधी राखवी.	टीप:–गणत्री करनारने गणत्री बुक आप्या पछी आ नमुना प्रमाणे पहोंच लेवी; अने एवी एकंदर तमाम पहोंचो जथा टुकडीना अनुक्रमवार गोठवी चार्ज सुपरिन्टेन्डन्टे बांधी राखवी.
थाणे मोजे कस्बे टुकडीनो अक्षर जथा अंक ने माटे गणत्री बुक अंक कुल स्लीपो (पुरुषनी स्त्रीनी) वाळी मने पहोंची छे.. ता. माहे जानेवारी सने १९३१ गणत्री करनारनी सही.	थाणे मोजे कस्बे टुकडीनो अक्षर जथा अंक ने माटे गणत्री बुक अंक कुल स्लीपो (पुरुषनी स्त्रीनी) वाळी मने पहोंची छे. ता. माहे जानेवारी सने १९३१ गणत्री करनारनी सही.

(g) After the final enumeration, the charge superintendents had to show in the circle summary of provisional totals the serial numbers of enumeration books for each block:—

Circle Summary

Prant__________ Mahal__________ Thana__________ Circle__________

Serial No. as shown in Form No.7	Name of village or ward and moholla of town	Serial No. of Slip books	Serial No. of Block	No. of inhabited houses	Population		
					Persons	Male	Female
1	2	3	4	5	6	7	8

(h) Then when the enumeration books were to be returned to the Central Office for tabulation, it was provided that a clerk from the mahal should be detailed with the circle distribution register so that each book as sent to the mahal was to be verified as being intact and properly returned.

63. Other Forms.—The enumeration books altogether contained 24,480 English and 3,006,000 Gujarati slips. The other parts of an enumeration book were (a) covers with instructions, (b) covers without instructions, (c) instruction pages and (d) specimen slip pages; besides the enumeration books, we had to have

(i) house hold enumeration books with covers,
(ii) travellers' passes,
(iii) sex enquiry books of two sizes–one containing 42 slips and another, with 84 slips,
(iv) block lists,
(v) books of unemployment slips each containing 12 slips–4 to a page with a cover of instructions,
(vi) sex enquiry *parwanas*,
(vii) circle and charge summaries, and
(viii) schedules for census of livestock and classification of homesteads (Form 6 A – *vide* para 54)

The following table gives the details of the forms printed under each of the above heads :–

Serial No.	Name of Form	English	Gujarati	Total
1	2	3	4	5
1	Enumeration Book Covers			
	(a) with instructions	250	13,000	13,250
	(b) without instructions	250	33,500	33,750
2	Instruction pages	210	13,000	13,210
3	Specimen slip pages	420	26,000	26,420
4	Household Enumeration Covers	100	...	100
5	Travellers' passes	...	31,000	31,000
6	Block lists (House lists)	450	80,000	80,450
7	Number of slips contained in enumeration books	24,480	3,006,000	3,030,480
8	Total number of enumeration books ...	210	46,500	46,710
9	Books of Unemployment slips each containing four slips to a page	...	8,000	8,000
10	Sex Enquiry Books ...			
	(a) each containing 42 slips	100	3,500	3,600
	(b) each containing 84 slips	...	2,500	2,500
	Total number of slips	4,200	3,57,000	361,200
11	Sex Enquiry Parwanas	...	5,000	5,000
12	Circle summaries	120	3,000	3,120
13	Charge summaries	...	500	500
14	Census of Livestock forms combined with block lists	1,000	30,000	31,000

H. Preliminary Record

64. Preparation for Preliminary Record.—As pointed out in para 61 above, the distribution of enumeration books to all the mahals was completed by about the 24th December 1930, and the preliminary count was not to start in the villages till the 15th January and in the towns till the 25th. Thus there remained a clear period of from three weeks to a month for the enumerating and supervising staff to be put through our intensive course of training. The steps taken by the Central Office in this direction have been already detailed; Mahal Charge Superintendents now held classes of their census staff in different centres in their talukas and in other ways tried their best to keep themselves abreast in census matters. Some of the sub-divisional officers were very zealous, but their uninstructed zeal in some places was somewhat embarassing to the Census Department. The district officers generally kept aloof at this stage; perhaps this was as well, as it has been always the policy of the State Census executive to centralise the direction of these operations in their hands. But it would be better for census work in future if the District Officers took the trouble of making themselves more instructed in census matters. One or two were undoubtedly helpful, in the matter of supplying notes of their impressions on demographic changes in their districts in the last decade. One or two others were prevented by the pressure of other urgent work to attend to details of census work. But it was surely inexcusable on the part of one Suba to show complete ignorance of the fact that a census of the educated unemployed was being taken along with the general census, or that an enquiry into the Size and Sex Constitution of Families was actually in progress. Ignorance in such matters showed an incapacity to appreciate matters beyond their desk routine which was unforgiveable in a Suba. I am forced to put these impressions on record, as they are strengthened by the experience of two censuses. It is hoped that District Officers will take in future a more enlightened view of their responsibilities.

65. The Census Conference at Delhi.—The most memorable event for the local census organisation was the calling of the Conference of Census Superintendents of Provinces and Commissioners of Indian States at Delhi on the 7th and 8th January 1931. I received the invitation of the Census Commissioner for India on the 20th November and I at once replied stating my full desire to cooperate in this matter. I proceeded to Delhi on the 5th January accompanied by my Personal Assistant. The Census Commissioner received us with the most distinguished consideration. We had a most fruitful three days of conversations and conferences. The formal Conference was held in Old Delhi on the 7th January and lasted for full two days. In addition, Dr. and Mrs. Hutton were most hospitable to all of us. Appendix D gives the whole proceedings of the Conference in full, corrected so far as my part is concerned. During the conference, the part taken by the Baroda Census in many matters, especially in regard to the Sex Enquiry, and the new system of the Enumeration Book drew much attention, and the Census Commissioner for India was pleased to refer other Superintendents of Census Operations to me for consultation and advice. Mr. Porter of Bengal, and Col. Cole of Rajputana were much interested in the enumeration slip book. As a result of the conference, which was unique within my experience in the Indian Census, a note of instructions was issued by the Census Commissioner of India for our use; it is hereby reproduced in full:—

" **Tabulation of castes.**—All castes of 2 per mille and upwards should be tabulated in each province of British India. Castes with a lower figure should be tabulated if for any reason they are of particular interest or importance.

" A list of castes required for all India purposes will be circulated and figures will be required for these castes, whether tabulated provincially or not.

" **Classification of new Castes.**—Many castes will be returned at this census under new names. Where it is merely a new name for a complete caste the name adopted by the caste as a whole may be given first in Table XXIII (new

Table No. XVII) with others, including the terms necessary for reference to previous figures, after it in brackets.

" Where the new caste name represents, as it will do in some cases this time, a consolidation of castes which appeared separately under different names last time, a reference will be necessary to show the separate groups of previous decades now combined under one new title.

" **Muslim Hindus.**—There are certain number of castes which it is difficult to classify definitely as either Muslims or Hindus. Where the Superintendent of Census Operations is unable to decide that they belong definitely to one or other category they should be excluded from both and returned under " other religions " and mention made of their numbers and religious practices in the report.

" **Earner and Dependent.**—Women and Children should not be shown as earners unless they actually receive wages in cash or in kind. This was made sufficiently clear in the instructions issued by me last year. The fact that child is a member of a joint family should not be held to constitute him an earner.

" The subsidiary occupation of dependents was never intended to be determined by the occupation of the person on whom they are dependent but by the work actually performed by them. The misunderstanding which has led to this mistake can only arise in the case of agriculture, and can be adjusted in the published tables by transferring female and child dependents shown as cultivating owners, etc., to the correct heading, *viz.*, agricultural labourer. This should be done in all cases where the adjustment is possible.

" **Backward classes and Illiterates.**—For the purposes of the Census of India I intend at present to retain the term Depressed classes to indicate untouchables, whether of the milder or more severe degree of untouchability. I have no objection to Provincial Superintendents using better terms if they can find or coin them.

" As regards the classification of castes into Advanced, Intermediate and Illiterate I propose to base them on a purely percentage scale. Three parallel lists may be made for each province based on Provincial Table II (*vide* Bombay Census Report 1921, Part II page ix) and including in the first column all castes which have more than 50 per cent of literates and in the third all those which have less than 10 per cent of the same, while those from 10 per cent to 50 per cent inclusive go to the middle column. If necessary the return " caste unspecified " may be treated as a specific unit for the purposes of these lists; in the Punjab the numbers who return no caste may be considerable.

" **Record of tribal religions.**—The discussion may be referred to. Generally speaking the best plan will be to show as tribals those who inhabit really jungly or inaccessible regions.

" **Religion of Chuhras.**—See Punjab Tribes and Castes, Volume I pages 182–sqq. Some of the Chuhras claim Rajput origin. Some even a Brahman origin and some a Muslim origin. Others apparently ascribe the caste to a Bhil origin. Generally speaking the caste is coloured by Hinduism, and uses degraded Brahmans as priests.

" **Organised Industry.**—The minimum number of persons required to constitute a case of organised industry is 3–one paying the wage and two others working for wages simultaneously. But this minimum will only apply when the wage payer is also working himself. If he does not work then one wage payer and three work men is the minimum under the definition already given. It is left to Superintendents of Census Operations to fix a higher minimum in accordance with local conditions if they are able and wishful to do so, but as there is no separate return of factories at this census the fixation of a higher minimum number of workers to constitute organised industry will involve special provisions.

" **Definition of European and Anglo-Indian.**—The following difinition may be taken for practical purposes in such cases as call for the use of any definition:–

An European is a person of pure European descent on both sides.

An Anglo–Indian is a person whose father, grand–father or other progenitor in the male line was an European.

Admittedly these definitions are faulty in some respects and cases will occur in which it would be difficult to apply them but they will cover the great majority of cases and will serve for census purposes.

The Feringhis of East Bengal and the East Indians of Bombay should be regarded an exception in so far as they appear to be Anglo-Indians by the above test. They should be returned as Indian Christians.

" **Natural Divisions.**—The use of Natural Divisions by which statistics of density of population were shown last census will be retained for that purpose in Provinces and States. Agencies dealing with a number of States should deal with density figures by States, but may disregard natural divisions which do not coincide with State boundaries if they desire to do so."

66. Objections in above instructions.—In regard to these instructions, objections were respectfully urged to two of the items included above. In the first place it was pointed out that the course suggested in respect of working dependents that the work in which they were occupied should have no relation to the occupation of the head of the family was open to the gravest objections. Working dependents whatever may be the form of their assistance to the head of the family should be placed in the same category as these latter. For instance, as to agriculture, if the earner was a cultivating owner, his wife merely because she helps him should not be classed with agricultural labourers, because an agricultural labourer was differentiated from other grades of agriculture, by his receipt of wages and by the fact that he does not occupy the land. It was further urged in respect of agricultural labour that properly speaking there should be no working dependents under this head, as all these working as agricultural labourers, would be ordinarily in receipt of wages and therefore shown as earners: and that if working dependents of cultivating tenants were shown under agricultural labour, a wholly false view of agricultural groupings would result. The second point that was urged by me in regard to these instructions was about the percentage scale fixed for backward classes and illiterates. It was pointed out that this scale was based on male literacy and was adopted at my instance from the Baroda Census report of 1921. In answer to my letter No. 433 of the 2nd February 1931, in which I put forward the above objections, the Census Commissioner in his reply of the 5th February (No. 33–Genl.) was pleased to agree to my second point about literacy; in regard to the first point, he held a contrary view but was good enough to let me have my interpretation provided I arranged the figures in such a form that they could be rearranged for the all–India report, and that in stating them in my own form, I was to draw attention in a footnote or otherwise to the different arrangement adopted.

67. The *Hijrati* question : the Bombay Superintendent's Request and its Sequel.—One other important point that cropped up about this time has to be noticed. As I pointed out in para 59 above, while discussing the wastage of slips, there were very hazy notions as to the extent of political immigration with which this State was afflicted due to the civil disobedience movement in British India. As these political immigrants began coming in towards the end of the house numbering period,–and even at the stage of the corrected return of houses, it could not be stated definitely what their number was. Probably influenced by a somewhat exaggerated estimate of the number of these people, Mr. Dracup, Provincial Superintendent of Census Operations of Bombay, wrote to me suggesting that in those villages of the State where immigrants from the British territory had temporarily built *mandwas* on account of the civil disobedience movement, we should exclude the figures of such persons enumerated from our totals, and hand over the enumeration books, etc. to him to be included in his own district totals. To this procedure, I stated my objections, in the first place because the Census was not of the *de jure* population, but of the actual number of persons residing in the State on the census date; secondly because the collection of such books and making up of special totals would unduly delay the despatch of provisional totals; thirdly because, it was neither necessary nor desirable to single out this special form of political immigration from other kinds of migration; and lastly because I thought that the movement was rapidly subsiding and that such a special step of excluding these immigrants from the enumerated totals—unknown to previous censuses—would bring down on us justifiable comment which we should avoid. Along with my objections, I assured Mr. Dracup however of my fullest co-operation about giving him figures of such immigrants per village and sex and even of their distribution by chief castes. I am glad to say that the Census Commissioner in his letter of the 12th February upheld my objections. In order to arrive at an accurate estimate of these immigrants I issued most elaborate instructions. Such immigrants were to be divided into 3 classes (a) those that came over to village sites and lived in hired houses or as guests with resident families within our towns and villages, (b) those that came over to village sites and built temporary hutments for their residence; and (c) those that squatted on *sim* lands and built themselves temporary leaf huts or *mandwas* for their temporary stay. During the preliminary count, every slip of such immigrant was to be marked out "ही" or हीजरती and the name of the village from which the person came was to be recorded if possible. On the final day, these slips were to be carefully revised and an estimate of their number by sex and their distribution by chief castes per village was to be made by the mahal charge superintendents. These instructions were carefully followed. Wherever there seemed the least possibility of an error, the lists were got revised through personal inspection and actual recount. At the tabulation stage, we will see how these estimates were subjected to further scrutiny and drawn up into tables.

68. Common Errors noticed in the Preliminary Record.—We return to our account of the general operations. My assistant and myself began our third Census tour and were travelling continuously from January till the middle of February. In the course of our inspections the commonest errors noticed were in regard to religion, caste and occupation. In this State, sects were recorded along with religions, and enumerators were often found negligent in this regard. In regard to caste and occupation, the most stringent warnings were issued so that vague entries might be avoided. Even then in many cases, gross negligence was seen and promptly punished. In this census however, as in the bulk of the entries, a simple tick or cross was necessary, the work was found much easier than in previous censuses. A large number of enumerators had experience of previous censuses, and it stood them in good stead. Occasionally however the tendency to indulge in perverse humour could not be resisted. For instance as to civil condition, a man was entered both as married and widowed, and when taxed about the entry, the enumerator gave out as the reason that as the man was twice married, he must have been widowed first and married a second time. A propagandist in teetotalism in another place entered a Muslim dealer in foreign wines as a christian because he could not think that a follower of the true religion could deal in such vile stuff ! More genuine and pardonable types of mistakes were in connection with "working dependent", the meaning of which was not clear to many. But on the whole my verdict is, after experience of two censuses, as that of Mr. Maganlal, the Assistant Census Commissioner, after three censuses, that the work was better and more neatly done in 1931, than ever before. The proportion of errors was very much less and the eagerness to vie with each other to turn out good work was keener than I had noticed on the previous occasion.

69. The Scheme of Prizes for good work.—One reason for this keenness of competition was due to the fact that the scheme of cash prizes to be distributed to the Census staff to the amount of Rs. 4,000 which was sanctioned by the Council at my instance (*vide* C. O. No. 1/1 dated the 23rd August 1930) was advertised well in advance of the preliminarycount. These prizes together with certificates of merit were most powerful incentives to good work to all ranks of the census agency from the charge superitendents down to the humble enumerators. The following scheme of prizes as finally revised by me was sanctioned:—

Name of Census Staff	No. of prizes	Value of each prize	Total amount
Mahal Charge Superintendents		Rs.	Rs.
(i) First prize	6	30	180
(ii) Second prize	9	15	135
Mahal office clerks	9	10	90
Municipal staff	3	10	30
Supervisors	31	10	310
Sex inquiry workers (women) ...			
(i) First prize	1	8	8
(ii) Second prize	9	6	54
(iii) Third prize	47	4	188
Enumerators			
(i) First prize	30	8	240
(ii) Second prize	553	5	2,765
Total ...	698		4,000

70. All Transfers Stopped.—In order that there might be no dislocation of arrangements or sudden loss of trained men from any place, it was ordered (*vide* C. O. Census No. 5/2 dated the 4th October 1930) that all transfers of census officers of and below the rank of charge superintendents should be stopped with effect from the 1st January 1931 till the end of February 1931. This order was operative on all departments, as all local offices of the different departments of State were requisitioned for census work. Everywhere heads of departments co-operated. Occasionally local officers here and there interpreted the Council Order as giving them a license to transfer their subordinates *before the 1st January*. As soon as this was pointed out to me, I issued a very strict warning to all such district officers, who were told that any such attempt to forestall the Council Order would be frustrated. (*vide* my confidential note No. 256 dated the 24th November 1930).

71. Appointment of Census Inspectors :—*In addition to these measures* devised to secure efficiency of the census staff, a further step was taken on this occasion to appoint a staff of census inspectors and to allocate to them specified talukas where they would be continually on the move, inspecting census books, correcting mistakes and generally keeping the enumerators and supervisors up to the mark. In view of the large saving we were hoping to effect by doing away with slip copying after the census, we thought a part of this saving could be well utilized in this way. The idea of having a staff of travelling census inspectors, independant of the ex-officio district staff is not new. The U. P. Census tried it with great effect in 1911 and recommended it continuance in their administration report. The marginally noted establishment was entertained from the 1st January. They were to report themselves at once to the charge superintendents concerned, and their tour programme was to be under their control and supervision. While on tour, they were to be given every help from the local talatis and patels. The persons selected for these appointments were given an intensive preliminary training in the Central Office and they were subjected to a stiff test before they were sent out to the districts. As will appear from the margin, only Savli, Petlad and Bhadran talukas were not comprised in the scheme and the Personal Assistant and other staff from the Central Office were sent direct to these places for inspection. As to Okhamandal, the Assistant Census Commissioner was doing an intensive tour there about this time and no separate appointment was made. The experiment of these census inspectors succeeded very well, and I have no hesitation to recommend its continuance in future censuses.

CENSUS INSPECTORS

Names of Talukas	No. of appointments	Pay sanctioned.
		Rs.
City and Baroda Mahal...	1	90
Amreli Prant ...	1	60
Visnagar Vibhag ...	1	45
Songadh, Vyara, Kamrej.	1	50
Navsari, Gandevi, Palsana and Mahuva ...	1	40
Patan, Chansma, Harij and Mehsana ...	1	50
Kadi, Kalol, Dehgam and Atarsumba ...	1	40
Vaghodia, Dabhoi Sankheda and Tilakwada ...	1	40
Karjan, Sinor, and Padra.	1	40

72. Census Holidays.—Finally to enable the Census Department to utilise to the fullest extent the staff borrowed from other offices, 25th, 26th and 27th were declared to be public holidays, under D. O. Census No. 4/3 dated the 23rd September 1930, passed on the Census Tippan No. 3 dated the 15th September 1930.

I. The Final Count

73. Preparations for the Final Count: Stopping of Cinemas.—A few days before the final census day, (i. e., on the 10th February 1931) a proclamation was issued that the final count would take place on the 26th February between the hours of 7 p.m. and midnight and directing that as far as possible no one should leave his village or town on that day and that the head of the family should sit up waking and keep a lamp burning till the enumerator called and revised the preliminary record. As a further help towards eliminating disturbing factors, the District Magistrate of Baroda at my instance stopped the working of cinemas from 5 in the evening till 12 o'clock midnight on the 26th in the City of Baroda. On a representation from the Proprietors of Cinemas, this was modified by me to the extent that they were allowed to open their shows *after* nine in the evening.

74. Further Disturbing Factors eliminated.—The final census date selected was the 26th February and the selection was governed by the considera-tion that there would be moonlight on that day and that there should be the least disturbance possible from marriages, fairs and festivals on that date. There were three places in the State, however, where such disturbances could be anticipated and prompt steps were taken to prevent their occurence in all cases, except one.

(a) At Sidhpur town, a Tapodhan Brahman called Nanalal Gopalji suddenly took it into his head to celebrate a post-mortem dinner which would have ordinarily meant an influx of 600 hungry Brahmans for a lavish feed of *ladus* to Sidhpur. At Upera, another village in Sidhpur taluka, a similar influx of 200 persons was expected. At both these places, prompt instructions were issued to stop them from this office but these instructions were not properly understood. The Mehsana Suba office instead of taking magisterial action, filed the papers. The Vahivatdar did not also try to forestall these events and use his personal influence to postpone them. As a result, the feasts at Upera and Sidhpur did take place, but an endeavour was made to send back the invitees to their homes before evening. This was successful at Upera, where, however, 15 males and 5 females who were unavoidably detained had to be enumerated. At Sidhpur, block No. 3 of Circle ख was affected. Instead of 16 inhabited houses with a normal population of 70 persons, the figures were at the final count, 37 inhabited houses, and 299 persons (191 males, 108 females). The effect of this disturbance will be discussed in the Census Report. It was fortunate that the number was not larger.

(b) In Dehgam Taluka, it was reported that the Vankars of the neighbour-ing villages were proposing to meet for a caste feast at Magudi. As soon as this information was given by the Census Inspector, the Vahivatdar was given instruc-tions by wire to stop the dinner and if necessary, to take magisterial action. The Aval Karkun and the Fouzdar were at once instructed by the Charge Superinten-dent to advise the Vankars to desist from their proposed caste feast, and it was reported that the leaders of the caste agreed to take the advice and stop the feast.

(c) From Mahuva in Navsari prant, the Vahivatdar reported that a *hat-wada* (market) was proposed to be held by the Raniparaj of surrounding villages on census day. This was also stopped by beat of drum. The Suba, who had to be impressed with the paramountcy of census arrangements, finally co-operated by issuing a prohibitory order.

It may be remarked in conclusion that in future, such disturbing factors should be met by the Census Commissioner by using his full powers as Sar Suba (under the Police Act) and forbidding such *hats*, fairs or caste feasts, so that peo-ple may be prevented under penalties from going to such occasions.

75. The Census Day.—On the final day, arrangements were made by the Census office to help the City, Camp and Railway census authorities by recalling all their Census Inspectors and detailing their central office clerks to different wards for casting up the provisional results. I was continuously on the move myself, and my assistant and staff who were given a State car to move out, were also continuously at work the whole evening. Particular attention was paid on this day everywhere in the State to the censusing of jails and hospitals, *vishis* (hotels), *dharmashalas*, rest-houses and camping grounds, wherever stragglers and wayside travellers were likely to be found. Instructions were issued to the effect that all enumerators should take a round in their blocks during day time and bring the preliminary record to date by scoring out the entries for those who had died or gone away and were not likely to return by night-time on that day, and by enumerating those who may have newly arrived or been born. All municipalities and local bodies were further enjoined to help the census staff by supplying them with lamps and candles.

J. Special Enquiries at the time of Preliminary and Final counts

76. Normal Size of the Household.—As pointed in para 15 above, *an attempt was made at the preliminary count to estimate the normally resident* population in the State by entering in column 5 of the block list the number of persons in the household normally residing at the time. From this reckoning, guests or servants were excluded and the facts so disclosed were later tabulated into State Table XI (Normal Size of the Household). As pointed out already, this can very well be done at the time of house numbering, and an estimate, if taken at that time, would have enabled us to eliminate wastage in slips in enumeration books much more than we have been able to do.

77. The Census of the Educated Unemployed.—Another enquiry, which was special to this census was the collection of statistics along with the general census, of educated persons, who were unemployed or not suitably employed. The information was collected for all male persons who were returned as literate in English and who were without employment. Each such person had to have his particulars recorded on to a separate slip in which the following items were to be entered :—

(1) Residence (Village and District)
(2) House number
(3) Name
(4) Age (nearest birth day)
(5) Caste
(6) Father's profession
(7) How long without employment ?
(8) University if any: if foreign, name of country
(9) Degree or other examination with date
(10) If now employed at all, in what capacity
(11) Employment for which fitted by education.

Books containing 12 such slips (four to a page) were printed and broadcasted throughout the State. The fact that such a census was to be taken, was widely advertised and that public interest was roused, was evinced by the persistent efforts of a group of young students who were perpetually seeking to give advice to the department about how the thing was to be done. In the City of Baroda and in all other towns, such books were given to every enumerator, and in rural areas, each supervisor was given one such book. While on their rounds during the preliminary enumeration, each enumerator was instructed to mark every such case of educated unemployment on the slip concerning such person with the words "E. U." and enter details regarding him in the special unemployment slip book. It was hoped through clause 10 of the questionnaire to draw every case of unemployed persons who thought themselves unsuitably employed. Having regard to this circumstance, and also to the loudly voiced complaints in public discussions regarding unemployment it was thought that the volume of unemployment was large, and a total number of 8,000 slip books was printed. From the actual number, as shown in Imperial Table XII, it will be seen how grossly in excess of the actual returns our calculations were. In the Census Report, an attempt will be made to appraise the accuracy of the return.

APPENDIX A

Calendar of Census Operations

No.	Kind of Census Operation	Time
1	2	3
1	Preparation of general village register and census maps	Latest by the end of June 1930
2	Appointment of Charge Superintendents ...	Beginning of July
3	Formation of blocks and circles	Latest by the end of July
4	Charge Register (showing blocks and circles) to be sent to the Census Commissioner, Baroda ...	15–8–1930
5	Report of change if any in the area of Mahals and Peta Mahals	31–8–1930
6	House Numbering	To be begun from 23–10–30 and completed on 15–11–30
7	Preparation of House Lists	Same as above
8	Maps for circles and blocks	15–11–30
9	Corrected return of houses to be sent to the District Census Offices	22–11–30
10	Corrected returns of houses to be sent to the Census Commissioner, Baroda	30–11–30
11	Testing of house numbering	From its commencement till the Census day
12	Appointment of Supervisors both for preliminary and final enumerations	1–12–30
13	Appointment of enumerators both for preliminary and final Census	1–12–30
14	Supply of forms	December 1930
15	Training of census staff	From September 1930 till the middle of November 1930 for House Numbering and then till the end of January 1931 for preliminary and final enumerations
16	Preliminary enumeration	
	In Villages	15th January to 10th February, 1931
	In Towns	25th January to 10th February, 1931
17	Testing of preliminary record	From beginning of the preliminary record till the Census day (26th February 1931)
18	Final Enumeration	26th February 1931 from 7 p. m. till midnight
19	Enumeaators' abstract	As early as possible after midnight of the 26th February 1931 but not later than 3 a. m. of the following morning
20	Circle summary	Latest by the morning of the 27th February 1931
21	Charge summary	As early as possible on the 27th February 1931
22	Provisional totals to be telegraphed to the Census Commissioner, Baroda	As early as possible after the Census

N. B. The time limit must be very punctually observed. Dated 21st June 1930.

APPENDIX B

Analysis of Touring Before the Census

Month	Days travelled	Towns visited	Villages visited	Inspection of Census daftars	House-numbers examined	Census books examined	Sex Enquiry books examined	Meetings, conferences held and lectures given	Talks, deputations or representations met	Remarks
1	2	3	4	5	6	7	8	9	10	11
A.—by the Census Commissioner										
1930										
July ...	9	1	...	1	...	...	...	1	1	Visited Bombay and Poona
August ...	6	4	...	2	...	...	...	3	1	
September...	13	5	1	...	...	...	...	6	4	
October ...	19	6	5	2	530 (in 10 blocks)	...	...	9	...	Visited Jamnagar, Bhavnagar, and Junagadh
November ...	19	4	28	22 (10 house lists)	1,974 (in 70 blocks)	...	...	5	3	
December ...	19	6	15	7 (4 house lists)	3,757 (in 70 blocks)	...	33	5	...	
1931										
January ...	22	10	13	5 (2 house lists)	20 (in 1 block)	455	30	8	3	Visited Delhi
February ...	12	8	15	2	...	497	12	1	1	
TOTAL...	**119**	**44**	**77**	**41** (16 house lists)	**6,281** (in 151 blocks)	**952**	**75**	**38**	**13**	
B.—by the Assistant Census Commissioner										
1930										
July ...	2	1	...	...	...	...	...	...	2	
August ...	2	2	...	...	...	...	...	1	...	
September...	2	2	...	1	...	...	...	...	5	
October ...	3	1	...	1	...	...	...	1	...	
November ...	13	4	4	2	1,150	...	...	2	1	
December ...	18	12	2	13	3,750	...	...	12	...	
1931										
January ...	10	6	1	...	...	282	3	10	2	
February ...	17	7	3	...	...	212	9	...	2	
TOTAL...	**67**	**35**	**10**	**17**	**4,900**	**494**	**12**	**26**	**12**	

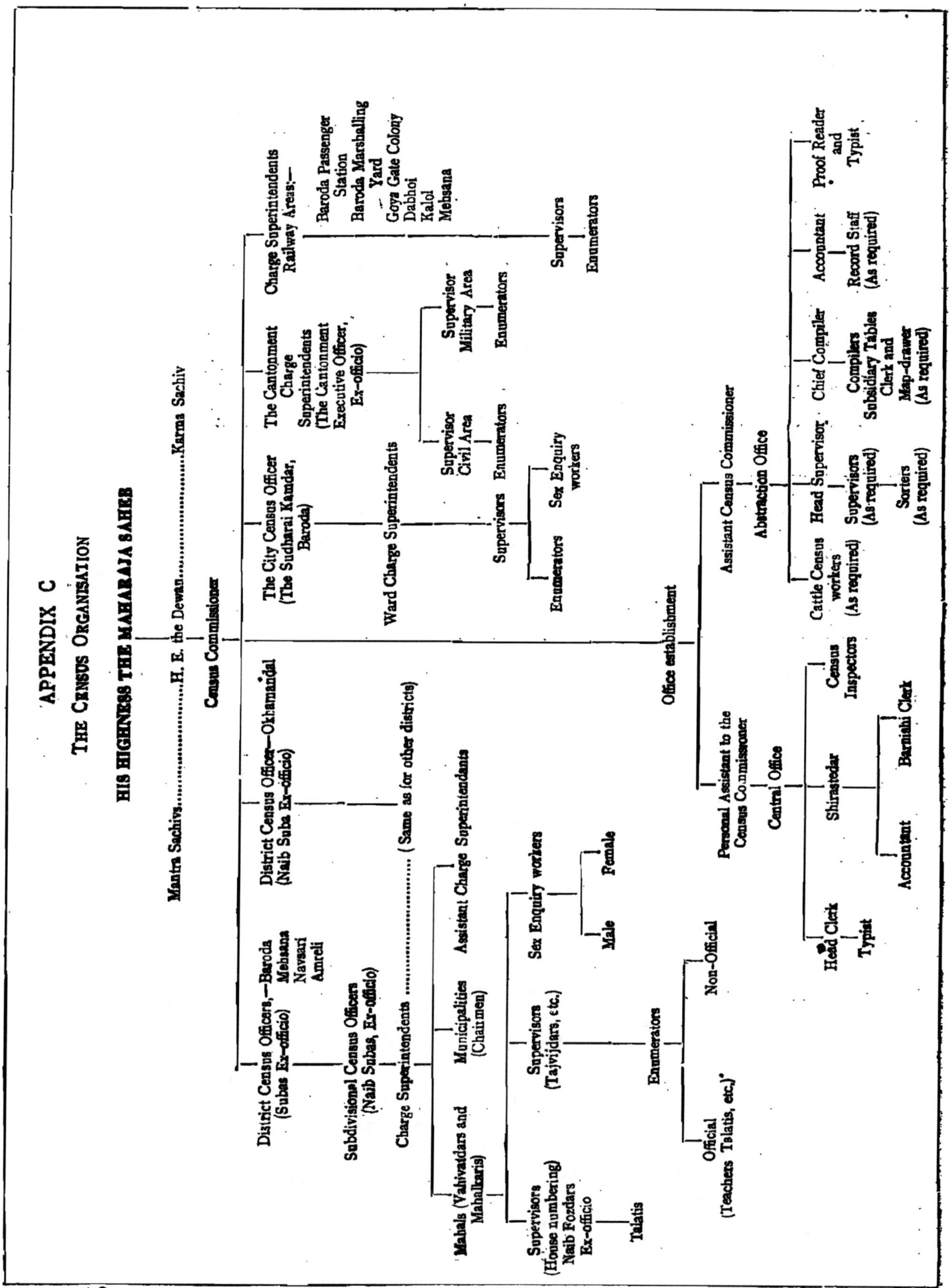
APPENDIX C
THE CENSUS ORGANISATION
HIS HIGHNESS THE MAHARAJA SAHEB
Mantra Sachivs..........H. E. the Dewan..........Karma Sachiv
Census Commissioner
District Census Officers,—Baroda Mehsana Navsari Amreli (Subas Ex-officio)
Subdivisional Census Officers (Naib Subas, Ex-officio)
Charge Superintendents ....
Mahals (Vahivatdars and Mahalkaris)
Supervisors (House numbering) Naib Fozdars Ex-officio
Talatis
Municipalities (Chairmen)
Supervisors (Tajvijdars, etc.)
Enumerators
Official (Teachers Talatis, etc.)
Non-Official
Assistant Charge Superintendents
Sex Enquiry workers
Male
Female
District Census Officer—Okhamandal (Naib Suba Ex-officio)
(Same as for other districts)
The City Census Officer (The Sudharai Kamdar, Baroda)
Ward Charge Superintendents
Supervisors
Enumerators
Sex Enquiry workers
The Cantonment Charge Superintendents (The Cantonment Executive Officer, Ex-officio)
Supervisor Civil Area
Enumerators
Supervisor Military Area
Enumerators
Charge Superintendents Railway Areas:—
Baroda Passenger Station
Baroda Marshalling Yard
Goya Gate Colony
Dabhoi
Kalol
Mehsana
Supervisors
Enumerators
Office establishment
Personal Assistant to the Census Commissioner
Central Office
Head Clerk
Typist
Shirastedar
Accountant
Barnishi Clerk
Census Inspectors
Assistant Census Commissioner
Abstraction Office
Cattle Census workers (As required)
Head Supervisor
Supervisors (As required)
Sorters (As required)
Chief Compiler
Compilers Subsidiary Tables Clerk and Map-drawer (As required)
Accountant
Record Staff (As required)
Proof Reader and Typist

APPENDIX D

CENSUS CONFERENCE

The Conference of Census officers met at the Old Secretariat Buildings, Delhi, on Wednesday the 7th January 1931, at 11 A. M. Dr. Hutton in the chair.

Present

Lieutenant-Colonel B. L. Cole, I. A., S. C. O., Rajputana and Ajmer-Merwara.
Mr. M. Venkatesa Iyengar, M. A., S. C. O., Mysore State.
K. S. Khan Ahmad Hasan Khan, M. A., P. C. S., S. C. O., Punjab.
Mr. Ghulam Ahmad Khan, Census Commissioner, Hyderabad State.
K. B. Gul Muhammad Khan, S. C. O., Baluchistan.
Mr. W. G. Lacey, I. C. S., S. C. O., Bihar and Orissa.
Captain G. L. Mallam, I. A., S. C. O, North West Frontier Province.
Mr. T. K. Sankara Menon, M. A., S. C. O., Cochin State.
Mr. S. V. Mukerjea, B. A. (Oxon.), F. S. S. (Lond.) Census Commissioner, Baroda State.
Mr. A. E. Porter, I. C. S., S. C. O., Bengal.
Mr. Rang Lal, B. A., Gwalior Government.
Mr. W. H. Shoobert, I. C. S., S. C. O., Central Provinces and Berar.
Mr. A. C. Turner, M. B. E., I. C. S., S. C. O., United Provinces.
Dr. N. Kunjan Pillai, M. A. B. Sc., Ph. D., Census Commissioner, Travancore.
Mr. C. S. Venkatachar, I. C. S., S. C. O., Central India Agency.
Mr. M. W. W. M. Yeatts, I. C. S., S. C. O., Madras.

Chairman.—I propose to start with the question taken up by Colonel Cole.—What exactly is meant by the words " The tabulation of castes will be as in 1911 " *vide* the Imperial Code of Census Procedure, Part II, page 34 ?

He explained that when he put those words in the Code, what he meant was this: in 1921 no castes were shown which were under a certain number per thousand of the population, whereas there was no such discrimination in 1911; but it might happen that a certain caste though small in numbers was relatively important and therefore he felt that such castes should not be omitted.

Colonel Cole explained what he had in mind when he sent in the question: if castes with an infinitesimal number of persons comprised in them had all to be put in, the tables would become very bulky, and proceeded to cite instances.

The Chairman said he was thinking only of castes and thought it would be better not to show them in the table of religion if they were very small.

Colonel Cole thought that there should be a minimum fixed in order to be eligible to go into the caste table—otherwise it would be very bulky indeed.

K. B. Gul Muhammad Khan agreed: as far as his province was concerned, caste related only to Hindus who numbered about 33 or 34 thousand coming from all parts of India : their numbers were very small whereas the number of castes was very large: last time they had all been lumped together as Hindus : if the Punjab wanted it, or if any other province wanted it, he could tabulate them-otherwise he would show them all as Hindus and not show them under caste: they were all there temporarily for trading or in government or railway service; the enumeration or tabling was not wanted for local purposes.

The Chairman said in that case there was no need : what he had in mind was conditions prevailing, say, in Assam where large numbers of people from Chota Nagpur had settled down.

Dr. Kunjan Pillai cited the instance of the Parsi families settled in Travancore, whose number was very small but who did not want to be left out in tabulating: there were other communities also like them.

Chairman.—It is really a matter of expense.

Mr. Mukerjea suggested they might have the option of either retaining all castes as returned or having a percentage basis: he cited the case of Baroda where even sub-castes had been tabulated including some very obscure castes of even 24 persons and so on. Several of them might be lumped together under miscellaneous with a resulting reduction in cost, but there must be option to retain such castes as are of local importance though their number might be less than one per mille.

The Chairman agreed.

Mr. Venkatesa Iyengar said in Mysore they had a limit of 4 per mille and they had 34 castes.

The Chairman summed up saying that all castes amounting to 4 per mille should be shown in the table and those with numbers below that should be left optional at the discretion of the census authority in each province according to the local importance of the caste concerned.

K. B. Gul Muhammad Khan cited the instance of certain Punjab tribes which were very important in the Punjab but of whom the figures might not be complete for all India unless other provinces also furnished the figures.

The Chairman pointed out that in that case all that would be necessary was to send the Census Commissioner for India the figures of a particular caste to be included in the total though the figures would not be shown separately in the provincial report.

Mr. Mukerjea asked if it would be possible for India to supply them with standard lists of castes having a proportion of 4 per mille from previous reports, which might be of all India importance: these would be tabulated and not the others. Going on the basis of 1921 was fairly safe. In Baroda they had figures of castes, like the Konkanastha Brahmans, who though not large in number were of very great importance and those figures would probably be required for the all India Report.

The Chairman thought the best plan would be, when his caste heads had been compiled, to send round the list and ask all provincial superintendents to give him figures.

Mr. Venkatesa Iyengar pointed out that there would be no saving in the sorting in that case and the Chairman agreed.

The Chairman finally said that he would compile a list of castes for which he would want all India figures and circulate it and leave it to Superintendents to give him figures for that list and to tabulate for their own provinces any castes under two per mille or not at their discretion.

The Conference agreed.

Mr. Venkatesa Iyengar thought that some agreement might be necessary between Superintendents of adjacent areas, like Madras, Mysore and Travancore in the case of communities like the Jains who were important though small in numbers perhaps less than two per mille.

The Chairman explained that two per mille would be the minimum above which it would be necessary to show all castes.

Mr. Gul Muhammad Khan.—There is one other point which I wish to bring to your notice, and it is this : In recent times castes have been divided. Don't you think it would be better to give details of all these castes ?

Chairman.—I don't think you can do it. The trouble is, details will not be reliable. The figures will be very very faulty. Personally, I don't think it is worth the trouble.

Mr. Shoobert.—In 1911, we had an Appendix, and in the Provincial and Imperial Tables they were all lumped together.

Mr. Gul Muhmmad Khan.—In the case of my province some people have gone to Assam and have settled down there, and unless their caste is given by the Assam Superintendent I cannot give the numbers nor can I place them in the proper category.

Chairman.—In a case like that you will have to write and ask the Superintendent to give you the castes of the Makranis that have settled in Assam. I don't think you can have a general principle for tabulating all castes like that.

Mr. Gul Muhmmad Khan.—The fact is in this country the caste or sub-caste or everybody is known to every man, and nobody can conceal his caste or sub-caste. It is only people of doubtful caste who will try to conceal their caste, not in their own area, but outside their area.

Chairman.—It is just an accurate statement of caste outside his own area, which is difficult to obtain.

Now, that brings me down to the second point raised by the Superintendent in Rajputana and Ajmer, as to the correct classification of such entries as Rohela Tank Kshatriya Brahmans, Nai, Brahman, etc., in order to avoid undue inflation of the list of castes. Now the question is as to how Rohela Tank Kshatriyas should be returned. The Rohela Tank Kshatriya means nothing or it meant nothing before this census but what we want is to correlate all these sub–castes. What I was going to suggest was that we should have a double table in which we could show the present name of the caste and the name used hitherto. Now, these Rohela Tank Kshatriyas are small in number, but they are all getting lumped together for caste purposes the darzis, calico printers, washermen and malis. I think a certain gentleman who came to see me recently told me that he was himself a *bona fide* Rajput, I think the gentleman belonged to one of the Rajputana States, I think he was from Jodhpur but I am not sure, he told me that he was recognised as a Rohela Tank Kshatriya by the Maharaja. Now, these people are all getting themselves lumped together and perhaps the Rajput community will ultimately accept the calico–printers, washermen, darzis and others.

If these people for some communal purposes want to be drawn in for caste and if they are going to be a consolidated community like that, then we should have for this year a consolidated name for darzis, washermen and calico–

printers, by whatever name they may choose to call themselves as a single caste corresponding to the combined numbers of the last census. It is a movement of very great interest.

Colonel Cole.—What exactly is the meaning of Rohela Tank Kshatriya?

Chairman.—They claim to represent one clan of Rajputs which they say could not be discovered. Unless therefore we show these people in the table in some way, they would feel that they are gradually being let down.

Dr. Kunjan Pillai.—There are some people who object to the old name of their caste being shown.

Chairman.—But we must have the old name in order to correlate, no matter what they call themselves.

Mr. Mukerjea.—The Nai Brahmans say that they do not mind being shown as Nai Brahmans with the word Barber in brackets but they object to be included as Hajams.

Mr. Venkatesa Iyengar.—There are some Vellalas in Mysore who want to be shown as Chauhans. They have passed a resolution to that effect. How should I show them?

Chairman.—I think you should show them as Vellala-Chauhans.

Dr. Kunjan Pillai.—What is the basis for accepting these changes?

Chairman.—We can only decide that according to the wish of the majority of the people.

Dr. Kunjan pillai.—Then there is another difficulty. A certain section of one caste wants to change its name while the other section does not want to change its name. What should we do in such a case?

Chairman.—Then you should put them down as in the last census. For instance, several castes were returned by alternative names.

Dr. Kunjan pillai.—For instance, in Travancore there are the Pulayas, a certain section of which wants to change their name to Cherumas, while the other section does not want to change its name.

Chairman.—Then you should show them as Pulayas and in brackets (Cherumas).

Mr. Mukerjea.—There are certain castes who tack on the Brahman name like Sonars, Salats, Panchals and Nai Brahmans. But the Brahmans have come to me and told me that these should not be included under Brahmans, while the Nai Brahmans themselves do not insist on being included under Brahmans. There are also Vishwakarma Brahmans who are presumably the same as the Rohela Tank Kshatriya. There are a number of castes like these. I think they should be allowed to come under one category, particularly if the castes are going to unite for the purposes of intermarriage and inter-dining.

Chairman.—The way we propose to classify them is to put several names as Kurmi-Kshatriya and so on. As a matter of fact, the Kurmi-Kshatriya is going to include Reddies.

Dr. Kunjan Pillai.—But will Vishwakarma Brahmans come under Brahmans?

Chairman.—Each caste will be taken according to alphabetical order.

Mr. Mukerjea.—Some States would rather like to have the total of Brahmans. For instance, my State would like to have the total of Brahmans separately shown.

Chairman.—Yes, I want a Brahman total of genuine Brahmans. What I want is not to get all Brahmans under one head, but we should get separate figures for the various classes of Brahmans in that classification.

Mr. Venkatesa Iyengar.—Supposing a Vishwakarma Brahman calls himself a Brahman, will he come under Brahman ?

Chairman.—All real Brahmans come under Pancha Dravida and Pancha Gauda.

Mr. Venkatesa Iyengar.—In Mysore there are three sub-castes in Brahmans, the Smarth, the Shri Vaishnava and the Shaiva. Except these three castes no others are treated as Brahmans.

Chairman.—Who is a Tuluva Brahman ?

Mr. Venkatesa Iyengar.—He is just like a Deshastha in the Bombay presidency, and among the Tuluvas you will find both Shivaites and Vaishnavites. It is a mattter for religious classification.

Chairman.—What I want to know is how far the regional names for Brahmans will go.

Mr. Venkatesa Iyengar.—There are three classes of people; there are the followers of Ramanujacharya, Shakaracharya and Madhwacharya.

Chairman.–Surely, there must be many others who claim to be Brahmans. There are the Saraswats in the South. What are they ?

Mr. Venkatesa Iyengar.–Saraswats are treated as Brahmans.

Mr Menon.–There is a set of Brahmans in the South called the Shiva Dwija Brahmans who are mostly working as priests in temples, but they are not allowed to inter-dine with Brahmans.

Mr. *Mukerjea.*—My point is, that so long as a certain community does not get itself recognised by the Brahmans themselves as a Brahman community, we should put them as a separate community.

Chairman.—We should show whether they are real Brahmans or degraded Brahmans.

The Chairman enquired for the purpose of division into Brahmans and non-Brahmans as to whom they take as Brahmans and whom non-Brahmans ?

Mr. Mukerjea said that those Brahmans who were not 'degraded' enough to lose their Brahmanhood were treated as Brahmans and shown in the Brahman total.

Colonel Cole suggested that in the provincial tables for the purpose of literacy, under the heading 'caste' it was better to deal with all the Brahmans under a single heading of 'Brahmans' at the top.

The Chairman said that he wanted to put them in the caste table. But it was not proposed to give any total in the caste table for Brahmans.

Dr. Kunjan Pillai enquired whether a classification such as Malayali Brahmans, Tamil Brahmans and Telugu Brahmans could be adopted in the census tables.

The Chairman thought that such a classification was perhaps possible in South India.

Dr. Kunjan Pillai expressed his difficulty in fitting in the South Indian classification into Northern Indian classification.

Mr. Venkatesa Iyengar was of opinion that no attempt should be made to bring in the South Indian classification into line with the North Indian classification.

But the Chairman said that they did overlap in Bombay and Central Provinces.

Mr. Venkatacher corroborated the Chairman's statement that they did overlap in Central Provinces.

Chairman.–The only thing to do is for each Superintendent to let me know how far he could fit in his classification with mine and then ask for instructions about others. I will try to fit his into my scheme.

Mr. Venkatachar referred to the existence of certain village priests who only mix with low classes. No other Brahmans will go and take food at their houses and it is difficult to bring them under either the Panch Gaud or Panch Dravid.

The Chairman said that Mr. Wilson's " Indian Castes " and Mr. Bhattacharya's book could be usefully referred to. The Chairman wanted to know the history of Hussani Brahmans.

Mr. Mukerjea said they were Musalmans and they were found in parts of Gujarat and their history could be found in one of the publications which form part of the old Bombay Gazetteer (Campbell's Gujarat Population).

The Chairman said that there were some Hussani Brahmans in Sind and Baroda.

Mr. Mukerjea then referred to the existence of certain classes of people in Baroda who could be called Hindu-Muslims. Amongst these Hindu-Musalmans, a large number bear opprobrious caste names like Shaikhdas. Indeed a separate clan of that name was opened in the Bombay Census of 1901, but this method was dropped later. Some of these call themselves Sheikhs, some trading Vohras and so on.

The Chairman enquired whether it would be possible to open a new heading such as Hindu-Muslim.

Mr. Mukerjea.—That was the case in 1901.

Chairman.—It is our business to record facts. I think we had better have a definite category in census as Hindu-Muhammadans.

Mr. Mukerjea.—It is too late now to do that.

Chairman.—We shall have to enter them as they call themselves

Mr. Mukerjea.—Perhaps we can enter them under " other sects '

Mr Ghulam Ahmed Khan.—They have got to be separated.

Chairman.—In the All-India table, we do not split up Hindus and Muhammadans. I should drop the splitting of castes-Hindus and Mohammadans. That is the best way to deal with it.

Mr. Mukerjea.—Those who call themselves Musalmans will be shown as Muslims, but the difficulty is with regard to falsification of returns. Muhammadans like Julahas, Pinjaras etc., call themselves Vohras or Pathans. But the Vohras or Pathans proper are anxious to retain their individuality and they do not want to be mixed up with these spurious claimants.

Colonel Cole said that there were some *Hinduised* Muhammadans. They were really Muhammadans but they followed Hindu customs.

Chairman.—It is a thing to be referred to in the report though it does not find a place in the Table. Under the caste heading you call them "Mers."

Colonel Cole:—They do not want to be called Hindus or Musalmans entirely.

Chairman.—They do not want to be called Musalmans because they could not then get Hindu wives.

Mr. Mukerjea.—What about the "Tadvis"? There is a vast difference in the actual religious condition of "Tadvis" in Bombay (Khandesh) and Baroda (Central Gujarat).

Chairman.—You have to treat them as you find them. You must write to the Bombay man and ask him how he classifies them, so that there may be uniformity of procedure.

Dr. Kunjan Pillai enquired about the classification of the different divisions of Kshatriyas.

Mr. Porter.—In question No. 3, you refer to the possible necessity of a double list.

Chairman.—Yes. In the tables there will be a double list to show reference to new names and to old ones. We can also put them in one table, possibly it is a question of which is more convenient.

Mr. Mukerjea.—When there are several synonyms for the same name, we can show all of them in the body of the report and not in the table.

Chairman.—For instance, it is not enough to show some as Rohela Tank Kshatriyas, because there are darzis, calico printers, etc., under that classification.

Mr. Mukerjea.—I do not think the tendency of occupational fusions is great in Bombay or Baroda.

Chairman.—It is definitely occurring in the Punjab.

Mr. Mukerjea.—There are definite occupational castes taking to other things, like Khedu Kumbhars etc. There are other functional groups, sections of whom are taking to the land. Same is the case with carpenters-Khedu Sutars.

K. S. Khan Ahmad Hasan Khan.—The carpenters in the Punjab are returning themselves as Moghuls.

Chairman.—Three cases arise definitely: (1) The case of Rohela Tank Kshatriyas in which case we have got distinct castes as darzis, calico printers, etc., who are going to return themselves under one caste name. (2) You have got the carpenters, the lohars and some others belonging to the artisan class who wish to return themselves again under one caste named Visva Brahmans. (3) You have got certain other carpenter castes in Bengal who want to be classed as Jangida Brahmans.

Mr. Porter.—Another section will say that must be classed as Visvakarma Brahmans.

Chairman.—It is a matter of policy. These people evidently think that they shoot as high as possible.

Mr. Porter.—What the Kurnims of Nepal did was the same. They formed the Kutria association. After some time they thought they did not go far enough and so they went a bit higher and they are now aiming to become Visva Brahmans.

Chairman.—But we have got to recognise all that. The important point is this, it may be necessary to work out some scheme with the two columns in or some scheme of separate columns to show how your consolidated castes will compare with the figures of the last census which were shown separately. For instance if you take an area in the Punjab and get all your darzis and calico printers shown under one caste named and if you have to refer to the figures of the last census, it will not be easy without some reference table.

Mr. Porter.—The best thing is to maintain divisions of last census and then give a supplementary table which will be a very small one showing what their present affiliations are, in the report. You show in your main table a collection of returns like their castes, beliefs, etc., as was shown in the previous tables, and you put in the last table a revised distribution of various castes according to the names which they now claim.

Chairman.—I think it is better to leave it to the Provinces as long as figures are available.

Mr. Shoobert.—In Provinces where it is not a complicated departure, they are put down in the alphabetical order. For instance in the case of Nai Brahmans, if we put them down as Nais or as Nai Brahmans, in both cases they come under "N".

Chairman.—I should not have separate figures for Nai Brahmans and Nais.

Mr. Shoobert.—In the last census we gave separate figures. The question is whether you want them in alphabetical order. For the purpose of marriage, etc., they do observe caste distinctions, I prefer to return them under Nai Brahmans. I do not think it fair to separate them.

Mr. Ghulam Ahmad Khan.—There are always representations made for change of old nomenclature. I have got a resolution which has been distributed all over the place in Hyderabad which asks that all the Yadhavas should be classified under one heading.

Chairman.—I do not think you can resist the change in nomenclature. It has become a habit. We must recognise it to this extent that you can give the nomenclature of the different names, about the old and the new names. I think we must recognise the new name as well. It is our business to keep a record of the change.

Mr. Ghulam Ahmed Khan.—We want a standard nomenclature. Each community adopts its own nomenclature.

Chairman.—The trouble is you cannot make a man call himself by a name which be does not like.

Mr. Venkatesa Iyengar.—In Mysore, the Yadavas are known as Goalas. The association of this community have asked for a change. Goala is the main caste and Yadava is the sub-caste in that community. In the case of Kammalas, there was a request that they should be called Visva Brahmans, some others wanted that they should be called Visva Karma Brahmans. The Government of Mysore changed the name into Visva Brahmans.

Chairman.—The position is this that we cannot resist these things except in the case where the name gives a definite confusion.

Mr. Venkatesa Iyengar.—Except in cases where the change is likely to lead to confusion, in cases in which we have allowed the change, I do not propose to give the old name in the tables.

Chairman.—We must have some means of reference to the old table.

Mr. Yeatts.—We should not give any discretion to the enumerators in the matter of translating the names.

Mr. Venkatesa Iyengar.—When the name is a recognised one as for instance Yadhava for Goala the enumerator can put it down himself. Mr. Porter pointed out that no claim to a change of name was ever put forward except as an accessory to appearing as a more distinguished caste. The Census Reports are invariably quoted as an authoritative statement of the claims of castes. Taking the case of Goalas who claimed to be called Yadavas because they belonged to the same race as Sri Krishna himself, they were claiming something which was merely a euphonious variation of their existing caste and to get an authoritative statement of that claim; but in the case of other people who wanted to pass off as one class or another of Brahmans, like the Nai Brahmans or the Savitri (?) Brahmans it was quite another thing.

The Chairman said they could not help that.

Mr. Porter pointed out that concessions of this kind in the past had accumulated difficulties for successive census officers; and the difficulties would go up in geometrical proportion by 1941.

Chairman.—Subject to the proviso that we are aiming at a time when we need not show any caste in the tables at all : the thing has been piling itself up and sooner or later the incubus must become so heavy that we cannot do it : but at present we have got to show it for certain purposes because we cannot record any social progress without showing caste.

Mr. Porter cited cases of subsidiary descriptions of castes such as Ugra Khatris (?) In some cases like Yadavas the change was justified as the castes were similar but not with all.

Mr. Mukerjea thought there was no harm in allowing those terms provided the movement behind them was genuine.

Mr. Venkatesa Iyengar pointed out that in the South the depressed classes were now calling themselves Adi-Karnataks as the name sounded more pleasant and thought it desirable that, that sort of thing should be encouraged.

The Chairman agreed.

K. S. Khan Ahmad Hasan Khan said that in the Punjab the hunger for change of names was connected with the Punjab Land Alienation Act under which only certain castes designated as agriculturists were able to enjoy certain privileges : he had issued a general instruction that the name of the changed caste should be accepted but that the traditional caste should be indicated in brackets.

The Chairman then passed on to the next item—proposed calendar for work in the post-enumeration stage.

In reply to Colonel Cole the Chairman said he had not laid down any calendar so far. The Imperial Code laid down a certain rate of work, but each province has its own system, say, in regard to slip copying by tahsils or in district headquarters. He would do his best to work out a time table based on the last census dates and let them have it.

Mr. Mukerjea.—They could send weekly progress reports and lists.

Mr. Venkatesa Iyengar said they would send copies of the totals as soon as ready, though in the last census the last tables were sent in August or September 1922.

The Chairman said what Colonel Cole wanted to have was a general scheme or the dates by which returns were expected on the basis of what took place during the last census: the time table would be for India as a whole.

The Conference then passed on to the next item—the precise definition of an earner among persons, whether male or female, engaged in all time agricultural occupations.

Colonel Cole explained that in one tahsil women working the whole time in their husbands' fields were put down as earners and in the next Tahsil as dependents.

The Chairman said he would put them down as dependents: it was a subsidiary occupation with them: unless of course they actually obtained receipts in cash or kind.

K. S. Khan Ahmad Khan.—Or by rent: if there are four grown up sons of a land owner working with their father but not paying any rent, they will also come in as dependants and their occupation shown in column 11.

Mr. Venkatesa Iyengar.—They have to be treated as land owners in Mysore.

K. S. Khan Ahmad Hasan Khan then cited the case of a minor boy whose uncle was working in the lands for him, and said that any one having a source of income must be shown as an earner.

Mr. Turner said that a man was an earner whether the income was earned or unearned and suggested that they should have uniform rules whether they were consistent or not. (He then proceeded to develop his argument and cited what he had done in his own province.)

Mr. Turner.—In the second case come the women and children under 10. I say they are earners if separately paid.

Mr. Venkatesa Iyengar.—In the occupation of agriculture you have to show them under one of those distinctions.

Mr. Turner.—Yes, but there are two or three rules that I would introduce. One is a woman or child under 10 whose name is entered either as a landlord or a tenant and must be treated as an earner whether she does any work or not. She must be shown as rent receiver. The last rule I had, was in the case of women and children under 10 whose names are entered along with the name of the male head of the family. People whose names are not entered and if they do any work at all, they must be shown as earners. It is only a question whether they are separately paid. If a woman gets any payment she must be shown as an earner.

Chairman.—I think we might accept what Mr. Turner says, but I do not accept the age limit, otherwise we can adopt a definite rule of that sort.

Mr. Venkatesa Iyengar.—How can a child under 10 be an earner ?

Mr. Turner.—If he is under 10, he is a dependant. As he is working jointly with his father, he has got a joint share, and if it is a joint family, he has got a share in the income.

Chairman.—Your entries under occupation should show so many as principal occupations, so many cultivating owners as dependants and so many as subsidiary.

Mr. Gul Muhammad Khan.—How can you call a man a cultivating owner when the person does not cultivate the land ?

Chairman.—If you take table 11, you will find a list of occupations, under column 2 of that table should be shown cultivating owner, cultivating tenant, non-cultivating owner and so forth. A dependant who is shown in column 11 of the general schedule will then come in column 6, as a male or female working dependent or the cultivating owner.

Col. Cole.—The feature of the present census is different from that of 1921 census where every name was shown as dependant. Every entry this time is appertaining to that entry alone. Therefore, when a woman is helping her husband in the cultivation, we cannot call her occupation as cultivating owner.

Chairman.—What is her subsidiary occupation ?

Col. Cole.—Agricultural labour.

Mr. Yeatts.—Here we are introducing a criterion which has no relation to the classification involved.

Chairman.—Quite right. It must be agricultural labour.

Mr. Mukerjea.—It is perfectly right to show the occupation in which she is assisting.

Chairman.—It is not the occupation on which she is dependant. It is personal occupation.

Mr. Mukerjea.—In the present form of occupation table, you show total number of people who show this particular form of occupation as earners or as dependents. What is the test ? A man may be a cultivating owner as a *pukka* earner or a cultivating owner as dependent.

Chairman.—If he is working as a dependant, he cannot be called a cultivating owner at all. The column will be blank for that.

Mr. Mukerjea.—She will be agricultural owner as wife.

Mr. Venkatesa Iyengar.—It is not desirable to class wife as labourer.

Chairman.—She will be agricultural labourer and working dependent.

Mr. Venkatesa Iyengar.—It is not correct from many points of view. She may be working in the field and get things done; it is not agricultural labour by any means. If you like, you may have some different classification for these cases, such as cultivation. Do not call an owner a non-owner.

Chairman.—Have you got your preliminary enumeration complete ?

Mr. Mukerjea:—Yes; we cannot change our instructions now.

Mr. Porter.—You did not define earner in your instructions. I define earner as a man who actually works or carries on business whether by himself or by sharing in co-parcenary property or business or concern of any kind and everybody else is dependent. In the case of women and children they are to be presumed as dependents unless they actually work and in addition receive a direct return in cash or kind outside. In the case of a woman or child, where the husband or the father is alive, the criterion whether she or the child is earner or not is whether the woman or child gets from outside some direct return in cash or kind. Take for instance the case of a herd boy of 15 years who takes out his father's cattle. Mr. Turner says he is an earner. I say he is a dependent. If he is dependent you put in column 11; if he goes out to a neighbour, he is an earner. The advantage of my system is this. According to Mr. Turner's system he will show in his figures for owners of property or tenants an enormously inflated number which will include people over 10 who have not really any title to call themselves owners, because their fathers will be shown as owners. I say if he is working as dependent put him down in column 11, the same entry which is entered in column 10 for a person who is an earner. In that way by comparing the figures of columns 10 and 11, I shall be able to show that these people who are regarded by contradictory terms as dependent cultivating owner or dependent land owners are actually people, who unless they have got some other principal occupation, are people who belong to the families of those other people who are regarded as cultivating owners or cultivating tenants shown in column 10. Therefore, I shall have some means of showing, though not to the same extent as in 1921, the real occupation of the earner on whom the dependent depends. I shall be able to show something at all events which is real whereas Mr. Turner's tables will not be real. Whether male or female, if you compare your figures with the actual record of your State, you will see that your landlords are enormously inflated.

Mr. Mukerjea.—In Table XI, the total population shows the total earners showing principal occupations. Under the total working dependents, you will get the class of dependents of cultivating owners who are in some way assisting. Really there is no inflation of real figures. The real figures will be under earners and you can quite possibly compare these figures with the revenue figures. Last time anybody who assisted in any shape or form went under earners. That was why the 1921 earners were unduly inflated, This time we shall have under working dependents people who belong to that class who assist not merely by agricultural labour, not by bird scaring for bird scaring may be one form of assistance, but all classes of people who assist in agriculture in some form or other.

Chairman.—The point raised by Colonel Cole is how should you classify a wife who works all the time in her husband's fields.

Mr. Mukerjea.—She may be assisting as agricultural labourer; but she should be shown as dependant on the cultivating owner or tenant, according as the husband is one or the other. That is column 11.

Chairman.—Her exact reference ?

Mr. Mukerjea.—Cultivating owner. If she is a whole time worker, then she will go as earner, otherwise she will be a dependant.

Chairman.—May I have your entry for this wife who is working all the time in her husband's field ?

Mr. Mukerjea.—Column 9: Earner.

Chairman.—I say dependant.

Mr. Mukerjea.—She is not receiving any wages but she is working whole time, and she cannot, therefore, be a working dependant. Receipt of wages is one of the tests. Working whole time is another; column 9 of my schedule will show her as working dependant. I have three different categories. Earner, working dependant and totally dependant. She will come under working dependent. Column 10 blank. Column 11, she will be shown as cultivating owner or rather as dependent on the cultivating owner.

The Chairman proceeded to collect opinions.

Dr. Kunjan Pillai agreed with Mr. Mukerjea.

Mr. Ranglal said that he would take the wife as a dependent — occupation as agriculture–according to the head under which her husband goes.

Mr. Yeatts said that he would class her as a working labourer.

Captain Mallam.—The woman who regularly works in the fields of her husband should be shown as dependant: subsidiary occupation cultivation.

The Chairman pointed out that it could not be shown like that and that it should be referable to column 2 of Table XI, when they said dependant, which of these four heads would they put him under ?

Mr. Lacey.—I should put "agricultural labourer" every time.

Mr. K. B. Gul Muhammad Khan.—I shall show her as dependent under column 11. I shall class under the occupation table with families. The last time we showed all these dependents by groups along with actual workers: we are going to lump all dependents and show them in separate tables only for their subsidiary occupations: I do not think there will be any difficulty if we show them as dependents with subsidiary occupation as field labourers: I do not think they can be treated as tenants nor can they be classed under non–cultivating owners or cultivating owners because they have absolutely no shares in the land.

Mr. Mukerjea said that in regard to other occupations besides agricultural labour, it would not matter so much but that it would be a real error to class the dependent of the cultivating owner as agricultural labour, because her assistance resembles in certain features agricultural labour. The test for agricultural labour for an earner is the cash nexus. It should be applied also to the working dependent as well. There does seem to be a very serious difference of opinion.

Mr. Turner agreed and said that they were practically concerned only with the dependent females of the family.

Mr. Shoobert pointed out that the proportion of such females who worked all the day in the fields was very little.

Mr. Porter.—You may say that in a certain province a certain classification has been adopted, and certain others in other provinces. The total of your sub-head (?) 1 (a) will be the same whatever the classification adopted.

Chairman.—I should simply group them under agricultural labourers–we are only dealing with dependents. The question is what you are going to refer to in the list of occupations. If you enter under occupation "cultivation" for a dependent, it will be interpreted in your particular case as agricultural labourer.

Captain Mallam.—Is there no distinction between a man and a woman who is actually an agricultural labourer ?

Chairman.—We should enter the figures as agricultural labourers.

Colonel Cole.—I suggest that we should write to the Director General, Posts and Telegraphs, and ask him to issue instructions that on the 26th February and succeeding days all telegraph offices should be asked to co-operate in the census work as regards hours, and that all census messages should be given priority.

Chairman.—Yes, certainly, it is a very reasonable proposition, we will write to the Home Department. I think census telegrams should be expedited and should have priority on the 26th February and succeeding days.

The Conference then adjourned for lunch till 2–30 p. m.

AFTERNOON PROCEEDING (7–1–1931.)

The Conference met again after lunch at 2–30 p. m. Dr. Hutton was in the Chair.

Chairman.—The next thing we have to consider to-day is the agenda of Central Provinces and Berar. The first point is the proposal of the Director of Public Instruction, Central Provinces, to substitute the term "Backward Class" or "Depressed Class" and to remove the word "untouchable" from usage for purposes of Census.

Mr. Shoobert.—The Director of Public Instruction has put up that proposal because he thinks, and I agree with him, that if you label a man in the census records as depressed class or an untouchable class, you do not give him a chance of raising his dignity for the next ten years, and he wants to call them backward classes. No doubt, that would need a certain amount of re-adjustment of other heads, but I do not think there would be any difficulty on that score.

Dr. Kunjan Pillai.—They may be a backward class, but they may not be an untouchable class.

Mr. Menon.—We have an unapproachable caste in Malabar, and not merely untouchables.

Chairman.—Yes, they have to observe a certain distance. There are 10 yards caste and 20 yards caste and so on.

Mr. Shoobert.—I suggest that if we adopt the term " backward class " for the untouchables, we should then be following your suggestion. We should carry on with hill and forest tribes for the hill and forest tribes, and for criminal tribes and others, we might call them wandering tribes or nomad tribes as most of the criminal tribes do wander. We thus do away also with the stigma of calling people criminal tribes.

Mr. Venkatesa Iyengar.—But there is a Regulation which calls them criminal tribes.

Chairman.—They object strongly to being classed as criminal tribes. One section may be criminal in one province, and another section settled in another province may have ceased to be criminal.

Mr. Shoobert.—This arose like this. The Education Department has just issued a fat memorandum on the education of the depressed classes, and they have been trying to get in as much uplift as they can. I entirely agree that if you label a man as a depressed class or an untouchable class, you depress them really.

Mr. Mukerjea.—But the depressed man wants to be called as such. He wants to make capital out of it. It is important that you should estimate fairly and accurately the strength of the depressed classes within a particular province or State.

Chairman.—We want an accurate return of the depressed classes if only for the compilation of that map in which I hope to show the proportion of depressed classes as compared with clean Hindu castes and with Brahmans. The difficulty has arisen in Bombay where the Bombay people have insisted. (Reads from correspondence). Of course, if we are not going to say anybody untouchable, we have to invent some name for them.

Mr. Venkatesa Iyengar.—By the term "backward class" you mean backward as distinct from depressed ?

Chairman.—The terminology apparently adopted in Bombay is that the communities should be sub-divided into three groups: (1) depressed class or untouchables, (2) aboriginal hill tribes, and (3) other backward classes.

Mr. Mukerjea.—I proposed a similar classification to you to which you had an answer, namely, that you cannot call a class backward where it has a very high percentage of literacy, and so you cannot lay down any uniform rule.

The solution is to have a uniform literacy percentage scale and apply it uniformly in each province. So that there will be different results in different provinces on that basis. Marathas in my State will be very advanced under that rule and will be backward in Bombay Deccan.

Chairman.—If it is a question of depressed class, you cannot very well classify them by literacy.

Mr. Porter.—What is a depressed class ?

Chairman.—People who are for instance unapproachable in Madras. A sweeper is untouchable and he is not allowed inside the house.

Mr. Venkatesa Iyengar.—Any person who is treated as little less than human is a depressed class.

Chairman.—I do not think the Punjab will accept that view at all. They claim that they consider nobody as less than human.

K. S. Khan Ahmad Hasan Khan.—I have seen sweepers embraced at election times by big men.

Mr. Venkatachar.—A Basawa (?) is depressed in Bundelkund and not in Malwa.

Dr. Kunjan Pillai.—Are you going to show the total of the depressed classes for India ?

Chairman.—Yes.

Dr. Kunjan Pillai.—Then you have to lay down some thing to guide us as to who should be classed a depressed class person.

Mr. Mukerjea.—With all the guidance in the world you cannot get correct figures. Even the official estimates differ by millions.

Chairman.—The Government of India official estimate included Mundas, and it is manifestly absurd to say that they are any more depressed than myself.

Mr. Venkatachar.—A high caste man will not touch anybody else.

Mr. Menon.—We are all untouchables to the Nambudri Brahman in Malabar.

Chairman.—Can anybody suggest a general definition which will exclude the extremes on both sides ?

Mr. Mukerjea.—I think it is pretty plain what is a depressed class.

Mr. Shoobert.—(Reads out the classification of the Census Commissioner.) In our province, even in every district it is different. A Chamar (?) in Raigarh is not untouchable, but he is untouchable in the rest of the C. P.

Chairman.—I think I have defined untouchability somewhere as a condition in which contact with the man necessitated ceremonial purification by a high caste man. But the question is what is a high caste. It involves all sorts of difficult questions as to the exact line which you must draw in regard to the subject.

Dr. Kunjan Pillai.—A Brahman, if he touches a non-Brahman, must have his bath before taking his food.

Mr. Venkatesa Iyengar.—Not all Brahmans.

Dr. Kunjan Pillai.—The orthodox Brahman.

Mr. Menon.—Strictly speaking, a Nambudri Brahman will not take his meal if he has touched a Nair, without a bath.

Mr. Venkatachar.—May I ask untouchable with reference to whom ?

Mr. Shoobert.—Our Education Department has drawn up a list.

Chairman.—The Bombay Government have drawn up a list.

Mr. Mukerjea.—I have seen Mr. Dracup's list and it is arbitrary.

Chairman.—Yes, it is.

Mr. Venkatesa Iyengar.—We have got only two castes which are treated as depressed, the Puliyas and the Madikas. They are both now called Adi Karnatakas. No other body is treated as a depressed class. There are other classes, such as the barber community which if a man touches he would go and bathe before taking his food, but the barber is not treated as a depressed class person.

Chairman.—He does not have to sit outside the village school, and is not debarred from using the village well. Those are the things which constitute the test of a depressed class.

Mr. Venkatesa Iyengar.—The Puliyas are not allowed to touch the well that other castes use, and Government have sunk separate wells for them. Generally they go to separate schools, though by orders of the Government every general school is open to those people.

Chairman.—The social feeling is such that though Government have officially allowed the use of the general school to such people, they cannot use it in practice.

Mr. Venkatesa Iyengar.—Yes.

Chairman.—I do not know how far it applies to the Punjab.

K. S. Khan Ahmad Hasan Khan.—Not on the same scale. A Chuhra has become a member of Council in the Punjab and he takes his seat with other members, but it is not so in the schools.

Mr. Venkatesa Iyengar.—Members of the Council are supposed to be educated enough not to observe those differences.

Chairman.—What about Bengal and Assam ?

Mr. Porter.—There are no untouchables in Bengal, no depressed class.

Chairman.—What about Namasudras ?

Mr. Porter.—They are not denied access to schools.

Chairman.—Are they allowed to sit in the same school with Kayastha children ?

Mr. Porter.—I think so. Government do not forbid them.

Chairman.—But the question is one of society.

Mr. Porter.—Government recently conducted an inquiry into that matter, and their opinion is that in Bengal there is no untouchable problem. The whole question is really one of backwardness of education, and speaking roughly that position is correct in Bengal.

Chairman.—I think that applies to Assam also.

Mr. Porter.—The question of access to wells is the only case where you have anything approaching untouchability. In certain districts access to well is determined by the size of the well. A man of low caste cannot go and use a small well but if it is a big well he can go and use it. In the case of a small well, he goes and stands there, and one of the higher castes draws water for him from the well.

Mr. Venkatesa Iyengar.—That is untouchability.

Mr. Mukerjea.—He suffers from untouchability in not being allowed to enter a temple.

Mr. Porter.—Except a certain Kali temple I have never heard of any such thing in any other place arousing bitter feelings. But that has been settled.

Chairman.—By the higher castes boycotting the temple in question now that untouchables use it, so there is a certain amount of untouchability.

Mr. Porter.—What is the meaning of "depressed"? Is it a state of mind ? Your Garo in Mymensingh district is not by any means a depressed class person; but if he comes in contact with an advanced Hindu he becomes depressed.

Chairman.—Your hillman in Assam is anything but depressed in his own hills, but he is apt to become depressed when he comes down to the plains and stays there. He acquires an inferiority complex very quickly and he is given all sorts of dirty jobs to do. The water which would be taken from him in the hills is regarded as completely unclean in the plains.

Mr. Mukerjea.—What about "unclean" ? Would that not be a better word than " untouchable " ? (Laughter).

Cries of " No " from the Conference.

One Member.—" Depressed " is bad enough and we should not use word " unclean ".

Mr. Mukerjea.—The problem is serious only in Madras, Gujarat, and the Bombay Deccan, and I do not think it is so serious in other parts of India. I think it is pretty safe to call the whole of the depressed classes under the heading " Backward classes ". That is the same as backward.

Mr. Porter.—The position in Bengal is this. They used to have two lists which were mainly intended to guide Government in making appointments to Government service. The first list was called the backward class list and it included Anglo-Indians, Indian Christians and so on. The other list was called the depressed class list and it included low caste people like Namsudras, Muchis Santhals, and others–all those people aboriginal as well as Hindu castes. Those lists were under revision recently and a revised list has been prepared, and the word " depressed " has disappeared altogether. The two lists have been comprised in one and there is a single list of minority groups and backward classes. And I do not think that a good many of these backward classes group are depressed classes at all.

Chairman.—If you have got people who have disabilities as regards wells and schools, I think you ought to class them separately as depressed. You are not bound to follow the Local Government's classification.

Mr. Porter.—They repudiate the idea that there are any depressed classes at all.

Chairman.—Are they correct in repudiating ? Ultimately I have got to take your ruling on the subject as far as Bengal goes, I have not got any criterion by which I can say who is who. We know there are people who are untouchable and water from whose hands will not be accepted by a higher caste.

Mr. Venkatesa Iyengar.—In Mysore there are two castes, Gurlas and (?) They will not take water from each other but neither claims to be better than the other.

Chairman.—I think we must recognise that certain provinces at any rate will have to have two divisions,—depressed classes and backward classes, the depressed classes being defined as those who are debarred in a greater or less degree from the public wells and public schools, not by Government orders but by social practice.

Mr. Venkatesa Iyengar.—But we should consider also the case where social practice allows these people to use the general wells and the general schools.

Dr. Kunjan Pillai.—As for entering the temple, there is the question of distance : certain castes are allowed to go a little nearer than others, while the highest Brahmans can go very near the Deity.

Mr. Venkatesa Iyengar.—But there are castes which are not allowed into the temple at all ?

Dr. Kunjan Pillai.—In our parts, Christians are not allowed to enter the walls of the temples.

Chairman.—We shall have to leave non-Hindus out of this quite clearly.

Mr. Turner.—Could we not substitute 'backward' for 'depressed'?

Chairman.—Let Bombay do that if it likes.

I think each province can make a list of people who suffer disability on account of their low social position, being debarred from temples, schools or wells. We need not worry about backward classes as such.

Mr. Shoobert.—The Director of Public Instruction, C. P., has drawn my attention to paragraph 5 of the Memorandum on the Education of the Backward Classes and has inquired if there is any objection to the substitution of the word 'backward' for 'depressed' and the removal of the word 'untouchable' from usage for purposes of the census. Paragraph 5 reads : "It has been suggested that the first step towards raising the status of the depressed classes would be to remove from official usage words connoting a stigma such as 'untouchable'. It is suggested that depressed classes might be called backward classes. As an example of the value of this change may be quoted the case of the Mahars of Chattisgarh who now desire that their caste should be removed from the list of untouchables."

Chairman.—There would be no objection provided you make it clear for general purposes. I think the term 'backward' is a little unfortunate. The whole thing started with the request of the Servants of India Society that at this census all classes might be divided up into three categories from the educational point of view, viz., advanced, intermediate and backward, simply from the literacy point of view. It would be a very simple thing for us to do that and also a convenient thing because it would show what tribes have moved up. There would be overlapping, of course. I want to find another term.

Colonel Cole.—I may point out that in the Indian States the standard of literacy is very much allied to the standard of administration. They are very loth to draw up any comparison which reflects on the administration.

Chairman.—In the case of the all India table the figures from Indian States for that particular class which predominated might drag the whole class for India down.

Mr. Mukerjea.—Take Sind. Their population is very low in the literacy scale and would probably come under the backward communities. It may be somewhat difficult for you to have an all India table on that basis.

Mr. Venkatesa Iyengar.—In Travancore every community other than Brahmans is classed as backward.

Mr. Mukerjea.—I think the best thing is to have a colourless classification, so that any one who wants to convert the tables can do so.

K. B. Gul Muhammad Khan.—Certain classes have recently been emancipated in Baluchistan. There is no distinction among Muhammadans but of course some classes would not allow their own men to mix with them. So I have adopted a new nomenclature.

Chairman.—That would meet the case.

K. B. Gul Muhammad Khan.—Should they come under backward or depressed ?

Chairman.—It may not be necessary to classify them.

K. B. Gul Muhmmad Khan.—There is also another tribe in Mekran of fishermen who are considered to be a low caste socially.

Chairman.—In the matter of education the whole province is backward ?

K. B. Gul Muhmmad Khan.—A big majority of my people are illiterate.

Colonel Cole.—I would reserve the word 'backward' for those classes who are backward socially.

Chairman.—We shall have to leave each province to use its own nomenclature.

Mr. Shoobert.—We have come very much into line with Bombay. We have got our three classes. We know what we want and we get what we want.

Chairman.—It is merely a matter of nomenclature. I do not think it matters very much.

Mr. Mukerjea.—Is it decided that 'backward' should be restricted to this meaning, *viz.*, backward socially ?

Chairman.—Not only to that. At any rate for the purposes of the all India report we retain both 'depressed classes' and 'backward'. 'Backward' would include all those who are backward educationally and socially other than the depressed classes.

Mr. Mukerjea.—What about hill tribes ? A Bhil is certainly backward but not untouchable.

Chairman.—It must depend on the local position and cannot obviously be a matter of general application. If they are as a regular practice denied access to temples, wells and schools, they become depressed. As for those who do not come down to the plains, there is no point arising in their case.

Mr. Mukerjea.—'Depressed classes' only mean Hindu depressed classes ?

Chairman.—Yes.

Mr. Porter.—If I understood the result of the discussion, we are going to have three divisions–depressed Hindus interpreted as being untouchable Hindus, and a second sub–division in the first class of which will be backward classes. Now that may be anybody and cannot be restricted to Hindus, and must include people who are not Hindus at all. What is the criterion, except literacy ?

Chairman.—There must be a literacy test among other things, but of course they overlap.

Mr. Mukerjea.—There may be non–Hindus who are depressed in one social category but who are in the intermediate state in the literacy category or due to economic conditions.

Chairman.—I shall have to write an appendix in the all India report dealing with the position of the depressed classes generally. There will be a separate division on Provincial Table II into illiterate, intermediate and advanced, but it will be necessary to deal separately with the depressed classes as a whole. I would like to keep a distinction in my mind between the terms 'backward' and 'depressed'. In what position would you put a criminal tribe?

Mr. Porter.—We have got a separate head of wandering tribe. I may mention that among Muhammadans there is a class which is in a very real sense depressed, *viz.*, Jolas, with whom Sheiks and Pathans will not intermarry, and those other people who are sweepers, who are looked down upon by the other Muhammadans.

Chairman.—Merely being despised by others does not amount to being classified as depressed. The social disability must be more or less severe and definite.

Mr. Porter.—I want to except certain classes which have been declared by my Government to be backward minority communities and give you figures for them as being socially backward.

Chairman.—You are going to take only the literacy test?

Mr. Porter.—Yes.

Chairman.—I shall have to accept your word for it as you represent Bengal but with a mental reservation, which I may refer to in my report. Namasudras for all practical purposes I think are depressed classes, although their position may have improved a lot since I knew them.

Mr. Mukerjea.—I think the literacy test may not suffice. In Baroda there are certain depressed castes which have almost come up to the intermediate stage while some, like the Rabari, are quite respectable and paying even income-tax, but are very low in the literacy scale. They would simply rebel if they were to be put down as "depressed", but they are certainly very backward educationally.

Chairman.—The Bombay Government has drawn up a list of backward classes which has been done purely arbitrarily. They put down under backward classes people who are fairly high in literacy on the score of social disability, and did not include people who occupy a much lower position on the ground that there is no social disability and cannot therefore be included as backward. It has been done most arbitrarily.

K .B. Gul Muhammad Khan.—I made a list in Baluchistan and sent it out to the local offices. In the last census a particular tribe recorded their occupation as plunder. Actually the whole tribe lives on plunder even now and therefore they ought to be recorded as a criminal tribe. The local Government say they cannot do it because politically it is an important tribe.

Chairman.—I would suggest that every Superintendent should be asked to make out a list of depressed classes in consultation with the Local Government and take their approval. I do not think the Census Commissioner can give a definition.

The method of dealing with demands made against census budget by district officers and by the A. G.

Mr. Shoobert.—I can withdraw that point and fight it out with my A. G.

Chairman.—A circular has recently been issued on that subject.

Mr. Shoobert.—I have seen that. I will see my Accountant General when I go back and I think I will be able to get it straight. It is not worth worrying the Conference about.

Mr. Turner.—In our province the Central Pay and Accounts Office has been wanting to know whether the Government of India have declared the Local Government to be an agency for the purposes of the census. If they make that declaration all our difficulties would be solved.

Chairman.—I do not think the Government of India will put it in that form.

Mr. Turner.—I have to go to the Government of India to get sanction for Rs. 3 for a sweeper in my office. I can sanction expenditure in a district office but not in my own office.

Chairman.—If the Government of India declare the Local Government to be an agency, it shuts out the Census Commissioner entirely and all their correspondence will have to come through the Local Government and the Government of India and come to me through the Home Department. I do not think the point has arisen in any other province.

Mr. Turner.—My Central Pay and Accounts Officer has repudiated this expenditure because he says we will have to be declared an agency.

Chairman.—If you send me the correspondence I will take it up with the Government of India.

The best means of attaining accuracy in recording tribal religions.

Mr. Shoobert.—My point is largely this. In the first instance I find that the district officers have displayed ignorance as to the occupations which are followed by their tribesmen. There is a great tendency to classify them all as Hindus and there is also the difficulty that our enumerators are practically universally Hindus who may be of a proselytising turn of mind, and it is going to be very largely according to the wish of the enumerator, whether a *Gond* for instance is going to be recorded as a Hindu or a *Gond*. They should all be recorded as tribal religions.

Chairman.—What has happened in previous censuses is a shift–over. what I would suggest this time is that where it is impossible to decide whether a particular tribe is entirely Hinduised or not, the best plan is to make a territorial division. Where the tribes have more or less kept to themselves and have not been in touch with the Hindus, they should be returned as belonging to tribal religions; and to return them as Hindus where they have been more or less Hinduised.

Mr. Mukerjea.—My instructions follow your method. In Songadh for instance, there are certain tribes who I have said should be entered by the name of the tribe in the Religion column. With regard to the others who say they are Hindus a supplementary question should be put to them whether they believe in such and such gods and if they believe in Hinduism they should be entered as Hindus.

Mr. Shoobert.—The Hindu Mahasabha in our parts has objected to my instructions. I have simply made an addition to the ordinary instructions that a tribesman who returns himself as a Hindu should be further questioned to find out whether he really has adopted Hindu manners and customs, whether he reveres the Brahman and the cow, and observes caste, and so on.

Chairman.—There again you will get into trouble. We should not discuss what constitutes a Hindu.

Mr. Shoobert.—There are so many who return themselves as Hindus with the idea of getting a social uplift.

Chairman.—Do you think that in the Central Provinces the solution I propose will serve the purpose?

Mr. Shoobert.—It may and I have adopted it to a great extent but I want to know whether there is any further solution.

Lt. Col. Cole.—Where they have not been in touch with Hindus they should be looked on as tribal. But in one of our States which is mainly inhabited by Bhils I got a letter saying that they all wanted to be returned as Hindus. This will make a complete change in the figures of 1921.

Mr. Lacey.—In the jungly areas they should all be returned according to their tribal religions, but there is a great deal of propaganda either to return themselves as Hindus or to get the enumerators to return them as such. Generally you will find that the enumerator will record them as Hindus because he is one himself.

Chairman.—This is a point in which we cannot trust the enumerator, and when it is definitely known that certain people follow their tribal religions they should be recorded as such.

Mr. Lacey.—Do you mean to say that we can change it ?

Chairman.—I should deliberately say that we can change up to that extent. It has been done at every previous census in the Central Compilation Office. The best plan is to take a territorial line, where you get a few Hinduised ones and a certain number who are not Hinduised at all.

Mr. Venkatesa Iyengar.—If they worship in Hindu temples they must be taken as Hindus.

Chairman.—Yes.

Mr. Shoobert.—I find most of our fellows following tribal religions who are willing to follow anybody else's God.

Chairman.—In Assam I know of a Naga who put on the Hindu caste mark in order to be cured of a disease. I would not dream of putting him down as a Hindu.

K. B. Gul Muhammad Khan.—In our parts there are Muslims whose Nikah ceremony is performed by Hindu pundits. Will they be classed as Hindus or Muhammadans?

Chairman.—They are Muslim–Hindus.

I do not see what we can do except to say that when these tribal people habitually worship in a Hindu temple, at the same time worshipping their own gods, the worship in a Hindu temple may be taken as bringing these people within the pale of Hinduism. We can leave it to the Census Superintendents.

Non–co–operation with the Census

Mr. Mukerjea.—I have found no actual difficulty on this score.

K. S. Khan Ahmad Hasan Khan.—In one fairly large town in the Punjab, a few days ago all the house numbers were wiped out. There is still time to re-number the houses.

Col. Cole.—In our parts we decide to take no notice. After all we have got the house list and the enumerators know what their blocks are.

There was some further discussion after which the Chairman took up the list of questions propounded by the Census Superintendent, Baluchistan.

Chairman.—No. 1 is Tabulation of alien castes—whether every non-indigenous caste should be shown in the Imperial Tables in full detail; if not, which castes should be shown separately besides the indigenous castes and tribes?

No. 2 is Chuhras,—how should those Chuhras be classed who return themselves simply as Chuhras?

I think the Punjab Government's orders are that they should be returned as Hindus if they do not come under any other denomination.

K. B. Gul Muhammad Khan.—In Baluchistan there are certain Chuhras who definitely return themselves as Hindus, Muslims or Sikhs. But there are others who simply return themselves as Chuhras and nothing else.

Chairman.—What does Chuhra connote in Baluchistan?

K. B. Gul Muhammad Khan.—They are all from the Punjab. I do not think they would like to be classed as Hindus. I do not think the Sikhs would like it. I have given instructions that if they do not return any religion they should be simply classed as Chuhras. In Baluchistan I have lumped the whole lot and shown them as Hindus, Sikhs and others. Chuhras come separately under others.

Chairman.—No. 3 is Depressed and Backward Classes.

No. 4 is Lines on which information should be collected regarding the cultural border zones.

No. 5 is appointment of Assistants and Establishments.

K. B. Gul Muhammad Khan.—We have got a seniority list of candidates and among those candidates you have got a list of those who have passed a certain test and those that have not. That means that you should be guided by your Local Government. It took me two months to get one clerk. I wanted to pay him Rs. 90 a month but the Deputy Commissioner would pay him only Rs. 80. Though I told him that the man would do the work of two people, he would not sanction Rs. 90 with the result that the man is dissatisfied and is not doing his work properly.

Chairman.—That is a question on which I should be very shy of interfering with the Local Government. I can sanction Rs. 90 of course, if necessary, and the Local Government cannot say anything.

K. B. Gul Muhammad Khan.—Then I withdraw it.

Again, I have provided Rs. 300 for the Deputy Superintendent of the Tabulation Office. I have not got a Personal Assistant but a Deputy Superintendent.

K. S. Khan Ahmad Hasan Khan.—I have got a Personal Assistant who is in charge of the compilation and the Deputy Superintendent will be in charge of the sorting. The P. A. only functions to run the compilation office.

Chairman.—Every province differs from every other province in arrangements of that sort and there is no general rule. What is the exact point of your raising the question ?

K. B. Gul Muhammad Khan.—Whether the appointments are done under Local Government's orders ? For this I will have to go up to the Government because it is more than Rs. 250, but when the appointment is sanctioned, am I competant to appoint my assistant, or is it for the Local Government ?

Chairman.—You simply say to the Government, " I want so and so, " and I do not think your Local Government will object.

K. S. Khan Ahmad Hasan Khan.—I selected my Personal Assistant.

Chairman.—I should say, " I select such and such a man" and if the Local Government objects, we would do our best to back you up. The general principle is that the Census Superintendent should appoint his own staff. If the men do not work properly it is the Census Superintendent who will suffer.

K. B. Gul Muhammad Khan.—I withdraw this question.

Chairman.—No. 7 Maps for the Report.

Mr. Lacey.—Did you say that the Central Compilation Office is not regarded as Census Superintendent's Office ?

Chairman.—The matter is under consideration, but I think that it is not your own office.

K. B. Gul Muhammad Khan raised the question of certificates required for journeys by road between stations wholly or partly connected by rail.

Chairman.—Does the Local Government raise any difficulty about giving you the necessary certificate ?

K. B. Gul Muhammad Khan.—They want a programme in advance. The area to be covered is so wide that it is not possible to give one.

Chairman.—Why should they demand a programme ?

K. B. Gul Muhammad Khan.—Because the Deputy Commissioner says " I am responsible for controlling the expenditure "

Chairman.—I do not see why a programme is necessary to be sent. Is that the Local Government's rule ?

K. B. Gul Muhammad Khan.—No. The Commissioner says, "When I give a certificate it means that I control the expenditure, and for that I must have a programme of your tour before you proceed".

Chairman.—That is rather an unreasonable position, but I cannot help you if he says that.

No. 8 is how is the number of occupied houses in strictly Military Areas to be ascertained in the absence of house numbering ? The answer is there should be practically no occupied houses in strictly Military Areas. You should exclude those houses as far as possible.

Captain Mallam.—The rules for strictly Military Areas say definitely that, houses within the Military Areas should not be numbered. (Reads.)

A Member.—Would not a greater number of residential houses be excluded then ?

Chairman.—A certain number will fall inside, but it will be a very small number and the omission of that will have no ultimate significance.

Mr. Mukerjea.—There is a difference in the instructions in this respect between 1921 and 1931, and it will make a difference in the number of occupied houses.

Chairman.—It should make a very small difference indeed, because for practical purposes they should contain no occupied house.

Mr. Turner and Captain Mallam referred to Rule 5, sub-rule (2) of Appendix II which says " Throughout the enumeration the military and civil population shall be kept distinct and distinguishable in the enumeration books ".

Chairman.—That is, I think, for administrative purposes only. It is the Army people who want to know, but I do not think we need tabulate further. The words " and distinguishable " were my addition in order to make quite clear that the distinction, if it was needed, could be easily obtainable.

Mr. Lacey.—Are the wives of military men civil or military ?

Chairman.—Civil.

A Member.—What about those officers who live outside the military area ?

Chairman.—All the officers of the regiment will be on parade and there is no difficulty.

K. B. Gul Muhammad Khan.—For instance, most of the military officers live in the Quetta club and they will be censussed in the parade. I have issued instructions to my men not to include the military officers in the club.

Chairman.—No. 9 is fertility and mortality schedule.

K. B. Gul Muhammad Khan.—I have found it difficult to get people to do that kind of work. I wrote to several persons in representative areas and only one of them is willing to undertake it.

Chairman.—What is the organisation that collects fertility statistics in Baroda ?

Mr. Mukerjea.—We have about 5,000 permits sent out. 350,000 slips have already been sent out to 5,000 enumerators of whom 500 will be women,-mostly women teachers and nurses. I induced them to do this work by promise of prizes, and the Education and Medical Departments co-operated cordially in this respect. In the last Census, I had no less than 160,000 slips filled in.

Mr. Venkatesa Iyengar.—I think I shall be able to cover 6, or 7 or 10 villages at the utmost. There is one area which is done by a missionary lady. She understands the language of the people and can collect information.

Dr. Kunjan Pillai.—I am trying to get it done by boys and girls in the higher classes in the schools–boys studying in the 5th, 6th or 7th class. The printed instructions are there, and they will do the work under the supervision of the Headmaster or Headmistress as the case may be.

Mr. Menon.—I have distributed the schedules to women teachers. That is the only agency available.

Dr. Kunjan Pillai.—I have sent out 100,000 slips.

Mr. Menon.—I have distributed about 50,000.

Mr. Lacey.—I should be very lucky indeed if I get 5,000. You may try and get 100,000 or 500,000 but there is not the remotest chance of any of them being accurate or valuable in any way.

Chairman.—I think it will be in South India where there is a high percentage of literacy.

Mr. Venkatesa Iyengar.—In our part of the country the difficulty is to put the question as to when they began to live together.

Chairman.—Could you not get that in some other way, such as, when such and such a ceremony happened and so on.

Dr. Kunjan Pillai.—In our part of the country no respectable woman would be willing to give the information.

Mr. Mukerjea.—But if you say that the enquiry is optional ?

Mr. Venkatesa Iyengar.—I do not expect people would be willing to give the information.

K. B. Gul Muhammad Khan.—I think it will not serve any useful purpose. I issued 50,000 slips. People wanted to know why I was making inquiries about their women and children. In one village about 100 men were sitting there. I took statistics. In one family 12 children were said to have been born and it was said all of them died, in another 10 were born and only one survived, and in another 8 were born and all died.

Dr. Kunjan Pillai.—You want figures about the different strata of society the different castes ?

Chairman.—About the different social occupations, which has a very considerable bearing, what we want to be able to arrive at is some general fertility rate as well. The present fertility rates are based on statistics taken 30 or 50 years ago and are very much out of date. The Government Actuary has been most insistent on getting some reasonable figures which will enable him to work out a general mortality rate.

Dr. Kunjan Pillai.—When you come to the compilation of these tables, you want to have them applied for the different communities ?

Chairman.—I would like a table for each area.

Mr. Mukerjea.—I would like to have your instructions about the kind of table.

Chairman.—I do not want to restrict you at all.

Mr. Mukerjea.—Some idea of the birth-rate is to be gathered from the ages of the children still living or dead. As to that, Mr. Thompson in Bengal took two entries,—the age of the eldest child and the age of the youngest; that would give some idea, a better idea than the age of the children still living. Then, for instance, the question is whether a disparity in the ages of the husband and of the wife has a marked effect on fertility, as I think it has, as brought out in the last inquiry.

Mr. Shoobert.—There is no column for caste, is that on purpose ?

Chairman.—Yes.

Mr. Shoobert.—Would not caste affect fertility in so far as it was dependent on occupation ?

Chairman.—The schedules I sent round were tentative. I have not had all the replies in yet. We can easily put in caste.

Then we want to know how many children died before they had a chance to reproduce another generation,—in the case of girls before they reached the age of child-bearing and in the case of boys before they reached the marrying age,—from the ages of children still living.

Mr. Lacey.—How would you obtain any information from the questionnaire on these points ?

Chairman.—Not directly; you get the ages of the children still living.
We want to know the total number of children born alive and the total number of children surviving and their ages. That will give you a definite rate of survival.

Q.—You do not want to know the total number of children born including those born dead. Surely that is required for the purpose of fertility statistics?

Chairman.—I do not pretend to know anything about the subject myself. I have forgotten where I got this from but it was I think in consultation with the former Government actuary; and the number of children born dead is not wanted. It is difficult to get and if the child is still born I think it is not a case of fertility.

K. B. Gul Muhammad Khan.—Why should it be difficult to get the ages ? I think there should be no difficulty. The mothers could at least say that such and such children died who had been so many years younger.

Mr. Lacey.—No. 5 concerns the sex of the first child. What is the idea ?

Chairman.—That is a purely side issue.

Mr. Mukerjea.—In my last report I discussed about the masculinity of the first issue being a probable indication of a greater masculinity in the subsequent issues, and interesting conclusions were drawn, for instance, that the sex of the first child tends to determine the sex of the succeeding children. As it was a first effort, I could not build very much on my data.

Chairman.—I would ask Census Superintendents to let me have their ideas on the subject. Perhaps Census Superintendent, Baroda, will suggest a form of table in which to tabulate these facts. We can take it up to-morrow.

K. B. Gul Muhammad Khan.—One of the editors of a local paper has asked me for a copy of this schedule, and I did not give it to him.

Chairman.—Yes, that is purely a departmental paper. As for maps, we are going to write to everybody later on.

The Conference then adjourned till 11 A. M. on Thursday, 8th January 1931.

CENSUS CONFERENCE

Proceedings of Thursday, the 8th January 1931

The proceedings commenced at Eleven of the clock, with Dr. Hutton in the Chair.

Chairman.—The first thing in my list for to-day is the question of the necessity or otherwise of bringing the inquiry into Educated Unemployment within the scope of the Indian Census Act. Personally I do not think there is any necessity. However as the question has been raised, I should like to know whether anybody had any views to offer.

K. S. Khan Ahmad Hasan Khan.—There is no compulsion on the part of anybody to fill up the form. There should be no compulsion.

Chairman.—The question is—is it necessary to make any alteration in order to make the Act cover this point.

It was agreed that it was not necessary.

Mr. Mukerjea.—Are we to include only matriculates and above or others also ? There seems to be some doubt about it. The practice differs in different provinces.

Chairman.—I should be inclined to go back to matriculates and above because that is the practice in several provinces and to my mind it is a better practice. Some provinces were consulted and Bengal replied that they should have literates in English.

Mr. Mukerjea.—I have with me an additional table for the occupation of English literates. Along with that it will be interesting to have the unemployment figures for English literates. To attempt to number the vernacular unemployed will be too big a task. What about Column 9 ?

Chairman.—You will get a certain number of people who are actually employed but who will say that they are unemployed and give you fanciful answers. The human being is not always logical or literal and exact. I have kept this in order to cover this particular case. For instance you will have a man who is a B. L. and who is only employed in agriculture and who may fairly be shown as unemployed.

Mr. Mukerjea.—There seems to be an apparent contradiction between Column 10 and Column 7. Column 7 says 'for how long unemployed' and Column 10 says 'whether employed in any occupation at all'. Really there is no contradiction. Section 7 relates to gainful occupations and section 10 relates to any kind of business which may not bring in any earning. The enumerator does not understand this distinction. I do not think we should get any very useful figures under Column 10.

Chairman.—There are individuals who will say that they are out of employment and yet have some sort of employment. That is why the apparent contradiction is left in. For instance, the actual case I had in mind is that of a boy who had left school. I asked him what he was doing. He said he had no work and that he was selling tracts for a missionary society. I asked him what they paid and he said he got some pay. You have to deal with cases like that.

Dr. Kunjan Pillai.—This is also the case in Travancore. A man is a teacher in an aided school and gets a small salary. He would like to get a job in government service and if you ask him what he was doing, he would say that he was unemployed.

Mr. Mukerjea.—The father's occupation is really the criterion of the whole thing.

K. S. Khan Ahmad Hasan Khan.—How would you find out unemployment among certain classes ?

Mr. Mukerjea.—You get that from the occupation table.

Chairman.—Caste and profession taken together will give you the necessary indication.

K. S. Khan Ahmad Hasan Khan.—My point is this. In Madras for instance a person in the 6th class can read and write a letter. In the Panjab a middle passed man cannot attempt that. If you accept a uniform standard for every place it will bring in false figures.

Chairman.—That is a matter for you to determine in the Punjab.

K. S. Khan Ahmad Hasan Khan.—I have suggested that headmasters should be consulted as to when a boy becomes competent to read and write a letter. Up to the 7th class, they should accept any declaration with much caution. Some intelligent boys may develope that capacity much earlier.

Chairman.—The next thing we shall take up is the question of statistics by natural divisions. I should very much like to know the views of the conference on that subject. Last time I think natural divisions were excluded entirely. Shall we leave them out again or not.

Mr. Porter.—What is a natural division?

Chairman.—Take Rajputana for instance. It is divided into three natural divisions. One is black cotton country, one is sandy country and the third is the fertile country. The density is greatest where the rainfall is greatest. The idea in 1911 and 1921 was that the whole of India should be cut up for census operations into natural divisions and the compilation was shown both by natural divisions and political divisions in order to deal with statistics of density.

Mr. Mukerjea.—I should not advise this method of treatment in an all India report. It may be desirable within a province where there are clearly marked areas.

Dr. Kunjan Pillai.—We would like to have such divisions in Travancore. We have a coastal area which is densely populated. We have a hilly tract which is sparsely populated. There are clearly marked natural divisions there, the midland and highland.

Chairman.—It may be useful wherever it can be used. The real point is that some provinces are too broken up geographically to be dealt with in this manner.

Mr. Menon.—From the point of view of natural divisions, Travancore, Cochin and British Malabar should be joined together.

Chairman.—I should certainly like to have a density map which will show the same conditions in all parts but there are difficulties in preparing a density map based on natural divisions for the whole of India. Different provinces contain entirely different areas within their own boudaries.

Mr Mukerjea.—My point about natural division is whether we should entirely depend upon rainfall as a test. There is the question of composition of the people, the crops and so on. The original scheme of natural divisions went too much by the rainfall, and geological formation and various other things. I do not know whether for presentation of statistics it is as useful as a demographic analysis.

Mr. Yeatts.—In Madras we have the 26 districts grouped roughly as Telugu, Tamili, the West coast and Canarese country. I think that ought to be continued.

Chairman.—You must have a minimum unit. That is the difficulty of the whole question.

Mr. Porter.—In Bengal we have 3 or 4 very clearly marked areas. We have got more or less high ground in the west. Then we have the Eastern Bengal area in some of which there are no roads at all. They go under water completely. Then we have northern Bengal with hills like Darjeeling. There are very clearly defined natural divisions. If you are going to go down to the natural divisions within a district I think you will be getting into great difficulty. On the other hand the broad natural divisions are fairly easy and all that you need to do is to group your districts.

Chairman.—That may be so in certain places but in a place like Rajputana it is quite impossible to deal with natural divisions which do not coincide with political boundaries.

Mr. Porter.—If you are going to apply a strict geographical classification even in Bengal you will have difficulties. Malda for example would be split up into 3, because it is composed of three different geological formations.

Chairman.—Your broad line of geological distinction does not pass through the middle of Malda.

Mr. Porter.—I think it would.

Chairman.—Would it not be possible to treat the sub-divisions of Malda separately ?

Mr. Porter.—We should have to. All I was pointing out is that you have such variations within a district even if it falls within the broad geographic division. The question is where you are going to stop.

Chairman.—Your definite view is that a unit smaller than the district can be dealt with.

Mr. Porter.—I would not commit myself to that. I was simply asking how far these divisions are to be taken. You have got 3 or 4 well marked natural divisions in Bengal which are thoroughly well understood. How far are you going beyond that ? Are you going to introduce complicated geological considerations ? For instance, take the river Hoogly and the river Ganges. They divide Bengal into three entirely different natural divisions. Each has a different kind of rainfall and different kind of climate ?

Dr. Kunjan Pillai.—In some cases natural divisions do not coincide with administrative divisions. Some of these administrative divisions will have to be broken up and that can be easily done.

Mr. Ghulam Ahmed Khan.—In the Hyderabad the northern half is Mahratta and the southern portion is Telangana. We have been discussing the figures so far as natural boundaries are concerned.

Mr. Venkatesa Iyengar.—We have got Malnad, that is rainy tract and Maidan, the dry part. Hitherto it has been usual to separate the taluq figures. This time I propose to leave out the dry taluqs and add them to the dry division. That will give a really correct figure in the rainy tract and also a correct figure of people living in the dry tract.

Chairman.—The position is this. The figures for natural division can be given pretty accurately in smaller units, particularly in Southern India and on broad lines in Bengal and not at all in Rajputana and Central India.

Mr. Venkatesa Iyengar.—What if you approve of a tahsil being taken as the unit ?

Chairman.—Where you can take a smaller unit, it is always advantageous.

Mr. Mukerjea.—The tahsil would be too small a unit, the provincial tables will show the figures by taluqs but in the discussion of figures, I have adopted an intermediate arrangement between taluq and district and thereby come nearer to natural divisions than in previous census reports of my State.

Mr. Venkatesa Iyengar.—I shall not show the taluq figures in the Imperial table. I shall use the figures in the compilation office for the reports, and not in the tables. Instead of showing western division and eastern division, I can simply show districts.

Chairman.—We cannot show natural divisions in the tables.

Mr. Venkatesa Iyengar.—Unless district units can go wholly.

Colonel Cole.—What happened in 1921 ? I think in the United Provinces and Bombay and Rajputana in the report volume practically every subsidiary t able was grouped by districts and those districts were grouped by artificial as well as natural divisions.

Chairman.—The natural division does not always coincide with district boundaries. Naturally by omitting those tables, you save a certain amount of labour. One can safely omit the subsidiary table showing by natural divisions unless those natural divisions really correspond to actual facts.

Now we proceed to the next item in the agenda: That is the standard to be adopted for the classification of literacy, as advanced, intermediate and backward. What percentage of literacy may we take as the standard ? Are we to fix any arbitrary standard ?

Mr. Mukerjea.—The list will vary with each province. But we must fix a uniform standard. What may be a high standard in a certain province may be very low in Baroda, but a uniform standard is desirable.

Chairman.—Or the standard that is considered low in Baroda may be impossible in Rajputana.

Mr. Turner.—Is this grouping wanted for maps ?

Chairman.—For provincial tables.

Mr. Turner.—Why do you want to call anybody advanced or backward ?

Mr. Mukerjea.—The provincial tables show the literacy figures along with taluq figures.

Mr. Turner.—You must have a uniform standard for the whole of India. You want to show percentage of literacy up to a certain standard and that is only for table. There is no point in grouping which is after all an artificial distribution.

Mr. Mukerjea.—These figures will be correlated with taluq figures under the total number of literates.

Colonel Cole.—The provincial figures are not going to show the number of Brahmans and other Hindus among the literacy percentage.

Mr. Venkatachar.—This is an optional one. In Central India, there are many backward tracts.

Mr. Yeatts.—If for instance you take the standard of Travancore and fix a proportion on that basis, the proportion will be rather a misrepresenting one. The standard varies with the general development of the area in question.

Mr. Venkatesa Iyengar.—What is the object of this classification ? The Government have, for the purpose of scholarships, got their own list of backward classes.

Chairman.—This is to show the conditions in the area. I should like to compare the figures of particular areas with on some definite all–India basis. Unless some definite standard is fixed, this cannot be done.

Mr. Yeatts.—It is spurious accuracy, if I may say so. You are suggesting general terms, such as advanced, intermediate and backward.

Mr. Porter.—The whole difficulty will, I think disappear, if you cut out the classification proposed and simply state three groups, that is those having attained a literacy percentage of over 50 per cent., over 25 per cent. or below 10 per cent.

Chairman.—Yes; 10 per cent literacy would mean the same thing in all provinces.

Mr. Porter.—The whole argument comes to this. What is advanced in Bengal may be backward in Baroda. But 10 per cent, is still 10 per cent in Baroda. I think it is better to have these three groups of percentages.

Mr. Venkatesa Iyengar.—There is another difficulty. If I group a particular sect of people as backward from the point of view of literacy in the census report, it would be given a different meaning in the official records.

Chairman.—Then you might use the word "illiterate".

Colonel Cole.—Speaking from the point of view of Rajputana, they are not at all anxious to have any comparison made with other parts of India as regards literacy. .

Mr. Lacey.—It may be that some areas or some States have not got the same wealth or the same advantage for advancement of education.

Mr. Porter.—We can divide castes accordiug to the degree of literacy. Group 1, those having attained a literacy percentage of 50. Group 2, those having attained a literacy percentage of 25. Group 3, those having attained a literacy percentage of below 10.

Mr. Mukerjea.—I adopted the following percentage during the last census. Group 1 : below 10 per cent. Group 2 : between 10 and 50 per cent. Group 3 : over 50 per cent, in male literacy amongst castes.

Mr. Gul Muhammad Khan.—In that case Baluchistan will be knocked out completely. The numbers there are so small that I can only give absolute figures. If I strike percentages, probably the percentages would be higher than the actual number.

Chairman.—Then I will take the Baroda percentages as standard for the whole of India so that we may have uniformity, that is Group 1 : below 10 per-cent. Group 2 : between 10 and 50 per cent; and Group 3 : over 50 per cent.

Mr. Lacey.—Does the grouping over 50 per cent include females ?

Chairman.—Males only. We are not giving any names to the grouping—we are only giving percentages for the different group.

(The next point, i. e., the grouping of Christians was left over to be discussed later on for want of some information).

Chairman.—The next item is tabulation of industries. My idea is to prepare a list of certain industries which I would tabulate for the whole of India from the provincial returns and in that case every province will have to tabulate those industries in order that all-India figures might be available. Even if the industry is a very small one in any province, figures must be tabulated for that. If an industry is most insignificant in any province, in that case the simplest procedure would be for the Provincial Superintendent to give me the figures and not show them in his table. What I propose to do now is to make my list of industries. But I would leave it to the Provincial Superintendents to tabulate those particular industries or not in their tables *as they find them important.* For instance, it seems probable that in the case of Assam, the Superintendent may not think it worth while to tabulate in his report gold washing, for the industry is of no importance there; but I may want that gold washing for my general industries table owing to its importance elsewhere. I do not know whether anybody has any particular views.

Mr. Mukerjea.—We were already given a list of industries. I presume that this standard list would not be interfered with. Do you want figures for any industries which have not been included in that list ?

Chairman.—If they have not appeared in that list, I do not want figures for them.

Mr. Mukerjea.—If you want figures for districts they can be easily got.

Mr. Porter.—It all depends on the list of industries.

Chairman.—I cannot tabulate by districts.

Mr. Porter.—If you are going to tabulate for 27 or 30 districts you will have an enormous number of entries.

Chairman.—I can tabulate by provinces.

Mr Porter.—Last time we did it by districts.

Chairman.—That is my impression.

Mr. Porter.—Last time the enquiry was restricted to factories.

Colonel Cole said that in the case of Rajputana the industries would have to be shown by States, and the Chairman agreed.

Mr. Venkatachar asked what would happen if a particular industry was confined to say only two States, like Indore and Rewa.

Chairman suggested that States should be shown separately with their industries, if it did not involve a great deal or space.

Mr. Venkatesa Iyengar said that with regard to Mysore he would like to show the information by districts.

Mr. Ghulam Ahmed Khan wanted to know if the scope of the inquiry covered cottage industries also.

Chairman.—No; the idea is to tabulate industrialised industries.

Mr. Ghulam Ahmed Khan.–What about combined factories such as rice-hulling and oil-pressing factories going together–the same machinery being worked by the same operatives during different seasons.

Chairman.—We shall have to show them as combined industries.

Dr. Kunjan Pillai.—The same thing happens in Travancore with rubber and tea.

Mr. C. S. Venkatachar also cited the case of the cotton ginning industry and such like seasonal industries which were conducted for about four months in the year while the same men worked in the fields for the remaining eight months.

Chairman.—Some sort of instructions ought to be issued. Can anybody offer me a definition of organised industry.

Mr. Porter.—There is no definition: it does not need any: it has got to be translated into something else which describes it properly.

Mr. Mukerjea said that he had retained the minimum limit of ten persons working in a factory to make it an organised industry.

Mr. Venkatesa Iyengar was of opinion that even where there were only three or four persons, paid by a man, it was an organised industry; there should be no limit : he had asked his Director of Commerce to give him supplementary statistics for Mysore State to be included in his returns.

K. S. Khan Ahmad Hasan Khan.–What about a tailor employing other men in his shop.

Chairman.—That would be an organised industry.

K. S. Khan Ahmad Hasan Khan.–What should be the minimum number of men employed in such cases ?

Chairman.—I cannot fix the minimum number: last time the minimum number was taken as ten; Bengal wanted to reduce it to five this time; that gives indication of perhaps how low we can go.

Mr. Porter.—I should like a distinction to be introduced between those who are organised employees and those who are not.

Mr. Venkatesa Iyengar.—Perhaps the phrase organised employee might be changed.

Mr. Turner.—What about the proprietor of a show who works himself in it ? He must be included.

Chairman.—Supposing a man employs his nephew alone and pays him a a wage, how can he be regarded as a workman in the industry? There must be a mechanic and some other person. You must have three people: you cannot get below three because there is one man to manage and you must have two men working.

Mr. Turner.—Three people similarly employed and receiving wages for the work they do is that it ? In the instructions I have issued, we have said, supposing there is a road-side cart repairing shop and one of the persons employed is a carpenter, he comes under column 10 (?) and not column 12.

Mr. Venkatesa Iyengar.—In Mysore you have got rural and cottage industry statistics as supplementary to the statistics given in column 12.

Colonel Cole.—There is a certain amount of doubt whether a railway employee is in an organised industry or not; the same argument would apply to the Public Works Department.

Chairman.—The same argument will apply to all of us; the reason why railways are omitted is one of policy. Does anybody want that railway transport and industry should come in?

Mr. Shoobert instanced the case of master weavers who employed people working in their own houses for a wage and brought in their outturn once a week or so: he had put them down as an organised industry although they worked in their own houses singly and got wages, either weekly or by outturn; the master weaver of course supplied the yarn.

Chairman.—If they are paid weekly they probably are but not if by outturn. It comes between cottage industry and organised industry.

Mr Shoobert then instanced the case of *biri* factories, notably in Jubbulpore where a lot of women did the work at home and got paid weekly: they had been classed as casual workers.

Mr. Mukerjea opined that they should be shown as organised, no matter whether they were paid weekly or by piece work.

Dr. Kunjan Pillai also cited the case of coir industry in Travancore.

Chairman.—It is certainly organised: it is an intermediate stage.

Mr. Turner wanted to know if these figures should be tabulated district-wise.

Chairman.—That question has already been raised the answer was that the industries should be tabulated and a remark added at the end as to the districts where the industries were carried on. You cannot tabulate the whole thing by districts.

Mr. Lacey.—Is it necessary to decide definitely now what industries should be tabulated in every province? They will be sorted and then we can decide.

Chairman.—You need not decide now what you are going to have, but I shall have to decide what I am going to tabulate and that is why I want lists from you.

K. S. Khan Ahmad Hasan Khan.—What about agricultural co-operative banks?

Chairman.—Agriculture is not included.

Mr. Mukerjea.—What about government servants' co-operative societies and so on which manufacture as well as sell?

Chairman.—I think they should be excluded since it is a profit sharing institution. On the other hand, I think it is difficult to lay down a hard and fast rule.

Mr. C. S. Venkatachar.—What about jail industries?

Col. Cole.—No inmate of a jail is going to be shown in any of these columns.

Chairman.—A man's principal occupation may be agriculture; but if he goes and works in an Indore Cotton mill for four months, he certainly comes under organised industry. If he does it as a subsidiary occupation we must show it.

Mr. Porter raised the case of typists in banks and salesmen in big shops and such like people who ought to be entered in column 12.

Chairman.—It is very difficult to find a definition of industrial organisation which was not open to objection.

Mr. Mukerjea.—But you definitely exclude agriculture by rule and you also exclude trade?

Chairman.—Yes.

Mr. Mukerjea.—Presumably commerce also. Therefore why not a bank?

Chairman.—I do not definitely exclude trade by rule.

Mr. Porter.—What is the criterion of difference between a person who is a salesman in a shop who gets a wage from his employer and an operative in a mill who gets his pay from his employer?

Chairman.—There are no criteria of difference; the question is do you want to tabulate it against trade or not? Is it worth our while?

Mr. Porter.—I suggest it may be interesting to do so.

Chairman.—You would include transport?

Mr. Porter.—Yes, and I want to include the whole of the railways as an

Mr. Porter.—Having abandoned the word 'industry' in my definition and having adopted this criterion, where a man gets a wage or not, I have told the enumerators to put down the column of the employer also.

Chairman—That was the basis on which I made up my specimen table which gave rise to some criticism. I included even services of the State without the least intention of tabulating, because I could not avoid including them in the only definition that I could make of an industry.

Mr. Shoobert.—For future reference I think it would be better to call it "organised empoyment" instead of "organized industry", because everybody does come under organized employment.

Chairman.—You have got to give the enumerators some general principle to work on. I think it is much better to give them more detailed than to miss out things.

Mr. Venkatesa Iyengar.—If a person is shown as clerk in a co-operative bank, I suppose we don't take it as an organized industry?

Chairman.—I don't think it is safe to tabulate bank as an organized industry. The question you really want to get at is the number of persons who are working under more or less factory conditions.

Mr. Porter.—From whatever point of view you look at the question of motor transport, coming to deal with this question, I think it is very valuable to have these figures tabulated if you could afford to do it. I understand that in the English census everybody has both an occupation and an industry, and upon that analogy everybody ought to have an industry in Bengal or in India. But the tabulation of all that material will probably be expensive. For the purpose of our present discussion, I think it is perhaps desirable to consider how far you have got things like motor services organised.

Chairman.—Do you include the drivers also ?

Mr. Porter.—My instructions are that if a man gets no wage from anybody at all, then there is no entry for it, but if he gets anything, there is an entry for him, and the entry is in the case of productive industry, the business or trade or manufactory in pursuit of which the man is employed by his employer, in the case of a distributive industry, the business or trade in pursuance of which the man is employed, and in the case of a public utility service, the public utility service which the man helps to ply. I have had an exception to that rule to the effect that agricultural labourers are not to be put down in column 12 unless they are employed in extensive agricultural operations as in dairy farms. My point is at this stage I have not obstructed the insertion of any material which I may want to put in. On the other hand, I have made sure that in cases of doubt there will be an entry which will be reasonably likely to be correct and that nothing will therefore be excluded. We must now consider how far it is possible to expand the amount of information which will be supplied so as to include these figures along new lines.

Chairman.—Supposing we include the motor drivers, what will be the effect ? Shall we be able to get the figures ?

Mr. Mukerjea.—I am afraid you won't get them from Baroda.

Mr. Venketachar.—You will get them from Central India.

Mr. Mukerjea.—You will get drivers of motor cars under general occupation.

Chairman.—I am afraid then I cannot get figures for motor transport for all India.

Chairman.—Now, the last thing is about the proposals from the Anglo-Indian Association. I think all that we can say is none of them would be acceptable. I think I have circulated copies of the Anglo-Indian representation.

Mr. Porter.—The only places where some difficulty might be experienced are the big towns, but if we employ Anglo-Indian supervisors the whole difficulty can be solved. But some of their proposals have been made on a complete misapprehension of the processes of working for instance, they suggest that the daily total should be scrutinised by a committee.

Chairman.—It is simply absurd; we can't do it.

Mr. Porter.—Now, there is some difficulty in regard to the descendants of the old Portuguese in some parts of Bengal. They are all Christians and have Portuguese names like D' Souza, D' Cunha and so on, but for all cultural purposes they have assimilated with the native population. I think some simple criterion should be imposed.

Chairman.—In the district of Backergunj there is a small community who are definitely called Feringis, and I have had some of them in my court and they were called Algy, Ferdy and Monty. They could not speak anything but Bengali.

Mr. Mukerjea.—We have got in Bombay as also in Gujarat some people with a definite status, and they are called East Indians. They are mostly Maratha Kolis and are converts. I always treated them as Indians, and the Bombay practice is also to treat them as Indians.

Chairman.—I think we must treat the Feringis in Bengal as Indians.

Mr. Venkatesa Iyengar.—How are you going to find out that a man was not of European extraction?

Chairman.—We can't find it out, because they have no birth certificates. The language they speak is the test. That won't give you the exact criterion, but it would be generally a test in many cases. What I would like to adopt as the criterion for Christians is roughly a community of 70,000 or thereabouts should get a separate head for itself. I shall send detailed instructions about this matter, giving you a complete list of sects in India. You can give more details for your respective provinces.

K. S. Khan Ahmad Hasan Khan.—There is some difficulty about persons coming to Railway stations to catch a train on the census night, there is a likelihood of their being re-enumerated. For example, people daily come to railway stations at 9-0' clock to catch a train. So any person who comes to the railway station at 8 might have been enumerated in his own house in the town and he will be re-enumerated at the Station, because passes will not be issued in the town.

Chairman.—Won't the platform enumerator catch him as he comes along on the platform?

K. S. Khan Ahmad Hasan Khan.—The platform enumerator's business is to get hold of everybody who gets into the train.

Mr. Lacey.—Those people who want to leave the town that night should not be enumerated in the house because they are not spending the night there.

Mr. Mukerjea.—Would not the difficulty be obviated by handing over a pass to every person who has been enumerated in the house before he comes to the station that night?

Mr. Turner.—That will be too big a task. If a person says that he has been enumerated, I think you must leave it at that.

Chairman.—I think the case is that house enumerators will strike out all persons who are not going to spend the night there. These persons will be enumerated by the platform enumeration. In most cases they will be at the Railway Station by the time the Enumerator reaches the house.

The next question on this list is the classification of converts from Hinduism to Islam and *vice versa.* I think there is no difficulty at all. If a Hindu becomes a Muslim, you classify him as a Muslim and if a Muslim becomes a Hindu, you classify him as a Hindu.

The next point is how to enumerate people going to cinemas and theatres.

Mr. Mukerjea.—I asked the District Magistrate of Baroda to have all the cinemas closed for a time at least up to 9-30 at night.

Chairman.—You can make the cinema manager or the proprietor the enumerator for the population inside the cinema at the time of the census. He will then close the cinema to avoid the trouble of enumerating.

Mr. Porter.—I do not think you can get him to do that under the Act. You want an order of the Local Government.

K. B. Gul Muhammad Khan.—If that could be done, it would be a very good thing. I will get it done in Baluchistan.

Mr. Shoobert.—I want to raise this question about the dialects. A man speaks Hindi and his mother tongue is something else.

Chairman.—We do not deal in dialects at all. The test is its classification as a language in the linguistic survey.

Dr. Kunjan Pillai.—What is the principle to be adopted in selecting castes. You leave it to the provinces?

Chairman.—It is a provincial table. In some cases it will be interesting to show whether there is any particular occupation. It is a purely provincial matter.

Mr. Mukerjea.—I want to raise a question about Table XX, Part 2. I do not quite follow what is meant.

Chairman.—That refers to the area we are taking, it may be a tahsil or a district.

Mr. Mukerjea.—It is very important to show how a general language like Gujarati is displacing a language like Kachchhi.

Chairman.—In many cases it will be imposing too big a burden.. The point is that all over India you have got a steady movement going on in the direction of the prevalent language assimilating or ousting the minor languages which are largely retained as domestic languages. When you have got your map you will probably be able to trace the former area of a language by the area in which it is spoken as a secondary languege. It is a case of one language overlaying another. For instance, Santali was at one time the only language in use in the Santal Parganas and a considerable area besides. It is now being overlaid everywhere by Bengali or Hindi.

Mr. Porter.—Would it be possible to save time and expense or compilation by laying down some rules of exclusion. For instance 90 per cent of the literate in Bengal will return Bengali as their mother tongue and English as a subsidiary language.

Chairman.—It may be useful for some other purpose but for the purpose of our particular inquiry, English as a subsidiary language is useless except conceivably in a place like Calcutta and some parts of Bengal in which English is coming in as a regular language.. I have often noticed that in Calcutta people will prefer to talk in English, though it is not their mother tongue.

Mr. Mukerjea.—Among Parsis there is a genuine movement towards that. It will be interesting to find out how far English is *transplating* even Hindi as a *lingua franca.*

Mr. Porter.—The object is to see how far indigenous languages are being overlaid by the current language of the area.

Mr. Lacey.—In some districts in Bihar and Orissa I find as many as 50 mother tongues

Chairman.—May we know some of them?

Mr. Lacey.—Hindu, Urdu, Bengali, Gujarati, Kachchhi, Marathi, Marwari, Nepali, Panjabi, Pushtu, Mundari, Santali, Tamili, Telugu, Arabic, Chinese, English and so on.

Chairman.—The only one that will be relevant fo the purpose of our enquiry is the indigenous language of the area.

you will have to exclude practically everything else.

Mr. Lacey.—If you wash out Hindustani, it will make it very simple.

Chairman.—Wherever Hindustani is the mother tongue, you cannot exclude it.

K. S. Khan Ahmad Hasan Khan.—In the Panjab the court language is Hindustani, though the mother tongue is Panjabi.

Mr. Venkatesa Iyenger.—In my part both Telugu and Kannada are spoken. The Government officers have got to know both languages.

Mr. Venkatachar.—Malvi is a branch of Rajasthani.

Chairman.—I think Rajasthani should not be regarded as a language for bilingual purposes.

Mr. Venkatachar.—Again there are the Eastern Hindi and Western Hindi in some states. These are fifty–fifty. Will that be a bilingual area?

Chairman.—Do any other languages come in?

Mr. Venkatachar.—There is difference between the two languages—Bandeli and Bagheli.

Chairman.—They should then be classified. If the two are reciprocally incomprehensible, we must treat them in practice as different tongues.

Mr Venkatachar.—Rajasthani and Hindi are so near that there is practically no difference.

K. S. Khan Ahmad Hasan Khan—In the Panjab, there is the Sarafa and Lahnda used by shopkeepers. Will these be covered by the term Hindi?

K. B. Gul Muhammad Khan.—There is the Sindhi and Lahnda in Baluchistan. The local people, that is the Muhammadan tribesmen know no other language. They write letters and keep all their correspondence in Lahnda.

Chairman.—What script is it?

K. B. Gul Muhammad Khan.—It is Panjabi and Hindi mixed.

Chairman.—Supposing you merely say as Hindi, what is the extent of difference?

K. S. Khan Ahad Hassan Khan.—It is absolutely different from Dev Nagari.

Chairman.—A man who can read or write Dev Nagari cannot read or write Sarafa or Lahnda?

K. S. Khan Ahmad Hasan Khan.—No.

K. S. Khan Ahmad Hasan Khan.—In the Punjab, the orders are we should enter Urdu, Hindi, Gurumukhi or Roman. Anybody knowing any of these languages simply put down as literate.

Chairman.—In the circumstances, it is very difficult for one like myself who does not know Hindi, to decide whether Lahnda or Sarafa should be classified as Hindi or not.

K. S. Khan Ahmad Hasan Khan.—They call it Mahajani Hindi.

Chairman.—It is what we call Kaiti in Assam.

K. S. Khan Ahmad Hasan Khan.—I think the term Hindi could cover such cases.

K. B. Gul Muhammad Khan—.I am getting Lahnda entirely separated.

K S. Khan Ahmad Hasan Khan.—Is it going to be specified in the column?

K B. Gul Muhammad Khan.—Yes; in Baluchistan it is important.

Chairmn.—You settle that with your own people. These are put in merely for the benifit of local Governments. If you think it is enough to show it as Hindi, I do not mind. I shall not use those figures for the all India returns. All I want is literate in English or illiterate in English.

The Chairman then expressed his gratefulness to all the members for having given him the benefit of their advice. The conference then adjourned *sine die.*

STATEMENT No. I
Census Divisions and Agency

Division	Number of			Number of			Average of numbered houses per		
	Charges	Circles	Blocks	Charge Superintendents	Supervisors	Enumerators	Charge Superintendent	Supervisor	Enumerator
1	2	3	4	5	6	7	8	9	10
Baroda State	96	1,216	12,138	106	1,255	9,409	7,692	649	86
Baroda City (including Cantonment and Railway areas)	10	55	595	15	104	589	3,255	469	81
Amreli Division	11	97	945	11	97	763	5,031	570	73
Baroda Division	26	362	3,411	26	364	3,136	8,634	617	71
Non-synchronous Area ...	...	*5*	*36*	...	*5*	*20*	...	*266*	*66*
Mehsana Division	28	500	5,381	28	489	3,313	13,621	779	115
Navsari Division	17	175	1,638	22	174	1,443	4,255	538	64
Non-synchronous Area ...	...	*63*	*580*	*5*	*53*	*406*	*2 848*	*269*	*35*
Okhamandal ...	4	27	168	4	27	165	2,925	433	70

STATEMENT No. II
Number of enumeration books, slips, and other forms issued and used

Division	Enumeration books		Block Lists		Slips		Slips per 100 houses occupied		Other forms issued		
	Issued	Used	Issued	Used	Issued	Used*	Issued	Used	Household Cards	Boat Tickets	Traveller's Passes
1	2	3	4	5	6	7	8	9	10	11	12
Baroda State ...	44,413	38,344	72,619	58,833	2,983,179	2,548,790	530	453	742	...	30,000
Baroda City ...	2,002	1,799	3,217	2,819	129,315	116,530	429	387	300	...	4,000
Amreli Division ...	4,715	3,889	5,014	3,953	215,172	183,537	594	507	...	...	3,000
Baroda Division ...	11,357	10,138	21,802	16,036	877,239	743,658	541	442	60	...	7,000
Mehsana Division..	16,753	14,039	30,936	27,242	1,243,500	1,051,194	515	436	262	...	9,000
Navsari Division...	8,997	7,922	10,454	7,808	477,534	421,978	595	526	...	...	5,000
Okhamandal ...	589	507	1,196	975	40.419	31,893	571	449	120	...	2,000

* Figures shown in column 7 is the actual population enumerated on the Census date plus those slips which were scratched out on that date on account of the persons concerned having died or left the place of enumeration.

STATEMENT No. III
District Census charges

Division	District Office Establishment	House Numbering	Remuneration of Census Officers	Travelling allowances of Census Officers	Local purchase of Stationaries	Postage	Freight	Miscellaneous	Total
1	2	3	4	5	6	7	8	9	10
Baroda City ...	4,452- 7-4	...	...	...	...	...	...	197-9-7	6,443- 0-11
Amreli Division ...	91- 2-1	...	...	...	...	...	...	...	91- 2- 1
Baroda Division ...	150- 0-0	...	...	...	...	...	...	...	150- 0- 0
Mehsana Division..	150- 0-0	...	...	...	...	...	...	...	150- 0- 0
Navsari Division...	107-10-1	...	...	...	...	...	...	...	107-10- 1
Okhamandal ...	...	...	...	...	...	...	...	...	...
Total ...	**4,951-3-6**	...	...	...	...	...	...	**197-9-7**	**6,941-13-1**

STATEMENT No. IV

Enumerators and Supervisors

Name of charge	Number of blocks	Enumerators: Total	Enumerators: Talatis	Enumerators: School Teachers	Enumerators: Other public servants including Railwaymen and Military men	Enumerators: Non-officials: Members of Gampanchayats including Patels	Enumerators: Non-officials: Other private persons	Number of circles	Supervisors: Total	Supervisors: Revenue department	Supervisors: Educational department	Supervisors: Police department	Supervisors: Other public servants	Supervisors: Non-officials
1	2	3	4	5	6	7	8	9	10	11	12	13	14	15
BARODA STATE	**12,138**	**9,409**	**958**	**5,485**	**1,721**	**724**	**521**	**1,216**	**1,255**	**197**	**483**	**71**	**442**	**62**
Baroda City including Cantonment and Railway Areas	**595**	**589**	...	**196**	**390**	...	**3**	**55**	**104**	...	**30**	...	**73**	**1**
Baroda City (Ex. Contonment and railway areas	549	549	...	190	359	...	...	49	98	...	30	...	68	...
Baroda Cantonment	27	27	...	6	18	...	3	2	2	...	...	...	1	1
Civil Area	*15*	*15*	...	*6*	*6*	...	*3*	*1*	*1*	...	...	...	...	*1*
Military Area	*12*	*12*	...	...	*12*	...	...	*1*	*1*	...	...	...	*1*	...
Railway Areas	19	13	...	...	13	...	...	4	4	...	...	...	4	...
B. B. and C. I. Ry. Area ...	*15*	*9*	...	...	*9*	...	...	*2*	*2*	...	...	...	*2*	...
G. B. S. Ry. Area	*4*	*4*	...	...	*4*	...	...	*2*	*2*	...	...	...	*2*	...
Amreli Division	**945**	**763**	**68**	**455**	**158**	**60**	**22**	**97**	**97**	**21**	**39**	**9**	**25**	**3**
Amreli (Mahal)	352	283	19	176	48	35	7	36	36	7	22	...	7	...
Bhimkatta	8	8	1	5	1	1	...	1	1	...	...	1	...	...
Damnagar	176	144	16	88	34	6	...	12	12	4	3	1	3	1
Dhari	100	99	9	67	19	2	2	22	22	4	4	4	9	1
Khambha...	77	55	8	24	12	5	6	7	7	3	1	...	2	1
Kodinar	200	142	13	83	42	4	...	16	16	3	8	2	3	...
Ratanpur	32	32	2	14	2	7	7	3	3	...	1	1	1	...

Baroda Division	**3,411**	**3,136**	**337**	**1,921**	**288**	**361**	**229**	**362**	**364**	**57**	**154**	**26**	**115**	**12**
Baroda (Mahal)	461	388	60	247	27	51	3	47	47	12	19	4	11	1
Bhadran	232	232	20	165	25	14	8	20	20	1	11	2	5	1
Dabhoi	341	319	33	177	43	61	5	35	35	11	11	...	13	...
Dabhoi Station	3	3	...	...	3	...	...	1	1	...	...	...	1	...
Karjan	300	300	39	139	19	36	67	34	34	7	12	...	15	...
Padra	421	421	40	230	28	61	62	43	43	2	31	...	10	...
Petlad	671	670	45	501	41	50	33	67	70	3	48	3	16	...
Sankheda...	304	233	29	139	36	13	16	35	34	7	6	4	14	3
Savli	282	230	26	113	19	43	29	33	33	3	8	...	18	4
Sinor	158	157	18	121	17	1	...	20	20	5	4	11	...	...
Tilakwada	56	39	5	20	14	3	...	7	7	1	2	...	4	...
Vaghodia	182	144	22	69	19	28	6	20	20	5	2	2	8	3
Mehsana Division	**5,381**	**3,313**	**312**	**2,097**	**510**	**172**	**222**	**500**	**489**	**84**	**215**	**13**	**142**	**35**
Atarsumba	161	161	12	59	19	23	48	12	12	4	2	1	5	...
Chanasma	462	272	35	173	46	11	...	46	46	6	15	2	17	6
Dehgam	352	178	26	127	25	...	...	31	31	5	21	...	5	...
Harij	109	47	11	15	12	7	2	10	10	4	2	2	2	...
Kadi	588	306	40	209	53	6	...	52	52	10	23	2	3	9
Kalol	520	452	29	228	35	56	102	51	51	6	22	4	14	5
Kalol Station	2	2	...	...	2	...	...	1	1	...	...	...	1	...
Kheralu	421	264	27	186	46	5	...	36	36	12	15	...	9	...
Mehsana (Mahal)	475	312	26	216	57	5	8	45	45	1	16	1	27	...
Mehsana Station...	10	10	...	...	10	...	...	3	3	...	...	...	3	...
Patan	638	345	40	202	63	...	30	58	48	3	28	...	10	7
Sidhpur	580	376	32	229	60	34	31	54	54	11	21	1	15	6
Vijapur	688	371	18	290	58	12	1	68	68	14	36	...	18	...
Visnagar	375	216	16	163	24	13	...	33	32	8	14	...	8	2
Navsari Division	**1,638**	**1,443**	**227**	**753**	**302**	**129**	**32**	**175**	**174**	**30**	**39**	**21**	**73**	**11**
Gandevi	157	157	15	124	18	...	...	16	16	1	12	...	3	...
Kamrej	178	178	33	127	13	5	...	16	16	2	6	3	5	...
Mahuva	153	153	26	91	15	13	8	17	22	6	2	3	5	6
Mangrol	229	159	35	60	39	25	...	31	31	4	2	5	20	...
Navsari (Mahal)	315	316	30	201	72	13	...	31	31	8	4	5	12	2
Palsana	116	116	23	73	4	16	...	14	14	2	7	2	...	3
Songadh	241	115	31	14	68	2	...	23	17	2	1	2	12	...
Vyara	249	249	34	63	73	55	24	27	27	5	5	1	16	...
Okhamandal	**168**	**165**	**14**	**63**	**73**	**2**	**13**	**27**	**27**	**5**	**6**	**2**	**14**	...
Beyt	21	21	...	9	10	...	2	2	2	...	1	...	1	...
Okhamandal (Mahal) including Port Okha.	147	144	14	54	63	2	11	25	25	5	5	2	13	...

CHAPTER III

TABULATION, COMPILATION AND REPORT

A. The Preparation of Provisional Results

78. Preparation in the Districts.—We will now describe the course of operations on and after the census day. An adequate supply of enumeration card books, travellers' passes, etc. was maintained at all mahal headquarters and the railway authorities were also amply supplied with enumeration card books and travellers' passes to meet the extra demand at the Final Cenus. Mahal Officers had made previous arrangements with their supervisors where to meet with the final results. It was ordered that each enumerator should move out in his block and bring his preliminary record to date during day time so that the writing work after 7 P. M. could be reduced to minimum.

79. Preparations in the City and neighbourhood.—My Assistants and the staff were provided with a car from the State garage from 9 A. M. of the census day till 6 A. M. of the next morning. All of us moved in the different wards of the city and saw the work of the enumerators bringing their record up-to-date in day time. My Assistants also saw the work at Vishwamitri station, Makarpura town and Baroda Passenger Station and other places. After 7 P. M., all the staff that could be available was utilised for seeing to the final count and my clerks and Census Inspectors whom I had appointed from 1st January last and who were called back to Baroda two days before the census day, all helped the City Municipal Staff and other people in preparing final totals after the enumerators had taken their final rounds in their blocks. In the Cantonment, I deputed two clerks from the Central Office to help in the preparation of provisional totals at night. There were 4 trains due to arrive at Baroda Passenger Station between 7-30 P. M. and 8-30 P. M. and six of my clerks and inspectors were kept ready to supplement the Railway enumeration staff on the occasion. The rush was so great that my assistants had themselves to write out particulars for many passengers. I myself supervised this platform enumeration and gave all necessary help.

80. Visit to the Marshalling Yard.—I then saw the final census of the Railway Marshalling Yard, the Cantonment and all the wards of the City. My Shirastedar went to the State military lines at 9 P. M. with the Mahal Vahivatdar and helped in the work of the final census. The City Municipality had arranged to ask all the enumerators and supervisors of each ward to meet at the fire brigade station of each ward and kept Petromax lamps burning to give enough light for the work of seeing new entries made on the final day and to prepare the provisional totals. Over a hundred men collected at each of these places and there was great eagerness among them to show speedy and accurate work. The police and the scout troops in the city gave useful help. Figures of each ward as they were ready were taken by my office staff and posted in the totalling registers.

81. Arrangements for Telephone.—As there was telephonic connection between Baroda, Dabhoi and Miyagam–Karjan railway stations and with various fire brigade stations at Baroda, the Railway authorities of Baroda State were asked to have the telephone working throughout the night.

82. The first Results.—The Vahivatdar of Padra sent men in a motor car with the provisional totals from Padra to Baroda at 0–20 and the Vahivatdar of Vaghodia, Mir Intejamalli Saheb rushed to Baroda in a special car and arrived at the Census headquarters at 1–25 A. M. with the figures of the final Census. The Mahalkari of Bhadran sent a wire from Borsad, but not feeling sure of its early reaching, he sent a special man on camel–back to Baroda, who reached here at about 6 A. M., the following morning. Figures of Dabhoi station, Dabhoi mahal, and Karjan mahal were received on the phone during the night.

83. The Preparation of the City Figures.—My office people were busy during the whole night, helping in the counting of provisional totals, the Municipal, Cantonment and Railway authorities and as the figures were being received, they were posted on the totalling forms kept ready for the purpose. As there were trains arriving at Baroda Railway till 5 A. M. platform enumeration had to be carried on till then, but all other figures were ready and only the platform enumeration figures of the two mail trains arriving at Baroda at 4–30 and 5 A. M. remained to be added. It was only after the trains left Baroda, that their figures could be had but the Baroda City figures were ready before 6 A. M. and were at once telegraphed to the Census Commissioner for India at Delhi. They were immediately published with the figures of all the past censuses in the City for the information of the public.

84. Mahal Provisional Results.—Figures from other mahals and railway charges began to arrive by wire one after another and my clerks and both my assistants saw their being compiled into totals by districts. After the last wire, which was received before 5 in the afternoon on the 27th instant, the totals for the whole State were immediately made up and forthwith telegraphed to the Census Commissioner for India at Delhi. They were all published in the City for the information of the public along with the last census figures, showing the actual increase and its percentage also. The Mahal Officers vied with one another in the preparation and despatch of provisional totals and generally their work was satisfactory.

85. Appreciations.—The promptitude with which these results were made known to the public broke all previous records and evoked high praise from all quarters. The Chief Secretary to His Highness wrote to me on the 10th March 1931 as follows :—

> " His Highness the Maharaja Saheb has read your letter dated the 28th February 1931 and the provisional census returns with interest and has asked me to thank you for bringing about the census enumeration so quickly."

and shortly afterwards, at a public gathering His Highness the Maharaja Saheb himself most graciously complimented me on this achievement. The Resident of the State (Lieut. Colonel D. G. Wilson) wrote on the 3rd March a letter to me in appreciation from which the following extract is given:—

> "......It is a great achievement and one of which you may be justly proud to have got the totals with such remarkable promptitude; permit me to offer you and your staff my congratulations on this proof of efficiency.............."

B. Preparation of Final Totals

86. Opening of Abstraction office.—The Abstraction office was organised on the 1st March 1931. The enumeration books of the Baroda Cantonment, Baroda Marshalling Yard and the Baroda Passenger Station were taken charge of by the central office staff on the census night after the provisional totals were compiled by the supervisors and the charge superintendents concerned. Books of the Baroda City and the Baroda mahal were received on the next day while books of all the other mahals and the railway stations in the Raj were received by the 7th March 1931.

87. Preliminary procedure: (i) *Covers etc. removed.*—As soon as the enumeration books were received, each book was examined, its eligibility for a cash prize or a certificate was appraised and the book was relieved of its covers, instruction pages and specimen slips.

(ii) Slips cut by guillotine in the State Press.—The books, which were received in bundles of circles and *thanas,* were arranged according to mahals and districts in separate rooms. A different method was prescribed in respect of enumeration books for the City of Baroda and the towns; and those concerning rural areas. The former were at once sent to the State Press where a picked staff of census clerks, directly superintended by the Assistant Census Commissioner, Head Supervisor and others worked night and day at putting the books under the guillotine and cutting them into slips. Very great care was taken to see that the slips of one area did not get mixed up with those of the other areas.

(iii) Town and Rural slips kept separate.—Enumeration books of hamlets (पेटापरा) and railway stations of towns were kept along with those of the town proper and cut up separately. Each town was treated as a separate unit throughout the sorting operations. Enumeration books of railway stations in rural areas were taken up with those of the rural areas of the mahal. Slips of rural area of each mahal were kept separate throughout from those of towns.

(iv) No sorting for sex as slips were of different colours.—Sex did not require any sorting as in the enumeration books, arrangements were already made to enumerate females on buff-coloured, and males on white slips. When the enumeration books were being cut up into individual cards at the State Press, male and female cards for each unit were put in separate boxes or bags.

(v) How register "A" was prepared for rural areas.—As soon as the City and town books were cut into slips they were assigned to specially selected sorters, who started sorting operations with sorting for Religion and Sects. With regard to rural areas, before the books were cut up they were carefully counted over again, and a general sorting by main heads of religion was also done and the results posted in sorters' tickets. One ticket for each circle with spaces for entries of each block was given to each sorter. From these figures, Register "A" was prepared by blocks and circles, and village figures were taken from this Register "A"

88. The Arrangement of Boxes and Bags.—Slips, as pointed out already, were white for males and buff–coloured for females, but no separate colours were adopted as in past censuses to distinguish the main religions. Distinctions of colour for religions required to be learnt and experience showed that there was always a possibility of mistakes on that score. These were obviated on the present occasion by the method adopted. Again, distinctions in colour for the different religions always required an estimate of the strength of each faith beforehand; this estimate is liable to be falsified when the actual count is taken, and there is always a large wastage of paper inevitable in the adoption of this procedure, which we were able to avoid on this occasion. But slips for Muslims, Jains and others were kept in separate bags, with the name of the religion and the number of slips marked on each bag. It was arranged also to have white bags for males and red bags for females.

89. Different Colours of Sorters' Tickets for Males and Females.—Sorters' tickets for males were similarly printed on white paper and those for females on buff–coloured paper, in order to avoid mistakes in posting of male or female entries or *vice versa.*

90. Time taken for cutting.—The entire operation of cutting the books into slips was completed on the 19th March, after only 16 working days. As will be shown later, even counting this period, the total time taken for arriving at final results was much less than under the slip–copying system.

91. Provisional and Final Totals.—Register ' A ' was prepared soon after and we got the final estimate of the total population by the 24th March 1931. We did not, however, accept it as final till the sorting for sects and age–periods was completed for all towns and rural areas. The sorters' tickets for both these operations were compared with each other and Register " A ", and finally on the 30th March the total mentioned below was arrived at as the figure of the population of the State :—

Name	Population		Difference	
	Provisional totals	Final totals	Actual	Per cent
Baroda City ...	112,862	112,860	–2	·0017
Cantonement	*3,221*	*3,221*	...	...
Amreli ...	173,924	173,948	24	·013
Baroda ...	711,499	711,481	—18	—·0025
Mehsana ...	1,009,978	1,010,007	29	·0028
Navsari ...	404,343	404,377	34	·0084
Okhamandal ...	30,318	30,334	16	·053
Baroda State ...	2,442,924	2,443,007	83	·0034

The difference between the provisional totals and final totals thus arrived at, is only 83, *i. e.* ·0034 per cent. Out of this difference of 83, 48 should be further deducted for the following reason. As the Salher *thana* is a non–synchronous tract and far away from the head–quarter town of Songadh taluka, only the figures of the preliminary count were reckoned in the provisional charge total, and the final count showed an increase of 48, the actual difference therefore due to mistakes in charge totals was only 35, or ·00143 per cent.

92. Accuracy and Promptitude in Provisional and Final Totals.—The extremely small margin of error and the promptitude with which the final totals were prepared are both unique in the history of the Census of Baroda. As it will appear from the following table, the present census in these respects broke all previous records :—

Census year	Census date	Date on which provisional totals were telegraphed	Time taken for despatch of provisional totals	Difference between provisional and final totals	Proportionate margin of difference	Date of completion of final totals	Total time taken for arriving at final totals
1901	1-3-01	6-3-1901	5 days	1,765	·09	16-7-01	4½ months.
1911	10-3-11	12-3-1911	48 hours	1,345	·07	30-4-11	1½ „
1921	18-3-21	20-3-1921	36 hours	4,147	·2	6-5-21	1 month and 18 days.
1931	26-2-31	27-2-1931	17½ hours	83	·0034	24-3-31	26 days.

93. Beginning of Sorting at once.—As mentioned in the earlier part of this Report, the entries were directly made on to the card and therefore no inter vening slip-copying was necessary before sorting could be taken in hand, with the result that immediately after the enumeration books were cut up into slips on the guillotine, sorting operations were begun.

94. Organisation of Units.—Baroda city, all towns and the rural areas of each division were kept separate in different rooms in the Saroj Bungalow, on the whole forming 89 units distributed as shown in the marginal table. Separate gangs were formed for each of these units. Six specially efficient sorters were placed in charge of the slips for the City and the Cantonment. Town slips were also entrusted to select sorters. The sorting establishment began to be formed as soon as the Abastraction Office was opened. We began with the nucleus of our inspecting staff, till such time as all the books had arrived and the books were made up into slips and the sorting operations were proceeding normally. Our total strength of sorters was 90. Over them there were 8 supervisors and a Head Supervisor. The Assistant Census Commissioner supervised the whole work throughout. The City and Cantonment formed 2 units while all towns and mahal rural areas formed separate units.

Area	Number of units
Baroda City ...	2
Towns ...	48
Rural areas ...	39
TOTAL ...	89

95. Average slips per sorter.—The average number of slips for a sorter in the city block was 18,810. For towns, the average per each sorter was 25,634 and for rural areas 28,235. The average for the whole population per sorter was 27,144 slips.

96. Facilities provided for a sorter.—Each city and urban area sorter was provided with a table and a chair, and a set of two pigeon-holes each having 6 x 5 holes with a number of adhesive labels and a big card board to cover his pigeon-holes whenever he left office. Rural area sorters were asked to share a table lengthwise between two. Every one was supplied with adhesive labels at each sorting.

97. Boxes for slips.—Boxes for keeping the slips were of wood in the past censuses; this time as the slips were the only material available and as it was essential to protect them from white ants, as well as from possible damage from rain or fire, we decided to have strong steel boxes. Wooden boxes and pigeon holes could not realise even one fourth of their value when they had to be disposed of; but these steel boxes, though costlier in the beginning, gave us thoroughly good service while in use and kept the slips in good condition. When they were disposed of, they fetched Rs. 334–0–0 or 28·7of their value, so that in this respect we did much better than in 1921. The boxes realised fairly good prices *i. e.* over 40 per cent of their value but the pigeon-holes being inconvenient for any other purpose, did not get a higher bid; they realised only 14·5 per cent of their purchase price.

98. Number and arrangement of boxes.—The boxes were of two sizes, one measurnig 24″ x 16″ x 12″ and the other 36″ x 16″ x 12″ so that they could conveniently accommodate four and six books at the bottom. Pigeon holes also required to be of greater size as the slips measured 7¼″ x 3½″ instead of the usual slips of 4½″ x 2″ size prescribed for and used by other provinces and states. The number of boxes used was as shown in the margin. Each box was serially numbered and a label (Form H) was affixed to it showing the area concerned, and the names of religions with the number of slips contained in each.

Area of uuits	Number of boxes
Baroda City ...	10
Baroda Dn. Rural ...	38
Mehsana „ „ ...	41
Navsari „ „ ...	22
Amreli „ „ ...	8
Okhamandal „ ...	1
Urban areas ...	28
TOTAL ...	158

C. *Scheme of Sorting*

99. The scheme of Imperial Tables.—The forms cf Imperial Tables are usually prescribed by the Census Commissiner for India. As in this State, there were additional columns provided in the schedule, the forms of these Tables had to be slightly modified to suit our requirements. These modifications were approved by the Census Commissioner for India in his letter No. 49–Rept dated the 8th April 1931. The following is the list of Imperial and State tables compiled for this census:—

1. IMPERIAL TABLES

I. Area, Houses and Population
II. Variation in Population during last fifty years
III. Towns and Villages classified by population
IV. Towns classified by Population with variation for fifty years
V. Towns arranged territorially with population by Religion
VI. Birthplace
VII. Age, Sex and Civil condition
VIII. Civil condition by selected castes
IX. Infirmities
  Part A. Distribution by age
  Part B. Infirmities by divisions
  Part C. Infirmities by selected castes, tribes and races
X. Occupation or Means of livelihood
XI. Occupation of selected castes, tribes or races
  Part A. Occupation of selected castes, tribes aud races
  Part B. Distribution of Earners in certain groups of Occupation by caste, tribe or race
XII. Educated Unemployment
  Part A. Educated unemployment by class
  Part B. „ „ „ degree

XIII. Literacy by religion and age.
XIV. „ „ selected castes, tribes or races
XV. Language
  Part A. Language
  Part B. Bilingualism
  Part C. Polylingualism
XVI. Religion
  Part A. Religion
  Part B. Sects
  Part C. Christians by race and sect
XVII. Caste, Tribe or Race
XVIII. Variation of Population of selected tribes during last fifty years
XIX. European and Allied Races and Anglo-Indians by race and age

II. STATE TABLES

A. Talukwar Statistics

I. Area, Houses and Population by talukas and peta mahals
II. Population of Talukas, etc., by religion and literacy
III. Variation in population by mahals
  Part A. Since 1891
  Part B. Adjusted population in talukas since 1901
  Part C. Variations in density since 1901
IV. Total area and village site areas by mahals
V. Age, Sex and Civil condition in selected towns
VI. Special Literacy Tables
  Part A. Literacy by script (Hindi and Urdu) by religion and mother tongue
  Part B. „ „ „ „ „ „ by religion and age
  Part C. „ „ „ „ „ „ for selected castes
  Part D. Literacy by talukas
  Part E. Literacy by towns
  Part F. Literacy by wards of the City
VII. Chief castes by talukas
VIII. Occupation in selected towns

B. Special Tables

IX. The Census of Livestock
X. The Tenement Census in the Baroda City; Statistics by wards and circles
  Part A. Classification of structures according to kind
  Part B. Classification of structures according to floors
  Part C. Inhabited structures by number of families
  Part D. Inhabited structures by number of occupants
  Part E. Inhabited structures by number of rooms and families
XI The Normal Size of the Household by divisions
XII. Classification of Homesteads
  Part A. State Summary
  Part B. Rural areas
  Part C. Urban areas
  Part D. Baroda city

XIII. Industrial Statistics
- Part A. Whole State Summary
- Part B. Details by divisions

XIV. Dependents by age-groups
- Part A. By certain castes
- Part B. By divisions

XV. The Infirm
- Part A. By mahals
- Part B. by age and civil condition

XVI. Annual Age-periods
- Part A. By divisions
- Part B. By religions

XVII. Sects by divisions

XVIII. Special Tables for Immigrants
- Part A. Immigrants by age periods
- Part B. Immigrants to City from selected areas
- Part C. Comparative literacy of local Immigrant population in the City

100. Imperial Tables curtailed this time.—The number of Imperial Tables was curtailed this time from motives of economy and the following tables were dropped by us :—

(a) Occupations subsidiary to Agriculture.
(b) Combined occupations.
(c) Occupations by religion.

But we decided to prepare as parts of Imperial Tables IX and XVI respectively, the tables regarding Infirmities of selected castes, and the Races and Sects of Christians although dropped in the All-India Tables, and to include statistics re: number and kind of factory establishments in the Tables Volume as State Table XIII. These statistics were prepared from the materials supplied by the Director of Commerce and Industries who was also good enough to send a general note on industrial development. As to the State Tables, in addition to the above list, a special table showing the occupations of persons literate in English was also compiled and published as a subsidiary table in the Report Volume. These tables formed part of the General Census. Others tables mentioned under B. above, were prepared in connection with the special enquiries carried on alongside of the Census. The Tables in connection with the Sex Enquiry formed part of the Report.

D. Sorting of Tables Reviewed

101. Imperial Tables I-V.—As the figures for these Tables could be had from Register "A", no special sorting was required for these.

102. Imperial Table XVI Parts A and B and State Table XVII.—The first regular sorting operations began with respect to these Tables. In rural areas there was no special sorting by religion, as the figures were obtained from Register "A". In respect of urban areas, the slips were sorted by sects and then finally bundled according to the different religions. The sorters were supplied with adhesive labels for sects and the sorters' tickets containing the names of the same sects. Some Nanakshahis were found to have returned themselves as Hindu Nanakshahi instead of Sikh; they were, therefore, included in the Hindu total and separately shown as Nanakshahi. Some Jains had returned themselves as Hindus and shown their sects "Swetambari", "Digambari" etc. in the sect column. These were tabulated as Jains and not as Hindus. Christian sects were not entered properly in the enumeration books and enquiries had to be made of the local officials and missionary agencies working in the State about the sect of Christians residing in particular villages. Some of the Molesalam Girasias returned themselves as Hindus and were tabulated accordingly. Sorters were required to sort the sects as appeared in the slips; any readjustment by them was totally forbidden. Satyakeval, Kuberpanthi or Kayampanthi were three sect names separately compiled in previous censuses. On this occasion, as they were found to mean one and the same sect, they were all included under one head at the compilation stage. While the same sects were being sorted, slips for main religions such as Muslim, Tribal, Jain, Sikh, Arya, Brahmo and other groups were separated from Hindu Brahmanic and kept in separate bags or packets and the Hindu Brahmanic slips were tied into bundles but kept uncovered and thus placed in the boxes. The sorting of religion was not finally accepted until the sects were sorted, as figures of these helped to settle the figures finally for main religions; these figures were compared with those in Register "A" and the discrepancies noticed were reconciled.

103. Sorting for Age.—Sorting for Imperial Table VII (Age, Sex and Civil condition) was taken up after Sects were sorted, according to the age–groups, 0, 1, 2, 3, 4 to 6, 7 to 13, 14 to 16, 17 to 23, 24 to 26, 27 to 33, 34 to 36, 37 to 43, 44 to 46, 47 to 53, 54 to 56, 57 to 63, 64 to 66, 67 to 73, 74 and over, prescribed for this Table. After the slips were sorted in the above age–groups into the pigeon–holes and noted in the sorters' tickets, the sorter took out the slips from each pigeon-hole and divided them into each annual age–period; this was a check on any wrong sorting that may have been made for Imperial Table VII and the figures of annual age–periods were written on separate sorters' tickets from which annual age–periods were compiled for the whole state by districts and religions. The slips for each age–group sorted were then divided into three heaps showing the civil condition, *viz.*, married, unmarried and widowed; the total of each age–group in the sorters' tickets for all the three civil conditions was to agree with the total of the annual age–periods of that age–group. In some slips, children and babies were entered as married and widowed in connection with which enquiries had to be made of the local officials and the entries corrected wherever necessary. Notes were kept of persons who claimed to be one hundred years old and over. These were specially enquired into. In most of these cases, their ages recorded were found to be mere conjectures. In four cases, the age was found to be more or less genuine, and photographs of the persons concerned were included in the full report.

104. Procedure regarding Infirmities.—After this table was sorted, each sorter was asked to go over his slips for the last column of infirmities and he copied all entries of these slips on to separate slips. These newly copied infirmity slips were given to select sorters for sorting. When the figures of infirmities were compiled, there appeared a very large increase under deaf–mutism. It was, therefore, necessary to make sure regarding each individual; and the slips for all deaf–mutes were re–copied and sent to each mahal for verification with a special stress on the fact that such as were only deaf were not to be included in the return but all those who had both these defects either congenitally or after birth were to be so entered. The reports of the mahals brought down the figures to 1266 from 2655. These tables were sorted by a separate staff under the direct supervision of the Head Supervisor.

105. Sorting for Literacy by age: Imperial Table XIII.—The slips sorted for Table VII were in bundles of the age-groups prescribed for that table. For literacy by age, there would be no literate in the age-groups 0, 1, 2, 3, and these age-groups slips were therefore put aside. In the age-group 4 to 6, there would be hardly any literate; but that age-group was sorted for this table. The test for literacy is "ability to write a letter and read the reply to it." This test was maintained, but along with that those that were "able to read printed matter only" were so recorded on the slips and they were, therefore, sorted for the purpose. In the sorters' tickets for the literacy table, the age-groups were 4 to 6, 7 to 13, 14 to 16, 17 to 23, 24 to 26, 27 to 33, and 34 and over. There were two sorters' tickets, one for recording literacy according to the standard definition and the other for recording the figures of ability to read printed matter only. The age-groups were the same in both the tickets.

106. Procedure described.—The sorter took slips of all the three civil conditions of each age-group by turn. He divided the slips into three pigeon holes labelled, 'literate', 'literate in English', and 'able to ready only' ; and the slips of totally illiterate were put on the table in heaps. Slips of literates in Vernacular languages who knew English were to be put in the pigeon-holes of literate in English; as also of persons who knew English only. As each age-group was finished, slips were counted and made into bundles of 250 slips. The figures were entered in the respective columns of the sorters' tickets. The total of literate, literate in English, able to read only and totally illiterate, tallied with the total of the three civil conditions of the respective age-group in Table VII. Each age-group from 4 to 6 up to 27 to 33 was taken separately for this table but from 34 and onwards, all the age-groups of Table VII were taken together.

107. Correction of Mistakes found.—Along with the entry of literacy or ability to read only, space was provided in the enumeration card for the entry of literacy in Hindi or Urdu if a person was literate in either of the two or both the scripts. In a few cases, it was found that although a person was entered as literate in the Hindi or Urdu column, he was shown as illiterate (*i. e.* with a X) in the literacy column. This was, of course, a mistake of the enumerator and was promptly corrected at the sorting stage. Very strict instructions were given to see that literacy figures were properly sorted. All slips of illiterates were carefully seen by the supervisors, to make sure that no literate person was wrongly sorted as illiterate. In the City slips, certain absurd mistakes were detected and corrected. The mistakes arose from the fact that some very careless enumerators were not familiar with the distinction between ticks and crosses. The City work with its horde of ill-trained enumerators picked at random at the time of the preliminary count was not found to come up to the standard of efficient work of the district staff. The City organisation was therefore weak. Supervision was slack and the training, not adequate. In future, it will be better to keep a trained nucleus of paid hands and reduce the remaining number of enumerators. There is no reason why the number of houses per enumerator should not be increased to 150, and the number of blocks reduced. The work in the City in 1931 was inferior in efficiency to that in 1921 in my opinion.

108. Occupations of Literates in English.—After the sorting of literates was completed, the bundles of English literate slips were taken up in the different units and sorted for the various occupations they followed. The following were the occupations selected :—

1. Teacher and Professor
2. Private tutor
3. Doctor
4. Pleader
5. Police Service
6. Millitary Service
7. Railway Service
8. Post and Telegraph Service
9. Telephone Service
10. Service of other kinds
11. Trade
12. Agriculture
13. Industries
14. Private Service.
15. Domestic Service
16. Independent means
17. Unproductive
18. Other occupations

109. Sorting for Hindi and Urdu scripts.—The slips of literates in Vernacular and literates in English were both afterwards sorted for literacy in Hindi, Urdu or both. They were sorted into three pigeon-holes labelled accordingly. The age-periods were kept up. These slips of persons who can read and write Hindi or Urdu script were then sorted by their mother tongue-Gujarati, Marathi, Western Hindi (Hindustani) and 'Other'. They were also sorted by important castes, tribes or races and the figures put in separate sorters' tickets provided for the purpose.

110. Sorting for Literacy by caste (Imperial Table XIV).—After the slips were sorted (for Imperial Table XIII) for literacy a slight change in the order of sorting was made; instead of sorting for birth-place and language as prescribed by the Census Commissioner for India, sorting for caste had to be taken up as His Highness the Maharaja Saheb wanted literacey figures by caste for municipal and other administrative purposes. For this sorting, slips of literates and illiterates were kept separate. In the sorters' tickets devised for the purpose, against caste names, separate columns were provided for the entry of figures of literates and illiterates. The caste names printed in the tickets included almost all castes of any importance. Generally all castes with a strength in each of 2 per mille, plus a few other castes of local importance were selected and first provisionally divided into Advanced, Intermediate and Illiterate according to a literacy percentage scale. The figures of literates in English in each caste were written in brackets below the name of the caste and they were included in the total of literates per caste selected. Caste names which appeared on enumeration cards but not printed in the sorters' tickets were to be written out by the sorter. This sorting gave the literacy figures by caste and also the strength of each caste, male and female. These figures in the tickets were compiled to give the total strength of each caste as well as its literacy. When the figures were finally compiled for each caste, they were finally classified into the three classes noted above according to the literacy percentage scale.

111. Civil condition by selected castes.—Next was taken up sorting for civil condition by age for selected castes. The castes selected for this as well as for the Occupation and Literacy Tables were the same as for Imperial Table XIV, and the caste names were printed in the sorters' tickets. For Table VIII literate and illiterate slips of each caste were put together and sorted into six age-groups such as 0–6, 7–13, 14–16, 17–23, 24–43, 44 and over. They were then divided into three heaps of unmarried, married and widowed according to the tick mark found against entries in column 9 of the enumeration cards. Total dependents were to have no entry in occupation columns 10, 11 and 12 and thus as their dependence on any particular occupation cannot be known, the total dependents were not at all required for any sorting for occupational tables which only deal with 'earners' and 'working dependents'. But these 'total dependents' were specially sorted for age-groups 0–16, 17–33, 34 and over, to have some idea as to dependence by age-periods. (It would be more useful next time to have the age groups 0–16; 17–43; 44 and over.) The slips of total dependents were then put aside. Working dependents of each selected caste were counted and their number entered in the proper column of the sorters' tickets against the name of the caste. As the table is intended to show the traditional occupation of each caste and its deviation therefrom, the traditional occupation of each caste was printed alongside the name of the caste. 'Working dependents' who followed the traditional caste occupation were separated and shown in the proper place in the sorter's ticket. They were not sorted for occupations other than the traditional occupation of the caste. The slips of earners were counted and those who had traditional occupation entered in column 10 of the slips with or without any subsidiary occupation in column 11 were taken out and the rest of the slips were sorted for the prescribed major heads of occupational classification scheme. The pigeon–holes were labelled with the names of the occupations and slips were sorted accordingly. Afterwards column 11 of the slips of earners was seen to find out if the traditional occupation of the caste was entered as a subsidiary occupation; and the number of them as had such subsidiary occupation was entered in the proper column of the sorters' tickets. Each selected caste bundle was taken separately for this sorting.

112. Non–working Dependents of all castes separated.—For castes, tribes etc. selected for the purposes of Tables VIII and XIV, non–working dependents were kept separate. The rest of the caste bundles were then all taken up and non–working dependents (shown as such in column 9) were taken out, in order to separate earners and working dependents needed for the sorting of the general occupation (Table X).

113. Imperial Table X – Occupation.—As mentioned above, slips of earners and working dependents were separated for the whole population and the non-working dependents' slips neglected as they were not required for this table. The groups of occupation to be sorted for this table numbered 195; out of these, those groups in which there were numerous entries, were selected for the first sorting. Each sorter was provided with two pigeon–holes, the holes numbering 60 in all, and such sixty occupations as had numerous entries were first taken up. The sorter then took each caste bundle in turn, and seeing the entry in column 10 only, distributed the slips in the appropriate pigeon–holes. Occupations not found on the pigeon-holes, were to be put aside for a second sorting. The pigeon holes had labels affixed to them in the same order as printed in the sorter's tickets. All castes bundles were thus sorted for the first sixty occupations.

114. Sorting procedure described.—The sorters were to take out slips from the pigeon-holes and divide them into two parts: (1) those in which there was an entry in column 10 only and (2) those in which there were entries in columns 10 and 11; and then to count those in which there was an entry in column 10 only and enter their number in column 2 of the sorter's ticket; also to enter the number of those having an entry both in columns 10 and 11, in column 3 of the sorters' ticket and put them aside for a third sort. Slips of working dependents (having an entry of occupation in column 11 only) were then taken up and sorted for the entry in column 11 for the first sixty occupations selected. The rest were kept aside for another sort. The second sort was for 60 more groups and the third and last sort for 40 odd remaining groups. The procedure was the same as in the first sort; and the occupations not found printed in the sorter's tickets, were sorted as appeared in the enumeration cards and written out in the sorter's tickets. After earners, working dependents were similarly sorted.

115. Procedure re: Subsidiary Occupations.—Earners with subsidiary occupations were kept separate throughout. Their number was entered in the sorter's tickets against each occupation. Their total for all occupations showed the total number of earners who had subsidiary occupations. These slips were then sorted by occupation entered in column 11, and the number was written for each occupation entry found below the name of the occupation in the sorter's ticket (as sorter's tickets had been already printed off and no column was provided for this, the figures were entered below the name of the occupation). The idea of printing group-numbers after the names of occupations in brackets in the sorter's ticket (Part I) for Occupation Table X greatly helped in the work of compilation. For slips of earners with subsidiary occupations, there was a separate sorter's ticket (Part II) prescribed by the Census Commissioner for India which had 195 columns horizontal as well as vertical. As this extra ticket was not at all necessary and only an addition of one column in the sorter's ticket Part I was enough, the matter was brought to the notice of the Census Commissioner for India for early instructions re: its adoption and he was kind enough to express his approval by wire. The following was the final form of the sorter's ticket adopted :—

Serial Number	Occupation	Workers		
		Earners		Working Dependents
		Without Sub sidiary Occupation	With Sub-sidiary Occupation	
1	2	3	4	5
1	Rent receiver Group No. (1)			
2	Cultivating owner " " (5)			
3	Cultivating tenant " " (6)			
4	Agricultural labourer " " (7)			
5	Market Gardener " " (16)			
6	Forest Department employe " " (17)			
7	Woodcutter and charcoal burners " " (18)			
8	Cowherd " " (21)			
9	Keeper of Pack animals " " (22)			
10	Shepherd " " (23)			
	(and so on)			

116. Sorters forbidden to classify.—Sorters were forbidden from making any classification of occupations. Each caste bundle was taken in turn with the result that the slips of each caste remained together. While counting the number of these slips, the sorter kept separate those of each caste and entered their number in the sorter's tickets for Table XI-B. The figures of earners and working dependents were put in separate columns in these sorter's tickets. The following nineteen important groups of occupations were selected for this purpose :—

Occupation.	Group No.	Occupation	Group No.
Army	(154)	Bank manager, money lender etc.	(115)
Police	(157)	Farm servants	(7)
Public administration	(159)	Agricultural and general labour	(191)
Lawyers of all kinds	(167)	Cotton ginning and pressing	(42)
Doctors and physicians	(169)	Cotton weaving and spinning	(43)
Professors and teachers	(174)	Printers, Engravers, Book Binders	(95)
Income from rent of land	(1)	Trade in Textiles	(117)
Cultivating owner	(5)	Owners and Managers of Hotels	(127)
Cultivating tenant	(6)	Grain and Pulse dealers	(129)
Persons living on their income.	(185)		

117. Imperial Table VI – Birthplace.—Sorting for birthplace followed that of occupation. All slips of earners (with or without subsidiary occupation), working dependents and total dependents were sorted for this table. Pigeon–holes were labelled with the names of five divisions and the city, and slips were sorted into them, the result being that the remaining slips represented foreign–born population. Pigeonholes were then lebelled with the names of contiguous districts and states in the same order as appeared in the sorters' tickets. The bulk of the slips was sorted by now. Another sorter's ticket gave the names of 44 important districts, states and countries for which slips were again sorted and entered in the sorter's ticket. Birthplace entries in the remaining slips were then sorted and written out in the blank spaces provided in the ticket. Where obscure place names (of villages etc.) occurred, against instructions, in the enumeration books, references were made back to the Mahals for correct details of districts and provinces. For the convenience of sorters, a standard list of districts and States of India and of the principal countries and towns was prepared and given to each of the sorters and supervisors.

118. Age–periods and Occupations of Immigrants.—The slips of immigrants from the five contiguous districts of British Gujarat, *viz* Surat, Ahmedabad, Broach, Kaira and Panch Mahals and Rewa Kantha and Mahi Kantha agencies and Kathiawar States, were specially sorted for certain selected occupations printed in the sorter's ticket designed for the purpose. These immigrants were further sorted by age–periods 0–9, 10–29, 20–39 and 40 and over.

119. Birthplaces by Mahals of Baroda State sorted for Baroda City immigrants.—For Baroda City, the slips of those born in the different divisions of the State were again sorted by mahals of each *prant*, and the result entered in separate sorter's tickets. It is printed on the title page of Imperial Table VI.

120. Table XV – Mother Tongue.—Slips were next taken up for sorting for mother tongue. As slips of Gujarati mother tongue formed the largest proportion, they were put aside in a heap and other languages mentioned in the sorter's tickets were sorted into pigeon holes lebelled with their names.

121. Subsidiary languages sorted.—The entry for subsidiary languages was made in column 15 of the enumeration card. For compilation for Table XV Part B, only Gujarati, Marathi, Kachchhi, and Western Hindi were the languages selected for sorting of subsidiary languages; for sort of each of the above as a mother tongue was correlated with the rest as subsidiary. In the sorter's tickets, against the mother tongue in column 14, as each subsidiary language was sorted, the figures of each were entered. For this sorting the first subsidiary language recorded in the enumeration card was looked to. The figures of second and third subsidiary languages were next sorted for and the entries were written at the back of the sorter's ticket provided for this sorting. No other subsidiary languages, nor subsidiary languages of persons whose mother tongue was not Gujarati, Marathi, Hindustani, Kachchhi and Bhil dialects care sorted.

122. **Sects of Christians and Races of Europeans etc.**—The Tables concerning sects of Christians as well as their division into Europeans, Anglo-Indians and Indian Christians and also the distribution of Europeans and Anglo-Indians by age were sorted by a special sorter.

123. **Procedure re: sorting followed.**—With the above quoted deviations, the procedure prescribed in the Imperial Census Procedure Code was scrupulously followed. Sex and Religion were kept separate throughout as also the towns and rural area in each mahal. Sorted slips were made into bundles of 250 each and not of one hundred as 250 appeared very convenient.

124. **Arrangement re: Minor Religions.**—Christian, Arya, Brahmo and other minor religions could have been conveniently sorted for the district as a whole for literacy, caste, civil condition and age-period, but were kept apart as separate statistics were required for individual towns.

125. **Sorting for Educated Unemployment.**—Slips re: educated unemployed numbered only 379 and were sorted by the Chief Compiler according to instructions given in the Imperial Census Procedure Code Part II.

126. **List of Selected Castes:**—Names of selected castes were printed in one and the same order in sorter's tickets for tables VIII and XIV and this list of castes with traditional occupation of each printed opposite it was supplied to all the sorters and supervisors for Table XI-A.

127. **Testing.**—While the sorters were going on with their work, the supervisors carefully watched whether they placed the slips into the appropriate pigeon holes and satisfied themselves that the work was properly done. When a sorter announced that he had completed his work of sorting for a table, the supervisors at once went to him and tested his work. Special care was taken to count all smaller items and all entries which seemed doubtful such as the entry of infants as married or widowed were specially checked and in some cases. Mahal Authorities were referred to for verification and the entries corrected if needed. While sorting for age was going on, slips of persons nearing 120 years of age was carefully seen and a note of the names of many of them was made by the Head Supervisor. For obscure caste names also, the Mahal Officers were referred to for proper enquiry and report.

128. **Training in sorting.**—The sorters and supervisors were supplied with the Census Code Part II which was in Gujarati; the whole system of enumeration cards as also details regarding sorting for each table or a part of it were also printed at the back of the sorter's tickets for that particular table or part of a table. They were all strictly enjoined to study these carefully and to get doubtful points cleared by personal reference to the Assistant Census Commissioner and Head Supervisor. Moreover before beginning sorting for every table, the exact procedure of sorting was explained to the sorters and supervisors by the Assistant Census Commissioner as well as the Head Supervisor. The work was therefore well understood; however the work was tested and inspected while it was being carried on by the sorters, by the above two officers and myself personally. The procedure for sorting different tables was grasped fairly easily by the sorters except that for Occupation Tables X and XI-A and B which appeared rather hard. But efforts were made to make the work of sorting easier by personal instructions given almost to every sorter, and the supervisors were taught in even greater detail. The sorters had to be specifically told that the entries in traditional occupation were exclusive of the other heads of occupations selected. Before a table was sorted, a class was held by the Assistant Census Commissioner and the staff were given detailed instructions.

129. **Time taken in sorting.**—The sorting was begun as the enumeration card books were being received and cut up by the State Press into individual cards. The cutting operations lasted till 19th March 1931 when the work of sor-

ting came into full working order. Sorting for all Imperial and State Tables was completed by 27th June 1931, *i. e.* in just 4 months from the census date. Here again it may be added that the Census of 1931 in this State has broken all previous records. In 1901, the work was slow and took nearly a year to be ready. In 1911, in spite of the fact that the volume of Tabular work was much less than in 1921 or 1931, sorting was not complete until the 22nd July, or about 4 months and a half from the Census date. In 1921, with a much larger volume of statistical work (28 new tables), sorting went on till the 10th September 1921 *i. e.* within six months of the census date. On the present occasion, the volume of statistical material was even more elaborate, and yet the work was over more expeditiously than before. From the Census Commissioner for India's tour notes dated 8th July (*vide* Appendix E) it appears that the work of sorting in this State was completed before any other State or Province.

130. Special sort re: Dependents.—As the unemployment slips were very few, and it was necessary to gauge the extent of unemployment, it was thought desirable to have the statistics re: the earning power or dependence among males between the ages 20–39 and male slips of these ages were divided into those of literates in the Vernacular only. literates in English and illiterates, and each heap sorted into earner, working dependent or non-working dependent. This work was taken in hand when the compilation work was nearing completion in the middle of September and it was finished on the 23rd October.

131. Comparative Statement.—A comparative statement showing the time taken in sorting for each Imperial and State Table in 1931 and 1921 is subjoined as Appendix F.

132. Out–turn of work. —The following was the daily average out–turn of work by each sorter for the main tables shown below :—

Name of Table	Rate of sorting	
	Male slips	Female slips
IMPERIAL.		
VI Birthplace	7,000	7,000
VII Age, Sex and Civil condition... ...	3,700	3,700
VIII Civil condition by Age of selected castes...	3,100	3,200
X Occupation	2,400	2,600
XI–A Occupation of selected castes... ...	2,700	3,500
XI–B Distribution of Earners and Working Dependents in selected castes ...	5,500	5,500
XIII Education by religion and age ...	6,000	10,000
XIV Literacy by selected castes	3,500	3,600
XV Language	13,000	13,500
XVI–B Sects	3,800	4,000
XVII Caste, Tribe or Race	2,500	2,500
OTHER		
1. Annual Age Periods	3,300	3,400
2. Able to read only		
3. Literates in Hindi and Urdu		
4. Castes of Literates in Hindi and Urdu	8,000	12,000
5. Occupation of English Literates		
6. Dependents by Age–periods... ...	5,500	5,500
7. Occupation of Immigrants from contiguous districts... ...	7,000	7,000
8. Immigrants by Age–periods ...		

E. Compilation of Tables

133. Compilation.—Compilation is the name given to the process of adding up the figures on the sorters' tickets to obtain district totals.

134. Office Arrangements.—Selected supervisors and sorters with a good knowledge of English, mostly matriculates and others with higher qualifications were engaged on this work under the designation of Compilers. In the beginning only one compiler was engaged for each district, and the number was increased when necessary in the larger districts after the sorting of slips was well advanced. Over a gang of ten compilers was a Supervisor and there was one Chief Compiler, whose principal duty was to give general instructions for the compilation of each table and compare the entries in the compilation registers with those in the sorter's tickets.

135. Caution regarding corrected Return of Houses (Form No 7).—From experience, it is necessary to mention that before compiling figures for a village or town, care should be taken to see that all its blocks including blocks of Railway Station areas if any or of adjoining hamlets are included in the total. Columns 1 and 2 of Register " A " were filled in before the Census from the corrected return of houses (*i. e.* Form No. 7) but mistakes were also found in that return, when it care compared with Register of blocks and circles (Form No. 4). It should be, therefore, enjoined that Form No. 7 when received should be carefully compared with Form No. 4 and discrepancies if any reconciled then. One cause of error is that the blocks of one village are likely to be added to another, when there are 2 or more villages in one circle and blocks are not distinctly shown for each village. As figures of each village are prepared they should be carefully compared with the figures of the previous census, and if there is a great divergence in the figures, it must be made sure that no block is omitted or no block (or blocks) of another village is included. As there is no slip–copying before Register " A " is prepared and all the slips of rural areas of a Mahal are thrown together, this care is specially necessary. It should also be enjoined that figures in circle summaries should show blocks of each village in such a way that no possibility of a mistake can arise, such as by straight lines separating one village from another in the same circle.

136. Care regarding Number of Occupied Houses.—The number of occupied houses has to be taken from circle summaries direct and there are no other data to check the figures. Great care is therefore needed, in preparing the totals and the number of occupied houses in each town should be compared with that of previous census and a thorough re–checking ordered if a great difference is found in the figures. Figures of towns by each religion – especially minor religions – should be compared with those of previous censuses to make sure that there is no misplacing of one religion figures for another in compilation. It will be very necessary to have columns for previous censuses in Imperial Tables II, IV and State Table I prepared in sufficient time before the Census. There is at present a difference in the order of columns for persons, males and females in Register " A " and in the form of village tables which causes inconvenience in posting the figures from one to the other. The order of columns in Register "A" should therefore be the same in both, as in Village Tables.

137. Preparation of Dehzada or Village Directory.—Side by side with the sorting operations was started the preparation of the *Dehzada* or village directory. The Head Supervisor gave over all the sheets of Register "A" for a charge to a staff of clerks appointed for the purpose, who had with them the blank forms of the Village Directory ready for the entries to be made. In this form were posted the population figures of each village by sex and religion and when the entries for three or four villages making up a circle were made these were compared with the circle total. If any discrepancy appeared, it was done again and the cause of error detected and removed. When the figures for all the villages of a taluka (which generally corresponded with a charge) were written out, a total was struck for the whole taluka and compared with the charge total prepared by the Record-keeper. The totals thus obtained were utilised for the preparation of the district total. The Village Directory (*Dehzada*) was thus being prepared as the sorting was progressing and was ready for the press on the 20th April 1931.

138. Size of Dehzada.—In the past censuses, the *Dehzada* extended to two bulky volumes and the particulars for each village included more than a hundred columns, on account of the figures for all the castes being shown separately. Most of the columns were blank and the size of the book was unnecessarily swelled by the inclusion of these figures. The distribution of the village population by religion ought to be quite sufficient for administrative purposes and would make the book handy and easy to carry about by the District Officers while on tour. It was decided in 1911 therefore to abridge the size of *Dehzada.* Following that practice, continued in 1921 also, the present one is a small volume of 317 pages only. It was ready in print on the 2nd December 1931, and copies were soon made available to all the local officers.

139. New Features of the Dehzada.--The present *Dehzada* volume contains certain innovations which have to be noted. The districts (*prants*) were arranged alphabetically and in each *prant* the talukas were similarly arranged. In each taluka, the villages were shown alphabetically as in 1921, but in addition on the first page for each district, the names of villages were arranged per mahal according to size with populations noted against each. In the Baroda, Navsari and Mehsana *prants*, the figures of *hijratis* were also shown per village and taluka. Again under each village, the population of hamlets and railway stations as also the floating population (of boats, platforms, trains etc.) was shown separately wherever found. At the end of the volume, a list of uninhabited villages has been given together with a list of villages which are included in the Revenue *Dehzada* but are not censused by the State, because they are not under the direct administration of His Highness's Government. Because of these additional features, the size of the present *Dehzada*, exceeds its predecessor by 105 pages. But it is claimed that the book has thereby become a handier publication and more useful for ready reference than before.

140. Compilation of Imperial Tables I–V, XVI (Religion) and State Table I.—Imperial Tables I to V and XVI (Religion) and State Table I were prepared soon after the slips were sorted for Religions and Sects. They were printed and sent to the Census Commissioner for India, Simla, where they reached on 22nd April 1931 and were the first to reach there.

141. Compilation of other Tables.—The rest of the tables were compiled as the slips were sorted for a particular table, and generally the instructions conveyed in Imperial Census Code, Part II were followed. The same distinction of colour—white for males and buff-coloured for females–in the printing of sorters' tickets was continued for compilation registers, also.

142. Imperial Table VII : the Process of Smoothing.—For compiling Imperial Table VII (Age, Sex and Civil condition), the ternary and septenary groups of every sorter's tickets were to be smoothed according to a prescribed formula as under:—

Sorter's Age Group.		Number of persons			Formula		Compiler's Age Group	Number of persons		
		Unmarried	Married	Widowed				Unmarried	Married	Widowed
0	A				A+½B	=	0– 1			
1	B				½B+½C	=	1– 2			
2	C				½C+½D	=	2– 3			
3	D				$\frac{1}{2}$D+$\frac{1}{6}$E	=	3– 4			
4– 6	E				$\frac{1}{3}$E	=	4– 5			
7–13	F				½F+½E	=	5–10			
14–16	G				½G+½F	=	10–15			
17–23	H				½H+½G	=	15–20			
24–26	I				½I +½H	=	20–25			
27–33	J				½J +½I	=	25–30			
34–36	K				½K+½J	=	30–35			
37–43	L				½L+½K	=	35–40			
44–46	M				½M+½L	=	40–45			
47–53	N				½N+½M	=	45–50			
54–56	O				½O+½N	=	50–55			
57–63	P				½P+½O	=	55–60			
64–66	Q				½Q+½P	=	60–65			
67–73	R				½R+½Q	=	65–70			
74and over	S				S+½R	=	70 and over			
Total ...							Total...			

In case of an odd number found when halving any group, the surplus odd number was always adjusted to the lower age group. The same principle was followed in the case of Group E. The sum of the divided totals with fractions omitted might differ by one or by two units from the undivided total. If there was one surplus unit only it was placed in the Age–group 4–5, but if there were two, the second was placed in the Age–group 3–4. These adjustments were only necessary in striking the final totals of the groups for districts.

Having obtained the figures for quinary age groups, compilation could be started. In regard to smoothing it was found to be a very laborious business to do this in respect of each unit (mahal or town). As only figures for the whole district were required for Imperial Tables, it appeared to be a waste of time and energy to do smoothing of ages for every sorter's ticket. It was therefore, ordered that the crude figures of age entries in the prescribed age groups of every main religion should be compiled for each division and the City and thereafter to smooth those figures by divisions and the city only. Thus there were two compilation registers for this table; one recording and totalling crude age–periods only, at the foot of which smoothing was done and figures entered, which were then taken up in a separate compilation register of quinary groups. This saved great trouble, time and expense and was therefore approved of by the Census Commissioner for India: this procedure of smoothing only the district figures of every main religion was followed for Literacy Table XIII and Infirmities Table IX also. Figures for State Tables by mahals and towns were prepared from unsmoothed figures of the sorter's tickets.

143. Annual Age Periods.—The compilation of annual age periods by districts and main religions takes a lot of time. Great care should, therefore, be taken from the beginning to check the entries with a view to avoid trouble at the end. For compilation of district totals for Imperial Tables VII and XIII, smoothed figures of each religion for the district should be totalled up to five district figures. It is no good to smooth the crude district totals of all religions as there is likelihood of small variations. In the same way, all main religions (smoothed figures) for each district should be totalled up to give the figures by religions for the State as a whole. The Annual Age Period Tables were prepared and sent to the Census Commissioner for India on 5th August 1931 and were approved by him.

144. Table VI–Birthplace.—The order of divisions of the State and the adjoining British districts and States in the compilation registers was the same as appeared in the sorters' tickets. A separate compilation sheet for the districts of each province was prepared. There was a column at the end of each province sheet for " Province—District unspecified. " The total of each non-contiguous province was taken for the Imperial Table and the figures by districts supplied to the Provincial Superintendents of Census and Census Commissioners of Indian States. Districts of States were not returned in the enumeration cards, except in a few cases only, where it was possible to do so.

145. General Compilation Form devised.—Instead of adopting the compilation register forms of certain tables prescribed by the Census Commissioner for India, we devised a general form on double foolscap paper and printed forty columns lengthwise, the first column providing space for the entry of caste names or any other item to be compiled. Columns 2,3,4, were for persons, males and females, *i. e.* total of the remaining columns 5 to 40, which were grouped in twos as below:—

Subject	Population						
	Persons	Males	Females	Males	Females	Males	Females
1	2	3	4	5	6	etc. till 39–40.	

This provided for entries of males and females of eighteen units, allowing space for their totals in columns 2–3–4. *The entries of male figures were made in blue ink and those of female figures in red ink* to facilitate horizontal totalling. These forms were printed without any headings, which had to be filled up according to requirements. The papers were ruled horizontally with thirty lines. This form sufficed for the entry of all towns and rural areas of Navsari, Amreli and Okha on one sheet. Baroda and Mehsana *prants* required one sheet each for rural and one for urban areas. One form was enough for the wards of the city, railway areas and the cantonment, for each religion compilation and one form more for the State totals.

146. Use of this form for Imperial Tables XIV, XVII, VI, XV, and State Table XVI.—This general form was used for the compilation of Table XIV–Literacy by selected castes, XVII–Caste, Tribe or Race, VI–Birthplace and XV–Language; as also for State Table XVI–Annual age periods by divisions and religions and State Table VI–A–Literates in Hindi or Urdu script combined with their caste, tribe or race and mother tongue.

147. Compilation Registers and Sorter's Tickets.—In compiling Table XIV–Literacy by selected castes, the order of castes in the sorter's tickets was exactly followed and for Tables XV–Language and VI–Birthplace, the entries in compilation registers followed the order in the sorter's tickets. For Language Table–Bilingualism, the first subsidiary language was compiled from the sorter's tickets, but the figures of that particular language as second or third subsidiary were compiled from the entries on the back of the sorter's tickets and were totalled up to give the whole number of the speakers of that language as a subsidiary one.

148. Compilation Registers for Imperial Tables XIV and XVII.—The sorter's ticket for caste figures and literacy of each was a combined one and the entries relating to caste strength and its literacy were copied into separate compilation registers for the two separate Tables XIV and XVII. When the figures of each sex were placed side by side for every town or rural area of a mahal, there was good material at a glance to check their comparative accuracy. In one rural area in Muslims, 139 females appeared in Gandhrap caste, with no entry in the male column. The female slips were referred to and found out to belong to village Balisana (Patan) with entries of " शेख गंध्रप ". The male slips of the village also showed the same entry but were sorted under " Shaikh ". The number was counted and the entry rectified. The Census Commissioner for India in his circular No. 38–Comp. dated the 16th July 1931 desired to have entries of each table for small units like towns and mahals compared with those of the previous census and to verify where there was a big difference. The method of compilation adopted here dispensed with the necessity of preparing separate statements for such a comparison. In Sidhpur and Patan mahals, the figures of Mumnas and Memons varied substantially from those of 1911 and 1921. The slips were referred to and this census figures were found to be correct—those of previous two censuses were wrongly compiled mistaking Momnas to be Memons.

149. Tables VIII and XI–A.—Separate sheets of the compilation register were provided for each caste. These compilation registers were of white colour for males and buff–coloured for females to avoid any chance of a mistake of one sex being wrongly posted for another. Instructions for compiling this table, given in the Imperial Census Code Part II were followed.

150. Tables XVI – C and XIX.—Table XVI – C (Christians by Sect and Race) and Table XIX – (Europeans by Race and Age) presented no difficulty as their numbers were very small. Where in the sorter's tickets the entries were only " Indian Christian ", the slips were sorted by villages and enquiries were made through the mahal officers for the correct record of the particular sect of them in that village. Indian Christians were further subdivided according to race, caste or tribe by a special sort.

151. Tables X–Occupation.—This table is really difficult to compile, but the arrangements made here rendered the work much easier. In the sorters' tickets devised for this table, group numbers were printed in brackets along with the description of the occupation, and only very few occupation names had to be written by the sorter. These hand–written entries only needed group numbers, which were given by the Assistant Census Commissioner. The entries in sorters' tickets were copied in compilation register forms separately for each religion. The compilation registers provided for the entry of the names of mahals or towns vertically and the group numbers with three sub–columns (1) earners (2) working dependents and (3) persons following the occupation as subsidiary to others were provided for in the headings. For compilation of district totals for this table, the names of religions appeared in the vertical column, and group numbers with the three sub–heads in horizontal columns. Thus while compiling for a district the figures by religion for the district were ready. The district totals were similarly compiled into figures for the whole State. Figures of religions by divisions per each group could thus be conveniently totalled up to give totals by main religions for the State as a whole.

152. **Table XI–A and XI–B.**—Table XI–A was compiled from the sorters' tickets according to the instructions conveyed in the Imperial Census Code, but its figures were also compared with those of XI–B for the group of occupations selected for each particular caste. If the caste figures showed divergence, the sorters tickets were referred to, to locate the discrepancy to any particular urban or rural area; sometimes the slips of caste were again sorted for this purpose. The number of agricultural rent receivers amongst Brahmans in Table XI–B exceeded the figure in XI–A. The discrepancy was located to Sojitra (Urban) and on sorting the slips, the number of 89 shown in sorters' ticket for XI–B was found to be not of the agricultural rent receivers but of the total of the caste and the entry was therefore rectified. Vohra (trading) females 139 appeared in the column of others under professions and liberal arts, in Kadi town females. On referring to the slips they appeared to fall under industry as they prepared अगरबत्ती and the entry was accordingly corrected.

153. **Compilation Staff.**—When compilation was in full swing, 40 compilers were engaged for the work, ten in each gang under a supervisor. At first, *i. e.* in March 1931, only 4 compilers were entertained. In April the number rose to 14, in May, to 26; and in June it fell to 19, but the number rose again to 40 in July. In August the work was getting lightened and we reduced 5 men. In September, we required only 21. In October, the number was 20. The compilation staff included also the special staff of sex enquiry compilers, who will be referred to in their special section later on. Separate tables were given to each gang, and the gang and its supervisor were responsible for that particular table. The supervisor himself did the compilation of a few units to explain the procedure to the compilers. The Assistant Census Commissioner and the Chief Compiler continuously watched the work carefully and gave instructions and cleared up ambiguities if any. They also compiled personally many of the final Imperial Tables.

154. **Despatch of work.**—The work of compilation was most expeditiously performed. In the Weekly Progress Report circulated by the Census Commissioner for India dated the 9th October, i. e. after the completion of the compilation work and the despatch of the last Tables to the Census Commissioner for India, it was found that this State had completed its work before any other Province or State had done. Ajmere–Merwara had indeed reported completion of this part of the undertaking before 2nd October 1931 but as it is part of Rajputana, it cannot be said that the work of the whole census charge of Rajputana and Ajmere–Merwara was completed in this respect. Compared to previous censuses, the work of compilation in this State has again broken previous records. In 1921, the Imperial Tables were all compiled by the 15th December; and in the present Census all the State Tables also were ready by the end of that month. There were in all 19 Imperial Tables and 2 State Tables to be prepared for the scrutiny of the Census Commissioner for India. In regard to Imperial Tables I–V, VIII, X XVI, XVII, XVIII and State Tables I (*i. e.* 11 Tables out of 21) this State was the first in all India. In regard to 7 other Tables, this State came second. As to the remaining three, this State ranked third. The Occupation Table is the most important of all and this had reached the Census Commissioner's office on the 16th September before any other State or Province.

155. **Completion of work of compilation.**—The compilation of all Imperial Tables was completed by the 7th October 1931, a small amount of work of some State Tables remained which was completed by the 28th October. The last of the Imperial Tables–XI–A and B–were sent to the Census Commissioner for India for scrutiny on the 7th October 1931.

156. **Printing of Tables.**—As each table was ready, it was sent to the State Press and after correcting the proofs etc., three copies of each table were sent to the Census Commissioner for India for scrutiny. As the tables were passed as correct, they were finally printed off in the State Press. No reprinting was nece-

sary in the Times of India Press as in the Census of 1911 and 1921. The following list shows the order of compilation of tables with the time taken from date of compilation to despatch of completed table to the Census Commissioner for India for scrutiny :—

Number and Name of Table	Number of days taken for compilation (approximate number of days)	Date of despatch to Census Commissioner for India	Date of passing by Census Commissioner for India
1	2	3	4
IMPERIAL TABLES			
I–Area, Houses and Population	5	1– 4–31	23– 6–31
II–Variation in Population since 1881	2	18– 4–31	23– 5–31
III–Towns and villages classified by population	15	14– 4–31	24– 6–31
IV–Towns classified by population with variation since 1881	7	18– 4–31	23– 5–31
V–Towns arranged territorially with population by religion	7	18– 4–31	23– 5–31
VI–Birth-place	25	8– 8–31	22–10–31
VII–Age, Sex and Civil Condition	30	20– 7–31	22–10–31
VIII–Age, Sex and Civil Condition by selected castes	15	31– 8–31	22–10–31
IX–Infirmities Parts A and B	10	10– 8–31	22–10–31
„ Part C	2	26– 8–31	
X–Occupation	30	14– 9–31	23–11–31
XI–Occupation of selected castes Parts A and B	20	2–10–31	8– 1–32
XII–Educated Unemployment	1	27– 6–31	19–10–31
XIII–Literacy by religion and age	30	28– 7–31	23–11–31
XIV–Literacy by selected castes	15	26– 8–31	17–10–31
XV–Language Part A	7	12– 8–31	30–11–31
„ Parts B and C	7	26–10–31	
XVI–Religion Part A.	3	18– 4–31	24– 6–31
„ Parts B and C	20	1– 8–31	13–11–31
XVII–Caste, Race or Tribe	30	2– 9–31	22–12–31
XVIII–Variation in population of Selected Tribes	3	17– 8–31	4–12–31
XIX–Europeans and Anglo-Indians by race and age	6	27– 7–31	31–10–31
STATE TABLES			
I–Area and Population of Mahals and Peta-Mahals	5	18– 4–31	1– 6–31
II–Population of Talukas by religion and literacy	7	14– 9–31	23–10–31

The completed Imperial Tables Volume was ready bound on the 26th December 1931 and a copy of the Imperial Tables Volume was despatched on the same date to the Census Commissioner for India. The State Tables were also ready on the same date: and a combined volume containing the abridged Report of the Census, together with all the Imperial and State Tables was also despatched on the above date to the Census Commissioner for India. In his reply dated 29th December 1931, he was pleased to observe as follows:—

> " Very many thanks for your D. O. No. 86/1 dated the 26th December and for the two volumes of Tables and abridged Report. You have been extraordinarily quick in getting your report out and I congratulate you on being the first to get the volumes of Tables printed and published. I have not yet had time to go through the Report but hope to do so very soon and meanwhile may express my approval to your maps. I like your map of literacy and hope that I may be able to find the money to produce a similar map for India. Your caste diagram of literacy likewise makes a very good illustration of comparative literacy in different castes.
>
> 2. I think the bindings of your census volumes are quite near enough to the sample I sent you and the general result is effective and just as good in appearance as the former bindings with gold lettering, if not better.
>
> 3. Many thanks again for the volumes and for many useful hints that I have got and expect to get from them and again many congratulations on your despatch in publishing. "

F. *Preparation of the Report and other publications.*

157. Some Results of the Census.—On this occasion the marginally noted publications besides the preparation of Tables were taken in hand. The first named was something in the nature of a summary report, somewhat more elaborate than the pamphlet issued in 1921, but less detailed than the summary Report of 1911. It was taken in hand as soon as the compilation of Tables was well advanced, in the last week of August, and the completed copy was ready in manuscript on the 13th September. It was sent to the Times of India Press soon after, and it was ready in print on the 8th December 1931. Advance copies were sent to the Chief Officers of the State and to the Census Commissioner for India on the 16th December.

1. Some Results of the Census
2. Census Report
3. Gujarati Summary
4. Administrative Volume

158. The Census Report:—The full Report was taken in hand while the abridged Report was in the Press. At first certain appendices were prepared including the Caste Glossary. Later the chapters on Language, Infirmities and Caste were taken in hand, after which the first and succeeding chapters were written. The last line was written on the 12th March 1932.

159. Number of Copies of Census Publications:—It would be useful to give here a list of publications undertaken by the Census Department and the number of copies printed on this occasion. Similar figures for the previous census are given for facility of reference. The publication of the full Census Report takes a long time after the census, before it is out. A handy book containing the first view of the results as disclosed by the absolute figures then compiled was deemed therefore necessary. As I thought this would be sufficient for the needs of the ordinary offices, I got 500 copies of this printed

Serial No.	Name of Publication	Number of copies printed	
		1931	1921
1	2	3	4
1	Census Report	350	1000
2	Imperial Tables Volume	1000	900
3	State Tables Volume	400	300
4	Dehzada	900	1000
5	Some Results of the Census	500	200
6	Administrative Volume	200	100
7	Gujarati Summary of the Report	1000	1 ,00
8	Census Procedure Code Part I	300	300
9	Census Procedure Code Part II	200	500

against 200 in the previous census, and got bound 400 copies of this with State and Imperial Tables together for circulation within the State, the remaining 100 copies being separately bound and distributed amongst principal officers of the State and to the Press, both here and outside. In view of the above arrangement I reduced the number of copies of the Full Report to 850, in order to save charges in printing. We had this time 100 more volumes of Imperial Tables as at least 6C0 were required by the Government of India. As to the Administrative Volume, I got 200 copies printed instead of 100 because the introduction of our new system of enumeration had created widespread public interest and I was requested by the Census Commissioner for India and Superintendents of Census Operations of the Provinces and the States to send them free copies of the Administrative Volume describing the new system in detail foı their guidance in future. I had also requested Government who passed the above list (*vide* Dewan Order No. 513 dated the 27th October 1931) to authorise me to make slight changes in the number of publications if circumstances so warranted. My request was sanctioned. All publications except the Full Census Report and Some Results of the Census which were printed at Bombay in the Times of India Press, were got printed locally in the State Press.

160. Prices of Publications.—The prices of Census Publications, if they are fixed in accordance with strict rules would become almost beyond the reach of ordinary persons. The Government cannot hope, and never intend, to recoup themselves for the cost through the sale of these books. In 1921 although the price of the Report came to Rs. 16–8–0 and for the Imperial Tables to Rs. 9 only Rs. 7–8–0 were fixed as the price for the set in respect of copies reserved for sale. On this occasion, too, I proposed to Government that with a view to bring the census publications within the easy reach of ordinary persons, their sale price should be suitably reduced. The Government was pleased to sanction my proposal as to prices as shown in the margin (*vide* Dewan Order No. 5/3 dated the 27th October 1931). I was authorised by the same order to make suitable arrangements for the sale of these publications. I have reserved for sale the marginally noted number of copies of these publications, and arranged to keep these in the State Press, which sells all government publications. So long as my office was open, a few copies were sold from the office.

Name of Publications	Number of copies reserved for sale	Price
1	2	3
The Census Report	50	6–0–0
The Imperial Table Volume	20	1–8–0
The Imperial and State Tables Volume	50	3–0–0
Some Results of the Census	20	1–0–0
Some Results with Full Tables Volume	100	4–0–0
Gujarati Summary	200	1–0–0
Dehzada	200	1–8–0
A set of Report and Imperial and State Tables Volume if bought together	...	7–8–0

161. The Gujarati Summary of the Census Report.—Last Census, the work of preparing a summary of the Census Report in Gujarati was entrusted to Mr. Gokaldas M. Shah, the Educational Inspector and he had very ably done it. This time also, a proposal was put up before to Government by me to have the report translated and published in Gujarati, suggesting as translator, the names of Messrs. M. N. Thakkar and Thakorbhai M. Desai along with that of Mr. Shah. The Government preferred to give the work again to Mr. G. M. Shah at an honorarium of Rs. 600/– (*vide* Dewan Order No. 2/1 dated the 6th October).

162. Free List of Census Publications.– It is a practice obtaining with the Government of India to arrange for free distribution of the Census Reports and Tables volumes between the Provinces and States that undertake independnt census operations since the inception of the first Census. The Government of India itself requires a large number of copies for its own use. This demand comes always in the vicinity of 600 volumes of each–the Report and the Tables Volumes. Besides this requirement of the Government of India, these reports are required to be sent to well-known Newspapers and Journals in the State and outside, as also to learned bodies outside India like the Royal Statistical Society and so on. Moreover the State correspondence rules (section 97–3) lay down a standard list of 254 copies for distribution of government publications to various government offices. I thought, however, this was not applicable to census publications. Moreover, a Full Report is hardly necessary for all government offices as I intended the circulation of the abridged Report (entitled "Some Results") bound with the Tables volumes to be adequate for the needs of mahal, vibhag and similar offices and minor libraries. I therefore approached the Government to leave the discretion for distribution of these books to me and they were pleased to grant my request. I then got 400 copies of my short Report bound together with the Imperial and State Tables for distribution to various government offices and also for free distribution and curtailed the printing list of 950 copies of the Full Report by 100 to 850 with a view to economise in printing.

G. *The Size and Sex Constitution of Families*

163. Preliminary Arrangements.—As in 1921, an enquiry into the Size and Sex Constitution of Families was undertaken along with this census, but on a much wider scale. The same agency as on the last occasion was employed, *viz*: the revenue staff, school teachers, doctors, nurses and honorary and other social workers. A considerable number of women assisted in the enquiry.

164. The Instructions and the Permit issued.—Circulars were issued early in November 1930 and the enquiry itself was started from the 1st of December, when slip–books containing 42 or 84 questionnaire slips each, were distributed all over the State with full printed instructions to the enquiry workers. The instructions emphasised that no names were to be asked and no compulsion employed to extract answers to questions and no police agency used except to gather information regarding the policeman's own women folk. The purpose of the inquiry was fully explained so as to leave no room for misunderstanding. Questions were to be asked as far as possible to women by women and to husbands or other relatives, by men enquirers. Permits authorising persons to enquire into these delicate questions were issued in the following form:—

પરવાનો

વસ્તીગણત્રી ખાતું—રાજ્ય વડોદરા સને ૧૯૩૧

રા. ______________ રહેવાસી ______________ ધંધો ______________

ને આ પરવાનો આપવામાં આવે છે કે આ વખતે આ રાજ્યમાં " કુટુંબનું કદ અને તેમાં સ્રીપુરૂષોનું પ્રમાણ (Size and Sex Constitution of Families)" સંબંધે થવાની તપાસના કામે માહિતી મેળવવા તમને આથી નિમવામાં આવે છે. માટે તમારે તે સંબંધે તમામ તપાસ કાયદેસર રીતે કરવી. આશા છે કે, તમે આ કામ પુરતી કાળજી તથા કુનેહથી કરીને જનહિતની આ ઉપયોગી તપાસમાં મદદ કરશો. તારીખ ૧ માહે નવેમ્બર સને ૧૯૩૦.

સેન્સસ કમિશનર,
રાજ્ય વડોદરા.

165. The Cases for Enquiry.—The enquiry being with reference to fertility of population, the information was collected for married women above the age of 13 years. Three kinds of women between the ages 13 to 45 only were considered for the enquiry:

(1) those effectively married to one husband who was alive at the time of enquiry,

(2) those widowed before 13 but remarried since and living with the second husband, and

(3) those effectively married since the age of puberty and widowed after the age of 45.

It is to be noted that widows below 45 years of age were to be excluded. In the case of married females, who had more than one husband after their 13th year of age, the particulars regarding the last marriage only were entered while divorced females living single were excluded altogether from the enquiry. Those women who were widowed after 13 and remarried to one or more husbands were at first purposely excluded from the inquiry, for the reason that the entries re: the duration of marriage and the number of children might not be correctly filled in. But it was pointed out that in all such cases where the woman was married to more than one husband the enquirer was to ask questions so as to establish the class to which the woman belonged and to decide whether or not to exclude her. Howerer, it was made clear that the enquirer was to take up such cases wherever the woman can state clearly the number of years she was married to her *present* husband, and the number of children born to her from the present marriage.

166. The Questionnaire.—The following details were to be inquired into, in reference to these women:—

(1) Name of village with Taluka
(2) House Number
(3) Caste, Tribe or Race of husband
(4) Occupation of husband
(5) Present age of husband
(6) Present age of present wife
(7) Duration of marriage with present wife
(8) Number of children born to present wife
Male Female Total
(9) Number of children surviving to present wife

Male **Female** **Total**

(10) Age of children still living (in order)

, , , , ,

, , , , ,

, , , , ,

, , , , ,

(11) Sex of first born (whether quick or still born)

Except Question No. 10 (Age of living children) the questionnaire was the same as in the last census. The house number was also to be shown on each slip. Only eight Tables were compiled in 1921; three more were added on this occasion as detailed below.

167. Sex Enquiry Workers.—The army of enquiry workers was constituted as under:—

Division	Total		Official		Non-official	
	Males	Females	Males	Females	Males	Females
Baroda State ...	**3,144**	**429**	**2,676**	**409**	**468**	**20**
Baroda City ...	174	131	164	127	10	4
Amreli ...	203	57	154	57	49	...
Baroda ...	1,065	91	929	91	136	...
Mehsana ...	1,083	103	950	93	133	10
Navsari ...	599	41	459	35	140	6
Okhamandal ...	20	6	20	6	...	...

168. Interim Progress Reports.—The enquiry lasted more than 6 months (from the 1st of December to the 15th of June) giving the workers sufficient time to collect information, the giving of which was necessarily optional and upon which therefore no pressure of time could be brought to bear. The following statement shows the monthly returns of filled-in slips during the above period, prepared from interim progress reports received every month from Charge Superintendents:—

Cumulative Figures

Division	Number of slips filled in and returned to Charge Office by				
	March 1st	April 1st	May 1st	June 1st	Total at the end of period July 10
Baroda State ...	**30,708**	**46,688**	**87,851**	**142,189**	**206,015**
Baroda City ...	928	1,395	1,395	2,765	7,260
Amreli ...	6,073	7,619	9,845	15,207	16,552
Baroda ...	11,107	14,472	26,257	41,020	63,430
Mehsana ...	8,500	15,827	34,254	53,306	78,177
Navsari ...	3,092	6,022	14,716	27,454	37,530
Okhamandal ...	1,008	1,353	1,384	2,437	3,066

Though the last date for receiving the slip-books containing the information was June 20, it was extended upto July 10, owing to the delay in sending the books by several Mahal Officers and strangely enough by the Baroda Municipal Office, which never seemed to have properly grasped the urgency of procedure in this particular enquiry. Throughout the State, the work of the City staff in this respect was most slack and inefficient.

169. Receipt of slip books and immediate start of sorting.—By the 20th of July all the Sex enquiry books were received in the Central Abstraction office. The process of dissembling them as soon as each lot was received, was entrusted to a picked staff of sorters. All slips were ready for sorting by the beginning of August. In all, there were 6 sorters engaged on this work.

170. Instructions for Sorting.—As soon as the slips of a division were liberated from their covers a select staff of specially instructed sorters pounced upon them and started their work according to the following instructions:—

After rejecting the blank, crossed out, incorrect and incompletely filled-in slips the sorters should divide all the slips into two heaps (A and B) as under:—

(A) Completed fertility cases, *i. e.*, where the wife had attained 45 years of age; and

(B) Continuing fertility cases, *i. e.*, where the fertility was still a continuing factor, *i. e.*, where the wife's age was below 45 years.

Separate sorting by division and religion;—In all eleven tables (8 from the completed, and 3 from the continuing and completed fertility slips) are to be prepared. In doing this work, the figures for Baroda City are throughout to be shown separately. In Table I, the figures should be given by divisions. Again, after the division of all the slips into heaps A and B the sorting will be by religion but when they are once sorted by castes, separate bundles for castes will be maintained thereafter.

TABLE I—Sex of the first born

This table should be prepared from slips of heap A, *i.e.*, completed fertility cases only. The sorter will first see column 11 and sort them according to the sex of the first born child whether male or female. He should then take the first born female slips and take out slips in which female children predominate, by looking at column 8 (total children born). He should then do the same thing for the first born male child slips also. Note that the number of children surviving (column 9) is not to be taken into consideration but the total number of children born (column 8) only is to be taken into account.

TABLE II—Number and sex constitution of families

This table is to be prepared from completed fertility cases only. Sorting for this table will have to be done in pigeon holes for the number of children born in column 8. *All the slips will be divided into 22 heaps.* The first heap will be of slips in which no children are born at all; the second will be of one child born; the third of two children; and so on till there are 21 children or more born in a family. All these heaps should then be counted and their number written in column 2 of the Sorters' ticket. Each heap will then be divided into two according to the sex of the first born. Then from each of these groups, find out the number of male and female children born. The total of these children will be equal to the number of children born to a marriage multiplied by the total number of marriages shown in column 2 of the sorters' ticket.

TABLE III—Size of Families by Occupation of Husband

This table is to be prepared from completed fertility cases only and for selected occupations. Column 4 of the slip shows the occupation of the husband. The slips will, therefore, be first divided according to occupations and their number shown in column 2 of the Sorters' ticket. Then from each *occupational heap* take slips one by one and see column 8 and find out the total number of children born. Again see column 9 and count the total number of children surviving.

TABLE IV—Size of Families by Caste or Religion of the Family (From completed fertility cases only)

Sort for each caste or religion first according to the standard list chosen. Then take the slips of *each* caste from the pigeonholes and count the total number of children born and also of surviving children. After this is done, the age of wife at marriage should be found out and tabulated as under :—

13–14, 15–19, 20–29 and 30 and over. (The age of wife at marriage is not shown in the slip and has, therefore, to be worked out by deducting the period of marriage (col. 7) from the age of wife shown in column 6, *e. g.*, if 46 years are shown as the present age of wife in column 6 and 30 years are shown as the period of marriage in column 7, then by deducting 30 from 46, the age of wife at marriage will be 16 years). The above age periods will be found for each caste and shown against it in respective columns. *Note* that the caste and age–periods sorted should be kept as they are.

TABLE V—Average size of family correlated with age of wife at marriage: (From completed fertility cases only)

The age of wife at marriage has been sorted for Table IV; it should be further sub–divided as under:—

13, 14, 15–19, 20–24, 25–29, and 30 and above, and their number shown against each age–period. Then from each age–period, find out separately the total number of children born from column 8 and the total number of surviving children from column 9 of the slips.

TABLE VI—Age of husband at last marriage: (From completed fertility cases only)

The age of wife at marriage is already sorted for the previous table. From the first group of those slips find out the age of husband at marriage (by deducting the period of marriage from the age of husband shown in column 5) as required per age–period given in the ticket. These will be 13–19; 20–29, 30–49, and 50 and over. Those cases in which the husbands have died after their wives have completed 45 years of age will also be found out and then for each of these groups the children born and those surviving will be counted and entered against their respective columns in the ticket.

TABLE VII—Duration of marriage correlated with caste or religion of family

It is to be noted that this table will be prepared from *both the completed and continuing fertility cases*. The castes and religions selected for Table IV are 40 in number but for this table only 12 castes and religions are to be sorted for as under :—

1	Brahman	7	Other Hindus
2	Vania	8	Jain
3	Patidar (all sub-castes)	9	Muslim
4	Baria and allied castes	10	Zoroastrian
5	Rajput	11	Christian
6	Vankar including Dhed	12	Tribal Religions

Then take each of these 12 castes in succession and sort for duration of marriage with the present wife, in the following periods of duration :—

Below 10, 10, 11–19, 20–31, 32, 33 and over

and again count the number of children born. The sorting by caste and religion will have to be done anew for continuing fertility slips, as it is not previously done.

TABLE VIII—PROPORTION OF FERTILE AND STERILE MARRIAGES

This table will be prepared from both the completed and the continuing fertility heaps, but the heaps will be kept separate and sorting will be done according to the age of wife at marriage as shown below :—

13–14, 15–19, 20–24, 25–29, 30 and over.

Then take each age-period and see column 7 for duration of marriage and divide them in the following periods of duration :—

0–4, 5–9, 10–14, 15 and over.

Then sort each heap whether fertile or sterile. Count them and put the number in your ticket in its proper place, *i. e.*, opposite and below the required age-period.

TABLE IX—AGE OF MOTHER AT FIRST BIRTH

This table will be prepared separately from each of the A (completed fertility cases) and B (continuing fertility cases) heaps and should, therefore, be done after preparing Table VI above. In this and the following two tables viz., X and XI only those slips in which the total children born (column 8) are *all* surviving (column 9) are to be taken into consideration. The castes and religions to be selected for this table will be the same as for Table VII.

After the castes and religions are sorted, take each heap, and find out the age of the mother at first birth by deducting the age of the first child (column 10) from the age of the wife shown in col. 6. Then sort these ages in the following age periods :

Below 13, 13–14, 14–15, 15–16, 17–20, 20 and over.

Count them and enter the figures in their proper places in your ticket.

TABLE X—FREQUENCY OF BIRTHS : (FROM COMPLETED FERTILITY CASES ONLY AND FROM SUCH OF THESE AS HAVE ALL THEIR CHILDREN BORN SURVIVING)

It will be done for the following groups :—

1. Hindu, Jain, and Tribal Religions

   A. Advanced
   B. Intermediate
   C. Illiterate

   } The castes in each of these groups will be the same as for Imperial Tables VIII, XI and XIV.

2. Muslim
3. Zoroastrian
4. Christian (Indian)

After the slips are divided into the above groups, take each group and find out the duration of time

(i) between the birth of the 1st and 2nd child
(ii) „ „ „ of the 2nd and 3rd child
(iii) „ „ „ of the 3rd and 4th child

This duration will then be sorted into the following periods :—

Below 2 years, 2–4, 4 and over.

The ages of surviving children are given in column 10 of the slips.

TABLE XI—Duration of childless period

This table will be prepared from completed fertility cases only and *that too* of cases in which all the children born are surviving. This period will be counted from the age of the last born child given in column 10 and will be sorted into the following periods of duration :—

1–3, 3–5, 5 and over.

This table, like Table X, will be done for the groups (Advanced, Intermediate and Illiterate) and religions separately.

SEX TABLE I

Sex of first born

Natural Division	Number of famales first born	Percentage of such families where female children predominate	Number of males first born	Percentage of such families where male children predominate	Number of females first born per 1,000 males first born	Number of Slips examined
1	2	3	4	5	6	7

SEX TABLE II

Size and sex constitution of families

Size of family (number of children born to a marriage)	Compiled from completed marriages only						
	Number of families			Sex		Number of female children per 1,000 males	Percentage of families to total
	Total	Having first male child	Having first female child	Male	Female		
1	2	3	4	5	6	7	8

SEX TABLE III

Size of Families by Occupation of Husband

Occupation of Husband	Number of Families examined	Total number of children born	Average per family	Number of children surviving	Proportion of surviving to total thousand born
1	2	3	4	5	6

31

SEX TABLE IV

Size of Families by Caste or Religion of Family

Caste or Religion	Number of Families examined.	Total number of children born	Average per family	Number of children surviving	Proportion of surviving to thousand born	Number of families with wife married at			
						13–14	15–19	20–29	30 and over
1	2	3	4	5	6	7	8	9	10

SEX TABLE V

Average size of Family correlated with Age of Wife at Marriage

Age of wife at marriage	Number of families	Number of children born	Average observed	Number of children surviving	Average observed
1	2	3	4	5	6

SEX TABLE VI

Age of Husband at last Marriage

Age of wife at last marriage		Age of Husband at marriage														
		13–19			20–29			30–49			50			Dead*		
Age Period	Number of wives	Number of husbands	Number of children		Number of husbands	Number of children		Number of husbands	Number of children		Number of husbands	Number of children		Number of husbands	Number of children	
			Born	Surviving		Born	Surviving		Born	Surviving		Born	Surviving		Born	Surviving
1	2	3	4	5	6	7	8	9	10	11	12	13	14	15	16	17

* These cases are presumably of husbands who have died after their wives have completed 45 years of age.

SEX TABLE VII.

Duration of marriage correlated with caste or religion of family

Caste or religion of husband	Duration of marriage with present wife																	
	Under 10 years			10 years			Between 10–19			Between 20–31			32			33 and over		
	Number of families	Number of children	Average number of children	Number of families	Number of children	Average number of children	Number of families	Number of children	Average number of Children	Number of families	Number of children	Average number of children	Number of families	Number of children	Average number of children	Number of families	Number of children	Average number of children
1	2	3	4	5	6	7	8	9	10	11	12	13	14	15	16	17	18	19

SEX TABLE VIII

Proportion of Fertile and Sterile Marriages

Age of wife at marriage	Duration of marriage years							
	0–4		5–9		10–14		15 and over	
	Fertile	Sterile	Fertile	Sterile	Fertile	Sterile	Fertile	Sterile
1	2	3	4	5	6	7	8	9

TABLE IX

Age of mother at first birth

(Completed and Continuing Fertility cases)

Serial No.	Caste or Religion	Age of mother at first birth					
		Below 13	13–14	14–15	15–16	16–20	20 and over
1	2	3	4	5	6	7	8

TABLE X

Frequency of Births

Serial No.	Name of Caste or Religion	Difference (in years) between the births of								
		1st and 2nd child			2nd and 3rd child			3rd and 4th child		
		Below 2	Between 2–4	4 and over	Below 2	Between 2–4	4 and over	Below 2	Between 2–4	4 and over
1	2	3	4	5	6	7	8	9	10	11

TABLE XI

Duration of childless period

Serial No.	Name of Caste or Religion	Duration (in years) of childless period after the birth of youngest child (for completed fertility only)		
		1–3	3–5	5 and over
1	2	3	4	5

171. Order of Sorting.—For completed fertility sorting, the order of sorting for various tables was as follows:—Tables I, II, III, V, VI, VIII, IV, VII, IX, X, XI. For continuing fertility slips, the age of wife at marriage was first written on them by deducting the duration of marriage from the present age. The slips were then sorted in order for Tables VIII, VII, and IX.

172. Average out-turn of work.—The average out-turn of sorting per day per sorter for these tables was as follows:–

	Number of Tables	Average number of slips sorted per day
I	Sex of First Born	1,800
II	Size and Sex Constitution of Families	1,500
III	Size of Families by Occupation of Husband...	1,000
IV	Size of Families by Caste or Religion of Family	1,000
V	Average size of Family correlated with age of Wife at Marriage	1,200
VI	Age of Husband at last Marriage	1,500
VII	Duration of Marriage correlated with Caste or Religion of Family	1,000
VIII	Proportion of Fertile and Sterile Marriages	1,950
IX	Age of Mother at First Birth (Completed and Continuing Fertility Cases)...	600
X	Frequency of Births	400
XI	Duration of Childless Period	800

The sorting operations were finished on the 16th October 1931.

173. Compilation of the results.—In addition to the first eight tables compiled for 1921, three additional tables were attempted as the scope of the inquiry was extended and an attempt was made to determine the prevalence of birth control through the frequency of births correlated with the caste and social strata of individual families. These three new tables are:–

IX Age of mother at first birth.

X Frequency of birth.

XI Duration of childless period.

No separate staff for compilation of these tables was engaged: as the sorting went on, the sorters became interested in the work and as all the units for a table were completely sorted they collected and compiled it themselves; it is therefore not possible to give the exact number of days required for compiling these tables. All the tables were, however, ready on the 20th October 1931.

APPENDIX E

Tour notes by the Census Commissioner for India. Baroda–3rd July 1931.

I visited the Baroda office on July the 3rd. Sorting was completed by June the 27th and compilation has got well ahead. Tables I–V, VII–IX, XVII, XVIII, and XXI are finished, XIX andXXIII are half finished, VI and XIII are in progress. Compilation is expected to be finished by the end of September. The *Bulletin Individuels* system has worked extremely well particularly as combined with the offer of rewards for the return of the best books of slips. Sex was dealt with by having male and female printed on different colours on alternate pages involving perhaps a slight waste, so slight as to be negligible as compared to the saving in the trouble of sorting. No other symbols were used. The same system of differentiating sex by colour is carried out in sorting tickets with great advantage. This might perfectly well have been done for India as a whole as the waste on tickets would probably be no greater than that under present conditions. The total saving involved by the abolition of slip–copying obtained by this process works out at almost 50% of the cost of abstraction in Baroda, though I do not think that this would be the case elsewhere. It also involves the elimination of one source of error and the danger from loss of slips is obviated by the treatment of slips as if they were Government treasure issued only on receipts and a receipt given for each book on its return.

189, 000 returns of the sex and fertility tables have been received and the Census Commissioner considers that returns may be relied on for their accuracy. They have nearly all been collected by women. 11 tables have been compiled which involved a staff of 10 compilers and one supervisor.

Returns of subsidiary languages have been adequate. The instructions given to enumerators were that no knowledge of language was to be regarded as an excuse for filling in the column. Only languages regularly used were to be put in. An improvement has been made in the sorter's ticket for Table XI by printing the group number after the name of the occupation printed on the tickets. The Census Commissioner has promised to send me specimens of filled–in tickets which may be useful to other Superintendents of Census Operations.

The unemployment schedule is a failure here, practically no returns received.

The Census Commissioner points out with regard to the smoothed age periods that he felt some doubt as to whether these periods are suitable for the table of education by age. The point is that literates may be expected to return their ages accurately and therefore they should not be smoothed as in the case of the general age periods for civil condition. I am inclined to doubt myself whether this would apply to the whole of the literate population but I think it certainly might apply for the school–going ages. Whether it would be desirable or not to show the literate population according to their return is a matter for considera-tion at another census. For this census it is too late to consider altering the procedure prescribed.

APPENDIX F

A Comparative statement of the number of Tables undertaken by the Census Department in the years 1921 and 1931

Serial Number of Table in		Name of Table	Days taken for Sorting		Date of Compilation		Remarks
1921	1931		1921	1931	1921	1931	
		IMPERIAL TABLES					
I	I	Area, Houses and Population	No Sorting required	No Sorting required	21- 5-21	15- 3-31	Tables I to V and XVI-A were compiled from register A.
II	II	Variation in Population since 1881			10- 5-21	17- 3-31	
III	III	Towns and Villages classified by Population			25- 5-21	24- 3-31	
IV	IV	Towns classified by Population with Variation since 1881			19- 5-21	28- 3-31	
V	V	Towns arranged territorially with Population by Religion			2- 6-21	31- 3-31	
XI	VI	Birthplace	5	5	22- 8-21	24- 7-31	
VII	VII	Age, Sex and Civil Condition	19	11	15- 7-21	18- 6-31	
XIV	VIII	Age, Sex and Civil Condition of Selected Castes	15	12	7-10-21	19- 8-31	
XII	IX	Infirmities	14	14	8- 8-21	4- 8-31	
	IX-B	„ by Division					
XII-A	IX-C	Infirmities by Selected Castes					
XVII	X	Occupation or means of livelihood	16	21	25-12-21	29- 8-31	

APPENDIX F—Contd.

Serial Number of Table in		Name of Table	Days taken for Sorting		Date of Compilation		Remarks
1921	1931		1921	1931	1921	1931	
XXI	XI	Occupation by Selected Castes, Tribes or Races	13	16	26-10-21	5-9-31	
...	XI-B	„ for certain groups of occupation	...	Sorted with Table X	...	6-10-31	Not compiled in 1921
...	XII	Educated Unemployment	...	1	...	26-5-31	
VIII	XIII	Literacy by Religion and Age	26	15	22-7-21	2-7-31	
IX	XIV	Literacy by Selected Castes, Tribes or Races	Sorted with Table XIV	Sorted with Table XVII	22-9-21	17-8-31	
X	XV	Language	Sorted with Table XI	Sorted with Table VI	6-8-21	31-7-31	
...	XV B & C	Bilingualism and Polylingualism	...	5	...	29-9-31	Not compiled in 1921
VI	XVI	Religion	No Sorting required	No Sorting required	19-5-21	26-3-31	
	XVI B	Sects	9 }	17	...	...	Printed as a State Table in 1921.
XV	XVI C	Christians by Sect and Race	4 }		25-7-21	18-7-31	
XIII	XVII	Race, Caste or Tribe	10	14	17-9-21	21-8-31	Table XIV was sorted with this Table
...	XVIII	Variation in Population of certain Tribes during last 50 years	...	Sorted with Table XVII	...	24-7-31	Not compiled in 1921
XVI	XIX	Europeans, Allied Races and Anglo-Indians by Race and Age	Not avilabie	2	25-7-21	21-7-31	

APPENDIX F—Contd

Serial Number of Table in		Name of Table	Days taken for Sorting		Date of Compilation		Remarks
1921	1931		1921	1931	1921	1931	
		STATE TABLES ***A-Talukwar Statistics***					
I	I	Area, Houses and Population by Mahals and Peta Mahals	No sorting required	No sorting required	Before June 1921	16-3-31	
II	II	Population of Talukas by Religion and Literacy	Not available	Sorted with Tables XIII and XIV	...	5-9-31	
		Number of days taken for sorting	102	93 (working days)			There was special separate sorting for Tables IX, XVI-C and XIX
III	III	Variation in Population by Mahals	No Sorting required	...	Ready before June 1921	Before March 1931	
...	IV	Total area and Village site area by Mahals	...	No sorting required	...	"	Not compiled in 1921
VII	V	Age, Sex and Civil Condition in selected towns	Sorted with corresponding Imp. Table	"	Ready before August 1921	Before October 1931	
X,XI,XII	VI	Special Literacy Statistics	Sorted with Table VIII	with Table XIII	15-12-21	"	Three additional parts A, B and C were compiled this time for Literacy by Script
XVI	VII	Chief Castes by Talukas	Sorted with Table XIII	with Table XVII	30-12-21	Before September 1931	

APPENDIX F—Contd.

Serial Number of Table in 1921	Serial Number of Table in 1931	Name of Table	Days taken for Sorting 1921	Days taken for Sorting 1931	Date of Compilation 1921	Date of Compilation 1931	Remarks
XXIV	VIII	Occupation in selected towns	Sorted with Imp. Table XVII	with Table X	15-12-21		
		B-Special Tables					
XXVI	IX	The Census of Livestock	No sorting required	...	June 1921	Before April 1931	
XIX-XXIII	X	The Tenement Census in Baroda City	By special staff within a month	No sorting required. Information collected while house numbering 20-11-30	Before 4th November 1921	Before June 1931	
XXIX	XI	Normal size of the Household	December 1921		20-2-22	...	
XVII, XVIII	XII	Classification of Homesteads	...		Before July 1921	Before March 1931	
XXXIX	XIII	Industrial Statistics	No sorting required	No sorting required	20-4-22	Before August 1931	
...	XIV	Non-working dependents by Age-groups.	...	Special Sorting 4 days	...	31-12-31	Not compiled in 1921
XIV	XV	The Infirm.	Special Sorting with corresponding Imperial Table		Before September 1921	Before August 1931	
VIII, IX	XVI	Annual Age-periods.	Sorted along with Table VII		Before August 1921	31-7-31	
V	XVII	Sects by Division.	Sorted with corresponding Imperial Table		Before June 1921	Before May 1931	

APPENDIX F—Concluded.

Serial Number of Table in		Name of Table	Days taken for Sorting		Date of Compilation		Remarks
1921	1931		1921	1931	1921	1931	
XV,XXV	XVIII	Special Tables for Immigrants (Parts A, B & C)	With Imperial Table XI	Special Sorting 5 days	Before 9-11-21	Before October 1931	Part C was not compiled in 2921
		C–Size and Sex Enquiry Tables					
XXX	I*	Sex of the First born		7			* For completed Fertility cases only
XXXII	II*	Number and Sex Constitution of Families		9			
XXXIII	III*	Size of Families by husband's Occupation		7			
XXXIV	IV*	Size of Families by Caste or Religion	Preliminary Sorting completed in December 1921	8			
XXXV	V*	Average Size of family correlated with Age of Wife		12			
XXXVI	VI*	Age of husband at last marriage		7	20-2-22	20-10-31	
XXXVII	VII	Duration of marriage correlated with Caste or Religion		22			Table VII, VIII and IX were compiled for completed as well as continuing fertility
XXXVIII	VIII	Proportion of Fertile and Sterile marriages		11			
...	IX	Age of mother at first birth	...	10			
...	X*	Frequency of Births	...	4			Not compiled in 1921
...	XI*	Duration of childless period	...	2			

1921 Imperial Tables Volume reached Census Commissioner of India on 30-3-22

1931 " " " on 28-12-31

CHAPTER IV

EXPENDITURE

174. The Census Expenditure.—There are two different ways–main and subsidiary–in which expenditure in connection with the census is incurred in this State. The main is that actually incurred in the special census office while the subsidiary is that incurred by other departments on behalf of the Census department such as paying of travelling allowance to their servants engaged on enumeration duty, etc. Before the Government Press came into existence, the whole of printing work was done by a contractor and its cost was not charged to several departments utilising it but was paid from the Accounts department direct to the contractor; and hence the expenditure on this account went under the subsidiary head. But now that the Government Press is started, it has been decided that the cost of printing should be met by the different departments from their own budget. So the principal item under subsidiary expenditure which was printing charges uptil now, now goes to the main head in the census office : and thus the differentiation between the two heads of expenditure is now practically abolished. For a suitable comparison with the figures of expenditure in previous censuses, the item on account of printing charges for forms, publications, etc., entrusted to the State Press should have to be omitted from the total of 1931. In 1921, and in previous years, the main publications of the census we entrusted to outside agencies; and the cost of each was shown under the main head. The *dehzada* and the enumeration forms, circulars and slips were alone printed in the State Press. On the present occasion, it was decided to entrust the onerous work of printing the Tables Volume, the Gujarati Summary, and the Administration Volume, besides the *dehzada* and the forms, circulars, etc., to the State Press. Only the Report and " Some Results " were given to an outside agency.

175. Comparison of Expenditure with Past Censuses.—In 1901, the total expenditure incurred on the census was Rs. 131,715 inclusive of the bonus to the census staff. It came to Rs. 58,000 in 1911. This rose to 1,17,000 in 1921, owing to post–war conditions and increased volume of statistical work done. On the present occasion, the total expenditure so far (31st May 1932) incurred comes to Rs. 102,158. To this will have to be added the salary of the small staff retained for closing the office, the printing charges of the Imperial Census Report, etc., and the bonus if sanctioned to the Census Commissioner and the staff. The total amount is thus expected to be in the vicinity of Rs. 112,700. This works out at Rs. 46·1 per 1,000 persons against Rs. 55 in the last census. The following statement gives the figures of budget and expenditure for the years 1929–30, 1930–31 and 1931–32 (estimated) per heads of expenditure :—

Serial No.	Head with Sub-head	1929-30		1930-31		1931-32		Total		Remarks
		Budget	Expenditure	Budget	Expenditure	Budget	Expenditure	Budget	Expenditure	
1	2	3	4	5	6	7	8	9	10	11
1	*Pay and allowance*	*5,475-0-0*	*4,068- 0-0*	*41,930- 0- 0*	*38,210-10- 6*	*30,806-7-3*	*28,997-14-4*	*78,211- 7- 3*	*71,276- 9-10*	
	Central Office	5,475-0-0	4,068- 0-0	24,090- 0- 0	22,776-14- 4	20,806-7-3	19,530- 3-0	50,371- 7- 3	46,475- 1- 4	
	Abstraction Office ...	...	...	17,341- 3-10	14,935- 1- 0	10,000-0-0	9,367-11-4	27,341- 3-10	24,301-12- 4	
	District establishments	...	...	498-12- 2	498-12- 2	...	...	498-12- 2	498-12- 2	
2	*Dead Stock*	*865-0-0*	*764- 8-0*	*4,100- 0- 0*	*4,065-11- 9*	*250-0-0*	*16- 0-0*	*5,215- 0- 0*	*4,846- 3- 9*	
	Furniture } ...	895-0-0	764- 8-0	4,100- 0- 0	2,657- 0- 0	250-0-0	16- 0-0	5,215- 0- 0	2,673- 0- 0	
	Miscellaneous }				1,408-11- 9				2,173- 3- 9	
3	*Travelling Allowance etc*	*50-0-0*	*16- 6-0*	*3,160- 0- 0*	*2,764-13- 0*	*1,000-0-0*	*460-11-0*	*4,210- 0- 0*	*3,241-14- 0*	
	Central Office	50-0-0	16- 6-0	3,000- 0- 0	2,740- 1- 0	1,000-0-0	460-11-0	4,050- 0- 0	3,217- 2- 0	
	District establishments	...	...	160- 0- 0	24-12- 0	...	...	160- 0- 0	24-12- 0	
4	*Contingency*	*1,610-0-0*	*610- 0-0*	*3,000- 0- 0*	*2,893- 8- 2*	*17,000-0-0*	*5,148- 1-6*	*21,610- 0- 0*	*8,651- 9- 8*	
	Books	...	...	3,000- 0- 0	105- 3- 0		26- 8-0		131-11- 0	
	Contingency miscellaneous	1,610-0-0	610- 0-0		2,788- 5- 2	17,000-0-0	5,121- 9-6	21,610- 0- 0	8,519-14- 0	
5	*Printing charges* ...	...	...	*7,810- 0- 0*	*7,754-14- 8*	*24,193-8-9*	*18,518- 6- 6*	*32,003- 8- 9*	*26,273- 5- 2*	
	Maps and Diagrams ...	...	...		29- 4- 0		2,993-11- 0		3,022-15- 0	
	Imperial Tables Volume	...	...		...		957-10- 8		957-10- 8	
	State Tables Volume ...	...	...		...		726-11- 9		726-11- 9	
	Census Report Volume	...	...		...		9,625-13- 0	32,003- 8- 9	9,625-13- 0	*Of these
	Dehzada	...	...	7,810- 0- 0	...	24,193-8-9	2,153- 6- 8		2,153- 6- 8	Rs.
	Some Results of the Census	...	...		...		1,117- 7- 0		1,117- 7- 0	2690-9-0
	Administrative Volume	...	...		...		480- 0- 0		480- 0- 0	were
	Miscellaneous	...	...		7,725-10- 8*		463-10- 5		8,819- 5- 1	spent on
6	*Total*	*8,000-0-0*	*5,458-14-0*	*60,000- 0- 0*	*55,689-11- 1*	*73,250-0-0*	*53,141- 1- 4*	*141,250- 0-0*	*114,289-10-5*	purchase
7	Less amount paid into the treasury from sale of furniture, books, etc, ...	...	...	...	107- 9- 0	...	1,530-13- 3	...	1,638- 6- 3	of paper for printing.
	Total Actual Cost ...	8,000-0-0	5,458-14-0	60,000- 0- 0	55,582- 2- 1	73,250-0-0	51,610- 4- 1	141,250- 0-0	112,651-4- 2	

176. Details Re: Census Staff.—The Census work being a temporary one it is necessary to keep a detailed record of hands employed at each stage of the operations and the salary paid to them so that it may be a useful guide to the future census office. Such statements were prepared both in 1911 and 1921, and were of much use in preparing budgets and making appointment of staff, etc. A similar statement is prepared this time also and is published as Appendix G.

177. Saving in Expenditure caused by the Adoption of the Bulletin Individuels system.—Hitherto the census information was recorded in the schedules and then copied on to separate slips for sorting purposes. This time, the Baroda Census adopted the Bulletin Individuels System referred to by Sir Edward Gait in his Census Report of 1911 for collecting the census details, taking full precautions against objections raised by him in the use of that system. It is needless to say that the system worked very satisfactorily and was helpful in saving of time and large amount of money. To give the average reader an idea of advantages of adopting the 'bulletin system' and abolishing the slip-copying system, it will be useful here to draw his attention to the brief note prepared for submission to the Census Commissioner for India when he last visited Baroda on the 3rd July 1931. It is printed at the end of this chapter as Appendix H and gives in the statement attached to it the details re: saving in time and money by its adoption in Baroda.

APPENDIX G—

PERIOD	CENTRAL OFFICE										
	Pay of Census Commissioner, Assistant Census Commissioner, and Personal Assistant		Other Office Establishment including menial establishment		TOTAL		Mathematical Assistant		Census Inspectors		
	Sanctioned	Disbursed	Sanctioned	Disbursed	Sanctioned	Disbursed	Sanctioned.	Disbursed	Number	Sanctioned	Disbursed
1	2	3	4	5	6	7	8	9	10	11	12
May 1930 to December 1930	3,266–10– 8 7,680– 0– 0	3,266–10– 8 7,680– 0– 0	1,299– 8– 0 2,485– 0– 0	801– 5– 4 2,401–13– 0	14,731– 2– 8	14,149–13– 0	...	...	...	...	...
	10,946–10– 8	10,946–10– 8	3,784– 8– 0	3,203– 2– 4							
January 1931	1,680– 0– 0	1,680– 0– 0	(21)509– 0– 0	452– 7– 3	2,189– 0– 0	2,132– 7– 3	...	...	9	470–0–0	449–3–1
February "	1,680– 0– 0	1,680– 0– 0	(21)509– 0– 0	489– 0– 0	2,189– 0– 0	2,169– 0– 0	...	...	9	470–0–0	455–0–0
March "	1,680– 0– 0	1,680– 0– 0	(20)494– 0– 0	386–11–10	2,174– 0– 0	2,066–11–10	...	...	...	...	...
April "	1,660– 0– 0	1,680– 0– 0	(20)494– 0– 0	403– 0– 0	2,174– 0– 0	2,066–11–10	...	...	...	...	...
May "	1,680– 0– 0	1,680– 0– 0	(20)494– 0– 0	439– 7– 9	2,174– 0– 0	2,119– 7– 9	...	...	...	...	...
June "	1,680– 0– 0	1,680– 0– 0	(20)494– 0– 0	449–12– 3	2,174– 0– 0	2,129–12– 3	100–0–0	100–0–0	...	...	...
July "											
July "	1,680– 0– 0 1,500– 0– 0	1,680– 0– 0 1,500– 0– 0	(20)494– 0– 0	459– 0– 0	–,174– 0– 0	2,139– 0– 0	100–0–0	100–0–0	...	...	...
August "	1.780– 0– 0	1,780– 0– 0	(20)494– 0– 0	438– 2– 1	2,274– 0– 0	2,218– 2– 1	100–0–0	100–0–0	...	...	...
September "	1,780– 0– 0	1,780– 0– 0	(20)494– 0– 0	419– 8– 0	2,274– 0– 0	2,199– 8– 0	100–0–0	100–0–0	...	...	...
October "	1,486– 7– 3	1,486– 7– 3	(20)494– 0– 0	331– 0– 0	1,980– 7– 3	1,817– 7– 3	100–0–0	100–0–0	...	...	...
November "	1,430– 0– 0	1,430– 0– 0	494– 0– 0	351–10– 2	1,924– 0– 0	1,781–10– 2	100–0–0	100–0–0	...	...	...
December "	1,430– 0– 0	1,430– 0– 0	494– 0– 0	327– 2– 1	1,924– 0– 0	1,757– 2– 1	...	...	...	...	...
January 1932	1,430– 0– 0	1.430– 0– 0	494– 0– 0	343– 8–10	1,924– 0– 0	1,793– 8–10	...	...	...	...	...
February "	1,430– 0– 0	1,430– 0– 0	494– 0– 0	344– 0– 0	1,924– 0– 0	1,774– 0– 0	...	...	...	...	...
March "	1,430– 0– 0	1,430– 0– 0	494– 0– 0	313– 0– 6	1,924– 0– 0	1,743– 0– 6	...	...	...	...	...
April "	430– 0– 0	430– 0– 0	494– 0– 0	203– 8– 6	924– 0– 0	633– 8– 6	...	...	...	...	...
May "	180– 0– 0	180– 0– 0	494– 0– 0	113– 3– 7	674– 0– 0	293– 3– 7	...	...	...	...	...

DETAILS RE: CENSUS STAFF

ABSTRACTION OFFICE

Head Supervisor		Supervisors			Sorters			Head Compiler		Compilers			Sorters for Size Normal of Household		
Sanctioned	Disbursed	Number	Sanctioned	Disbursed	Number	Sanctioned	Disbursed	Sanctioned	Disbursed	Number	Sanctioned	Disbursed	Number	Sanctioned	Disbursed
13	14	15	16	17	18	19	20	21	22	23	24	25	26	27	28
...	...	...	...	...	...	...	...	...	...	...	...	...	...	...	...
...	...	.	...	...	...	...	...	...	...	...	...	...	...	...	...
...	...	...	...	...	...	...	...	...	...	...	...	...	...	...	...
100-0-0	90-0-0	4	200-0-0	195 -0-0	50	1,000-0-0	909-11-2	...	...	4	100-0-0	91- 2- 0	3	75-0-0	63-11-4
		4	180-0-0	164-13-5	20	500-0-0	494- 0-8								
		4	160-0-0	110- 5-2	10	300-0-0	259- 0-6								
					10	350-0-0	300- 0-0								
		12	540-0-0	470- 2-7	90	2,150-0-0	1,962-12-4								
100-0-0	95-0-0	4	200-0-0	195- 0-0	15	525-0-0	482- 8-0	...	...	4	160-0-0	134-13- 4	...	...	...
		4	180-0-0	175- 0-0	15	450-0-0	416- 1-8			5	150-0-0	131- 5- 4			
					40	1,000-0-0	926- 3-2			5	125-0-0	118-12- 0			
					20	400-0-0	399- 5-4								
		8	380-0-0	370- 0-0	90	2,375-0-0	2,224- 2-2			14	435-0-0	384-14- 8			
100-0-0	100-0-0	4	200-0-0	195- 0-0	20	700-0-0	622-11-11	85-0-0	85-0-0	8	320-0-0	248- 9- 7	...	...	...
		4	180-0-0	175- 0-0	20	600-0-0	529-10-10			8	280-0-0	252-11- 4			
					35	875-0-9	783- 7- 9			10	300-0-0	223- 2- 1			
					15	345-0-0	310- 3- 7								
		8	380-0-0	370- 0-0	90	2,520-0-0	2,246-2-1			26	900-0-0	721- 7- 0			
100-0-0	100-0-0	4	200-0-0	200- 0-0	20	700-0-0	543- 2- 8	85-0-0	85-0-0	4	160-0-0	128- 0- 0			
		4	180-0-0	175- 0-0	20	600-0-0	457-14-11			5	175-0-0	173- 0- 0			
					50	1,250-0-0	856- 7- 5			10	300-0-0	244- 5-10			
		8	380-0-0	375- 0-0	90	2,550-0-0	1,875- 9-0			19	635-0-0	545- 5-10			
													10	56-0-0	24-10-0 (for seven days only)
85-0-0	85-0-0	1	50-0-0	50- 0-0	...	...	...	85-0-0	80-0-0	5	200-0-0	195- 0- 0	...	...	...
		3	135-0-0	135- 0-0	...	...	...			10	350-0-0	331-11- 4			
										25	750-0-0	653- 5- 9			
		4	185-0-0	185- 0-0						40	1,300-0-0	1,180-1- 1			
85-0-0	85-0-0	1	50-0-0	50- 0-0	...	...	...	85-0-0	85-0-0	5	200-0-0	171-12- 5	...	...	...
		3	135-0-0	135- 0-0						10	350-0-0	305-12-10			
										20	600-0-0	479- 7-10			
		4	185-0-0	185- 0-0						35	1,150-0-0	957- 1- 1			
85-0-0	85-0-0	1	50-0-0	50- 0-0	...	...	...	85-0-0	85-0-0	3	129-0-0	120- 0- 0	...	...	...
		2	90-0-0	90- 0-0						5	175-0-0	15 - 5- 4			
										8	240-0-0	217- 8- 6			
										5	125-0-0	125- 0- 0			
		3	140-0-0	140- 0-0						21	660-0-0	618-13-10			
...	...	2	90-0-0	78- 6-2	...	...	...	80-0-0	80-0-0	3	120-0-0	114-13- 5	...	...	...
										4	140-0-0	104- 5- 7			
										8	240-0-0	163- 9-10			
										5	125-0-0	91-14-11			
										20	625-0-0	474-11- 9			
...	...	...	...	...	...	...	...	...	...	2	80-0-0	80- 0- 0	...	...	...
...	...	...	...	...	...	...	...	...	...	2	80-0-0	56-12- 5	...	...	...
...	...	...	...	...	...	...	...	...	...	...	...	...	...	...	...
...	...	...	...	...	...	...	...	...	...	...	...	...	...	...	...
...	...	...	...	...	...	...	...	...	...	...	...	...	...	...	...
...	...	...	...	...	...	...	...	...	...	...	...	...	...	...	...
...	...	...	...	...	...	...	...	...	...	...	...	...	...	...	...

APPENDIX G-

Period	Abstraction Office													
	Accountant		Subsidiary Tables Clerks			Typists			Proof-readers		Map-drawer		Actuary clerk	
	Sanctioned	Disbursed	Number	Sanctioned	Disbursed	Number	Sanctioned	Disbursed	Sanctioned	Disbursed	Sanctioned	Disbursed	Sanctioned	Disbursed
1	29	30	31	32	33	34	35	36	37	38	39	40	41	42
May 1930 to December 1930	...	...	...	...	...	...	...	...	...	...	...	...	...	...
January 1931	...	...	...	...	...	...	...	...	...	...	...	...	...	...
February ,,	...	...	...	...	...	...	...	...	...	...	...	...	...	...
March ,,	65– 0– 0	50– 0– 0	...	...	...	...	...	...	...	...	...	...	...	...
April ,,	65– 0– 0	50– 0– 0	...	...	...	...	...	...	...	...	...	...	...	...
May ,,	60– 0– 0	55– 0– 0	2	100–0–0	91–14–11	...	...	...	...	...	40– 0– 0	40– 0– 0	...	...
June ,,	55– 0– 0	55– 0– 0	2	100–0–0	48– 5– 4	...	...	...	...	...	40– 0– 0	40– 0– 0	60– 0– 0	60– 0– 0
July ,,														
July ,,	60– 0– 0	55– 0– 0	1	65– 0– 0	60–12–11	...	...	...	...	...	40– 0– 0	40– 0– 0	75– 0– 0	75– 0– 0
August ,,	60– 0– 0	55– 0– 0	1	65– 0– 0	65– 0– 0	...	...	...	...	...	40– 0– 0	40– 0– 0	75– 0– 0	75– 0– 0
September ,,	60– 0– 0	55– 0– 0	1	65– 0– 0	24– 2– 8	...	...	...	...	...	40– 0– 0	40– 0– 0	75– 0– 0	75– 0– 0
October ,,	...	...	1	65– 0– 0	27– 4– 2	1 1 2	55– 0– 0 50– 0– 0 105–0–0	55– 0– 0 50– 0– 0 105–0–0	60– 0–0	60– 0–0	40– 0– 0	40– 0– 0	75– 0– 0	62–14– 5
November ,,	...	...	1	65– 0– 0	58– 8– 0	2	100–0–0	67–8–0	105– 0–0	105– 0–0	40– 0– 0	40– 0– 0	75– 0– 0	75– 0– 0
December ,,	...	...	...	...	...	2	85–0–0	85–0–0	60– 0–0	42– 9–3	40– 0– 0	40– 0– 0	...	...
January 1932	...	...	...	...	...	2	85–0–0	85–0–0	...	...	40– 0– 0	40– 0– 0	...	...
February ,,	...	...	...	...	...	2	85–0–0	85–0–0	...	...	40– 0– 0	40– 0– 0	...	...
March ,,	...	...	...	...	...	2	85–0–0	71–7–3	...	...	40– 0– 0	24– 8– 3	...	...
April ,,	...	...	...	...	...	1	50–0–0	50–0–0	...	...	...	...	...	...
May ,,	...	...	...	...	...	1	50–0–0	50–0–0	...	...	...	...	...	...

DETAILS RE: CENSUS STAFF—*(concluded)*

ABSTRACTION OFFICE

Chief Record Keeper		Compiler Report Materials		Menial Establishment			Police Guard			Total		
Sanctioned	Disbursed	Sanctioned	Disbursed	Number	Sanctioned	Disbursed	Number	Sanctioned	Disbursed	Number	Sanctioned	Disbursed
43	44	45	46	47	48	49	50	51	52	53	54	55
...	...	...	...	2	30-0-0	28- 1- 0		...	...	2	30-0- 0	28- 1- 0
...	...	...	...	2	30-0-0	30- 0- 0	...	...	...	11	500-0- 0	479- 3- 1
			...	2	30-0-0	30- 0- 0	...	...	...	11	500-0- 0	485- 0- 0
... ...	... ...	... ...	... ...	5 5	75-0-0 70-0-0	142- 9- 3	...	...	...	121	3,175-0- 0	2,870- 5- 6
				10	145-0-0							
...	...	...	...	1 3 5 1	20-0-0 45-0-0 70-0-0 10-0-0	20- 0- 0 45- 0- 0 70- 0- 0 10- 0- 0	...	...	...	124	3,500-0- 0	3,269- 0-10
				10	145-0-0	145- 0- 0						
...	...	...	...	1 3 5 1	20-0-7 45-0-0 70-0-0 10-0-0	20- 0- 0 44- 8- 3 68-10- 4 4- 3- 1	...	...	...	140	4,330-0- 0	3,849-13- 8
				10	145-0-0	137- 5- 8						
...	...	...	...	1 3 5	20-0-0 45-0-0 70-0-0	20- 0- 0 40- 0- 0 68- 2- 2	...	March 79-0-10 April 79-0-10 May 79-0-10 June 79-0-10	79- 0-10 79- 0-10 79- 0-10 79- 0-10	134 10 3	4,240-0- 0 56-0- 0 316-3- 4	3,390- 6- 4 24-10- 7 316- 3- 4
				9	135-0-0	128- 2- 2	3			13	372-3- 4	340-13-11
							12	316-3- 4	316- 3- 4			
...	...	...	...	1 3 5	20-0-0 45-0-0 70-0-0	20- 0- 0 40-10- 4 65-15- 0	3	79-0-10	79- 0-10	63	2,209-0-10	2,058- 9- 1
				9	135-0-0	118-10- 3						
...	...	...	...	1 3 5	20-0-0 45-0-0 70-0-0	20- 0- 0 40-10- 4 65-15- 0	3	79-0-10	79- 0-10	55	2,059-0-10	1,852-11- 3
				9	135-0-0	126- 9- 4						
...	...	...	...	1 3 5	20-0-0 45-0-0 70-0-0	20- 0- 0 45- 0- 0 49-14-11	3	79-0-10	79- 0-10	43	1,524-0-10	1,417- 0- 3
				9	135-0-0	114-14-11						
85-0-0	85-0-0	...	...	1 3 4	20-0-0 45-0-0 56-0-0	20- 0- 0 42- 9- 3 29- 5- 8	3	79-0-10	79- 0-10	42	1,525-0-10	1,284- 4- 3
				8	121-0-0	91-14-11						
85-0-0	85-0-0	80-0-0	80- 0- 0	5	79-0-0	50- 0- 6	3	79-0-10	79-0-10	20	888-0-10	820- 1- 4
85-0-0	85-0-0	80-0-0	80- 0- 0	...	...	...	3	79-0-10	79-0-10	11	509-0-10	468- 6- 6
85-0-0	85-0-0	80-0-0	80- 0- 0	...	...	...	3	79-0-10	79-0-10	8	369-0-10	369-0-10
85-0-0	85-0-0	80-0-0	80- 0- 0	...	...	...	3	79-0-10	79-0-10	8	369-0-10	369-0-10
85-0-0	85-0-0	80-0-0	80- 0- 0	...	...	...	3	79-0-10	79-0-10	8	369-0-10	340-0- 4
85-0-0	85-0-0	80-0-0	80- 0- 0	...	...	...	...	...	...	3	215-0- 0	215-0- 0
85-0-0	85-0-0	80-0-0	54- 3-10	...	...	...	...	...	...	3	215-0- 0	189-3-10

APPENDIX H

Note on the Advantages of Abolition of Slip-copying

In his Census Report for India 1911, on page 9 of the Introduction, Mr. (afterwards Sir) E. A. Gait has mentioned his objections to the system of "Bulletins Individuels" or direct entries on a card for each individual. His first objection is about the danger of the forms "being damaged, destroyed, lost or mixed up with other areas." This can be guarded against by careful supervision. This danger was foreseen and the danger of loss of slip-books is treated by the Census Commissioner for India not greater than in the case of enumeration books under the present system (vide Census Commissioner for India's letter No. 35 Enumeration dated 25-7-30). If care is taken while the card books are cut into slips, there is no chance of being mixed up and after sorting is begun, if a few slips are missing, it is not possible to find out which are lost; and even if the books are in existence, there is no advantage.

The second point urged by Mr. Gait is that books are useful for reference and ambiguous entries can be cleared up by reference. But such a reference is rarely necessary and if Supervisors take care while the original record is being made, there will be hardly any need of clearing up doubtful entries.

The third objection is the difficulty of handling cards for individuals though rather larger in size than slips are perhaps more desirable. No difficulty is found in handling them for sorting. All entries are in full and being in ink they are more legible than slips copied in abstraction office in haste with pencil and with abbreviations which are likely to be improperly understood. On the whole, the "Bulletins individuels" system eliminates one important source of error—the errors due to abstraction.

The fourth objection advanced is that enumeration work would be more difficult and the books will be very bulky. Now our enumeration card books used in this census were very handy and though entries were made on one side only, the enumerators found them much better than schedules. In schedules the enumerators had to write all entries for all persons and never a ditto. In the card system introduced by Baroda, the enumerators' work of writing is much reduced and he has only to put crosses or ticks in about 5 columns out of 18 and during our district tours, we noted how enumerators expressed their relief in as-much as the new system was easier to work.

Fifthly, it is mentioned by Sir Edward Gait that symbols and colours are of great assistance in sorting for sex, religion and civil condition. On the present occasion, we adopted this principle on its simplest basis, having white slips for males and buff-coloured for females and there was no chance of the two being mixed up. But we avoided over-elaboration in having no colours for religions or symbols for civil condition, as experience has shown that copyists in the earlier stages make many mistakes in selecting colours and the symbols. Here as we have facts distinctly written on the slips, there is no chance of mistake.

Lastly, there is the question of net gain in time and money. Though the cost of papers for enumeration cards is rather more than the price of small slips, the saving in time is at least six weeks, and in that saving, not only the pay of the copyists is saved, but the pay of the whole office (Central and Abstraction) for the period is saved and the operations can be brought to an end by that much earlier, which is a great saving in time and money; and the work of direct entries on to enumeration cards is more accurate than what could be had under the schedule and slip-copying system, where there are wilful or accidental mistakes done by copyists.

In the accompanying statement, the actual comparative cost of the two systems is detailed, whereby it can be seen that by operating on the new system of enumeration by cards (Bulletins individuels) we have been actually able to effect a saving of Rs. 11,800. On the side of the system we have adopted, we have taken the actual cost of paper and printing and in respect of the slip-copying system, we have taken as the basis, the establishment necessary for a population of 2,443,007 and 3 million slips. The slip copying establishment necessary for this purpose has been estimated on the basis of one copyist doing about 425 slips for 35 working days (the actual time taken in 1921). Our experience of the 1911 and 1921 Census shows that the standard of 500 slips per day is rarely reached until the very last stages of slip copying. Even if we assume the daily average to be 500, then the slip copyists will number 140, and our estimate of the cost of establishments will only be reduced by Rs. 1,125. Even then, there will be a clear saving of over Rs. 10,600.

Statement showing the comparison of expenses between the "Bulletin Individuel System and the System of Schedules and Slip-copying"

Bulletin Individuel System	Actual cost incurred Rs. As. Ps.	*Schedules and Slip-copying System*	Rs. As. Ps.
(1) Papers for slips and covers:—			
(i) Allibhai Akbarali ...	727-15- 0	(1) Papers for general schedules (450,000 in number) i. e. 150 Reams @ 7-1-4 per ream	1,062- 8- 0
(ii) Bombay Stationery Mart	948-13- 6		
(iii) Asok Brothers ...	1,013-12- 6	(2) Papers for covers (30,000 pieces for 15,000 books) 9 Reams @ 6-9-0 a ream	59- 1- 0
(iv) Papers from State Press	49-13- 2 95-15- 3	(3) Papers for block-lists (31,200 pieces) 10½ reams @ 7-1-4 ...	74- 6- 0
	2,836- 5- 5		
(2) Printing, numbering, stitching. etc. of Enumeration Card Books	1,327-10- 5	(4) Papers for 3 million slips (44 from a sheet of 18x22) 137 reams @ 5-2-0 ...	702- 2- 0
(3) Printing of covers ...	29- 4- 0	(5) Freight from Lucknow 110 Maunds 2 seers @ 1-8-2 (for bales) ...	167-10- 6
(4) Specimen slips:— Paper, binding, etc. ...	104-14- 8	(6) Printing Charges ...	1,347-14- 0
(5) Instructions to enumeraters:— Paper, printing, etc....	72- 5-11	(7) Central Office establishment charges for a month and a half	3,261- 0- 0
(6) Enumeration Card Books in English (500 five hundred)	236-14-11	Rs. 1,150 Census Commissioner's pay Rs. 350 Assistant's pay Rs. 180 Personal Assistant's pay Rs. 494 staff and menial establishment	
(7) Instructions for the above.	9-13- 0		
(8) Household Card Books (100)	11- 4- 2	Rs. 2,174-0-0	
(9) Cutting charges	50- 0- 0		

"Bulletin Individuel System and the System of Schedules and Slip-copying"—*continued*

Bulletin Individuel System	Actual cost incurred Rs. As. Ps.	*Schedules and Slip-copying System*		Rs. As. Ps.
		(8) Slip-copying establishment...		9,802– 8– 0
(10) Carting charges from and to the Press	30– 0– 0	1 Head Supervisor @ Rs. 125/	125	
Total Rs.	4,708– 8– 6	171 copyists @ Rs. 25/	4,250	
		15 Supervisors @ 35/	525	
		15 Assistant Supervisors @ 30/	450	
		5 Record keepers @ 45/	225	
		5 Assistant Record keepers @ 30/	150	
		1 Accountant @ 65/	65	
		5 Peons @ 15/	75	
		5 Peons @ 14/	70	
		Contingencies	600	
			6,535–0–0	
		Total Rs.		16,477– 1– 6

NOTE:—From the above, it will appear that there is a clear saving of Rs. 11,768–9–0, *i. e.*, Rs. 11,800 in round figures. If the Slip-copying average be taken at 500 per day per copyist instead of 425 average attained in Baroda in 1911 and 1921, there will be a reduction of Rs. 1,125 in the saving which will then be Rs. 10,600–0–0.

CHAPTER V

MISCELLANEOUS

178. Census Record.—The Census Record was, in 1901 placed in the charge of the Sar Suba Office but in 1911, it was kept along with the dead stock, books, furniture, etc., with the Assistant Fadnis. Bafore the time of handing over the records arose in 1921 a Statistics Branch had come into existence in the office of the Director of Commerce and Industries. The collection of census material being typically of a statistical nature, it was thought desirable to entrust the charge of the census records, books, furniture, etc., to that office. This time, however, the Government was approached, in this office tippan No. 9 dated the 18th March 1932, with a proposal to entrust the census records consisting of account and census preliminary operations files to the Raj Daftardar and the dead-stock including census reports, etc., to the Commerce Department, Statistical Branch and it was sanctioned under Dewan Order No. 8/6 dated the 31st March 1932. I was also authorised to decide as to what papers should be preserved and what should be destroyed. Arrangements were therefore made immediately to hand over the charge to the respective departments.

179. Words and Phrases used in Census Work.—Under Huzur Order No. 5/3 dated the 19th August 1931, all the departments have been asked to prepare a glossary of technical words and phrases in common use in the respective departments and to record it. In consequence, a glossary of such words (both in Gujarati and English) was prepared and is published herewith as Appendix I.

180. Closing of the Census Office.—Finally it must be mentioned that on completion of writing the Census Report, I was posted to work as Suba, Baroda District, which charge I took over on the 7th April 1932, and on that date the Census Office may be said to have closed, though a small staff was still working under my direct supervision. My Personal Assistant looked to final printing of the Report and the Head Clerk and record keeper were making preparations to hand over the charge to the respective departments. The printing of the Census Report was completed on the 18th June 1932 and a copy of it was immediately despatched to the Census Commissioner for India, Simla.

APPENDIX I–

A

Above comfort house	संपूर्ण सगवडवाळुं घर
Abstraction Office	वर्गीकरण कचेरी
Adjustment	बंधबेस्तु करवुं ते
Administrative volume	(वस्तीगणत्री संबंधीनो) कारोबारी हेवाल
Advanced '	आगळ पडता
Age	उम्मर
Age group	उम्मरवारी जथो
Age period	उमरवारी
Anglo–Indian	आंग्ल–भारतीय
Annual age period	वर्षवार उमरवारी
Area	क्षेत्रफळ
Assistant Census Commissioner	नायब वस्ती गणत्री अधिकारी

B

Below comfort house	अगवडवाळुं घर
Birthplace	जन्मभूमि
Blind	आंधळां
Block	जथो
Block List	जथापत्रक
Brown	तपखीरी
Brahmanic (Hindu)	सनातनी (हिंदु)

C

Calculating machine	सरवाळा करवानुं यंत्र
Caste	न्यात
Cattle Census	ढोरनी गणत्री
Census	वस्तीगणत्री
Census Act	वस्तीगणत्री निबंध
Census Procedure Code	वस्तीगणत्री संबंधी काम करवानी रीतनो निबंध
Census Commissioner	वस्तीगणत्री मुख्य अधिकारी
Census Commissioner's Office	वस्तीगणत्री कचेरी
Census Record	वस्तीगणत्री खातानुं दफतर
Central Office	मध्यवर्ती कचेरी
Charge	हकुमतनो प्रदेश
Charge summary	हकुमतना प्रदेशनो टुंक हेवाल
Charge superintendent	हुकमतवाळो (वस्तीगणत्री) अधिकारी
Checking	तपासणी
Christian	खिस्ती
Circles	टुकडीओ
Circle summary	टुकडी पत्रक
City	शहेर
Civil Condition	सांसारिक स्थिति
Class	वर्ग

MISCELLANEOUS

Classification of Homesteads	घरोनुं वर्गीकरण
Combined occupations	एकसाथे करवामां आवता धंधा
Compilation	एकीकरण
Compiler	एकीकरण करनार
Correction	दुरस्ती
Cover board	आच्छादन पत्र
Cover	आच्छादन, पुठुं
Correlation	परस्पर संबंध
Comparison	सरखामणी
D	
Deaf–mute	ब्हेरां–मुगां
Decrease, Decline	घटाडो
Density	वस्तीनुं गाढपणुं
Dependent	आश्रित
Diagrams	प्रमाणदर्शक चित्रो
Distribution	वहेंचणी
District Census Officer	प्रांतना वस्तीगणत्री अधिकारी
Division	प्रांत
E	
Earner	कमानार
Emigrants	आ हदमांथी बहार जनार
Entry	दाखल करवुं ते
Enumeration book	गणत्रीनी चोपडी
Enumeration Card	गणत्री पत्र
Enumerator	गणत्री करनार
Enumerator's Abstract	गणत्री करनारनी टुंकी हकीकत
European	युरोप खंडमां जन्मेला
F	
Family	कुटुंब
Female	स्त्री
Figures	आंकडा
Final	छेवटनुं
Form	नमुनो
Formation of Blocks and Circles	जथा टुकडीओ पाडवी ते
G	
General Schedule	सामान्य गणत्री पत्रक
General Village Register	गामोनी हकीकतनी नोंधवही
Group	जथो
Guillotine	कागळ कापवानुं यंत्र

H	
Hamlet	परूं
Head Clerk	अंग्रजी शाखानेा मुख्य कारकून
Homestead	घर
Household schedule	घरधणीए भरवानुं पत्रक
House List	घरोनुं पत्रक
House numbering	घरो उपर अनुक्रम अंक नाखवा ते
I	
Illiterate	अभण
Immigrants	परहदमांथी आवेला
Imperial Tables	शाहेनशाही पत्रको
In comfort house	साधारण सगवडवाळुं घर
Increase	वधारो
Individual	व्यक्तिवाचक
Industry	व्यापार, उद्योग
Infirmity	खोड खांपण
Insane	गांडा
Inspection	तपासणी
Inspection of house numbering	घरो उपर पाडेला अनुक्रम अंकनी तपासणी
Intermediate	मध्यम
Inverse correlation	व्यस्त संबंध
L	
Language	भाषा
Leprosy	रक्तपित
Literacy	भणतर
Literate	भणेला
M	
Male	पुरुष
Married	परणेलो अथवा लग्न थयेलो
Mistake	भूल
Mother–tongue	मातृभाषा
N	
Natural Population	राज्यमांज जन्मेली
Normal Population	स्थायी वस्ती
O	
Occupation	धंधो
Organisation	व्यवस्था, गोठवणी
P	
Perforation	छिद्रीकरण

Personal Assistant	अंगत मदद्नीश
Persons	माणसो
Pigeon-holes	पत्र वर्गीकरणनां खानां
Platform enumeration	स्टेशन गणत्री
Population	वस्ती
Preliminary enumeration	प्राथमिक गणत्री
Principal	मुख्य
Procedure	काम करवानी रीत
Progress report	थयेला कामनु निवेदन
Proportion	प्रमाण
Proportionate	प्रमाणबद्ध
Provisional total	प्राथमिक सरवाळो
R	
Race	वंश
Register	नोंधवहो
Religion	धर्म
Result	परिणाम
Rooms	ओरडा
Rural	ग्राम्य
S	
Schedule	पत्रक
Sects	पंथो
Selected Castes	मुकरर करेली न्यातो
Sex	लिंग, जाति
Size and Sex enquiry	कुटुंबना कदनी अने स्त्रीपुरुषना प्रमाणनी तपास
Slip	पत्रिका, पत्र
Slip Copying	पत्रिकानो उतारो
Smoothing	सरळ करवुं ते
Sorter	वर्गीकरण करनार
Sorting	वर्गीकरण करवुं ते
Sorters' Tickets	वर्गीकरण पत्रिका
Specimen schedule	नमुनानुं पत्रक
Square mile	चोरस माईल
State Tables	राज्यनी माहितीनां पत्रको
Statistics	आंकडा
Sub-divisional Officer	विभागना अमलदार
Subsidiary	पेटा, गौण
Subsidiary language	गौण भाषा
Subsidiary occupation	गौण धंधो
Supervisor	देखरेख राखनार
Supplementary	पुरवणी
Surplus	वधारो

APPENDIX I—

T	
Table	पत्रक
Tabulation	पत्रकरुपे गोठववुं ते
Tenement Census	घरोनी गणत्री
Testing	खात्री करवी ते
Total	सरवाळो
Town	कस्बो
Travellers' Tickets	मुसाफरो माटेनी पत्रिका
Tribal	रानी परज संबंधी
Tribe	रानी परज
U	
Unemployed	उद्यम सिवायना
Unmarried	कुंवारा
Urban	शहेरी
V	
Variation	तफावत
Verify	खात्री करवी ते
Village	गाम—गामडुं
Village Tables	गामडानी माहितीना पत्रको (देहझाडो)
W	
Wards of City or Town	शहेरना जथा
Widowed	रांडेला
Working dependents	काम करनार आश्रित

MISCELLANEOUS

अ	
अगवडवाळु घर	Below comfort house
अभण	Illiterate
आ	
आगळ पडता	Advanced
आच्छादन	Cover
आच्छादनपत्र	Cover card-board
आंकडा	Figures / Statistics
आंग्ल-भारतीय	Anglo-Indian
आंधळा	Blind
आश्रित	Dependent
आ हद्दमांथी बहार गयेला	Emigrants
उ	
उद्यम सिवायना	Unemployed
उमर	Age
उमरवारी	Age-period
उमरवारी जथो	Age-group
ए	
एक साथे करवामां आवता धंधा	Combined occupations
एकीकरण	Compilation
एकीकरण करनार	Compiler
ओ	
ओरडा	Rooms
अं	
अंगत मददनीश	Personal Assistant
अंग्रेजी शाखाना मुख्य कारकुन	Head clerk
क	
कमानार	Earner
कस्बो	Town
कागळ कापवानुं यंत्र	Guillotine
काम करनार आश्रित	Working dependents
काम करवानी रीत	Procedure
कुटुंब	Family
कुटुंबना कदनी अने स्त्री पुरुषना प्रमाणनी तपास	Size and Sex enquiry
कुंवारा	Unmarried
ख	
खात्री करवी	Verify
खात्री करवी ते	Testing
ख्रीस्ती	Christian
खोडखांपण	Infirmity
ग	
गणत्री करनार	Enumerator
गणत्री करनारनी टुंकी हकीकत	Enumerator's Abstract
गणत्रीनी चोपडी	Enumeration book
गणत्री पत्र	Enumeration card
गाढपणुं (वस्तीनुं)	Density

APPENDIX I—

गामडु	Village
गामडानी माहीतीनां पत्रको (देहझाडो)	Village Tables
गामोनी हकीकतनी नोंधवही	General Village Register
गांडा	Insane
ग्राम्य (वस्ती)	Rural
गौण	Subsidiary
गौण धंधो	Subsidiary Occupation
गौण भाषा	Subsidiary Language
घ	
घटाडो	Decrease, Decline
घर	House
घर धणीए करवानु पत्रक	Household schedule
घरो उपर अनुक्रम अंक नाखवा ते	House numbering
घरो उपर पाडेला अनुक्रम अंकनी तपासणी	Inspection of house numbering
घरोनु पत्रक	House List
घरोनुं वर्गीकरण	Classification of homesteads
च	
चोरस माइल	Square mile
छ	
छिद्री करण	Perforation
छेवटनुं	Final
ज	
जथो	Block Group
जथा टुकडी पाडवी	Formation of Blocks and Circles
जथा पत्रक	Block List
जन्मभूमि	Birth place
ट	
टुकडीओ	Circles
टुकडी पत्रक	Circle summary
ढ	
ढोरनी गणत्री	Cattle census
त	
तपखीरी	Brown
तपासणी	Inspection Checking
तफावत	Variation
थ	
थयेला कामनु निवेदन	Progress report
द	
दाखल करवुं ते	Entry
दुरस्ती	Correction
देखरेख राखनार	Supervisor
ध	
धर्म	Religion
धंधो	Occupation
न	
नगर विभाग	Wards of a City or Town
नमुनो	Form
नमुनानुं पत्रक	Specimen schedule
नायब वस्तीगणत्री अधिकारी	Assistant Census Commissioner
नोंधवही	Register

MISCELLANEOUS

प	
पत्रक	Table Schedule
पत्रकरुपे गोठववुं ते	Tabulation
पत्र वर्गीकरणना खाना	Pigeon-holes
पत्रिका	Slip
पत्रिकानो उतारो	Slip-Copying
परु	Hamlet
परस्पर संबंध	Correlation
परहद्मांथी आवेला	Immigrants
परिणाम	Result
प्रमाण	Proportion
प्रमाण बद्ध	Proportionate
प्रमाणदर्शक चित्रो	Diagrams
प्राथमिक गणत्री	Preliminary enumeration
प्राथमिक सरवाळो	Provisional Total
प्रांत	Division
प्रांतना वस्तीगणत्री अधिकारी	District Census officer
पुठुं	Cover
पुरती सगवडवाळुं घर	Above comfort house
पुरवणी	Supplementary
पुरुष	Male
ब	
बहेरां मुंगा	Deaf-mute
बंध बेस्तु करवुं ते	Adjustment
भ	
भणतर	Literacy
भणेला	Literate
भाषा	Language
भूल	Mistake
म	
मध्यम	Intermediate
मध्यवर्ती कचेरी	Central office
माणसो	Persons
मातृभाषा	Mother tongue
मुकरर करेली न्यातो	Selected Castes
मुख्य	Pricipal
मुसाफरो माटेनी पत्रिका	Travellers' Tickets
य	
युरोप खंडमां जन्मेला	European
र	
रक्तपित्त	Leprosy
राज्यनी माहितीनां पत्रको	State Tables
राज्यमांज जन्मेली	Natural Population
रानीपरज	Tribe
रानीपरज संबंधी	Tribal
रांडेला	Widowed
ल	
लग्न थयेल	Married
लिंग	Sex

વ	
વર્ગ	Class
વર્ગીકરણ કચેરી	Abstraction office
વર્ગીકરણ કરનાર	Sorter
વર્ગીકરણ કરવું	Sorting
વર્ગીકરણ પત્રિકા	Sorters' Tickets
વધારો	Increase / Surplus
વર્ષવાર ઉમરવારી	Annual age period
વસ્તી	Population
વસ્તીગણત્રી	Census
વસ્તીગણત્રી મુખ્ય અધિકારી	Census Commissioner
વસ્તીગણત્રી કચેરી	Census office
વસ્તીગણત્રી ખાતાનું દફતર	Census Record
વસ્તીગણત્રી નિબંધ	Census act
વસ્તીગણત્રી સંબંધી કામ કરવાની રીતનો નિબંધ	Census Procedure Code
(વસ્તીગણત્રી સંબંધીનો) કારોબારી હેવાલ	Administrative Volume
વસ્તીનું ગાઢપણું	Density
વહેંચણી	Distribution
વિભાગના અમલદાર	Subdivisional officer
વંશ	Race
વ્યક્તિ વાચક	Individual
વ્યાપાર, ઉદ્યોગ	Industry
વ્યવસ્થા	Organisation
વ્યસ્ત સંબંધ	Inverse correlation
શ	
શહેર	City
શહેરી	Urban
શહેરના જથા	Wards of a City or Town
શહેનશાહી	Imperial
શહેનશાહી પત્રકો	Imperial Tables
સ	
સનાતની (હિંદુ)	Brahmanic (Hindu)
સરખામણી	Comparison
સરવાળો	Total
સરવાળા કરવાનું યંત્ર	Calculating machine
સરળ કરવું તે	Smoothing
સાધારણ સગવડવાળું ઘર	In comfort house
સામાન્ય ગણત્રી પત્રક	General schedule
સંપૂર્ણ સગવડવાળું ઘર	Above comfort house
સાંસારિક સ્થિતિ	Civil condition
સ્ત્રી	Female
સ્થાયી વસ્તી	Noraml population
સ્ટેશન ગણત્રી	Platform enumeration
હ	
હકુમતનો પ્રદેશ	Charge
હકુમતના પ્રદેશનો ટુંક હેવાલ	Charge summary
હકુમતવાળો વસ્તીગણત્રી અધિકારી	Charge Superintendent
ક્ષ	
ક્ષેત્રફળ	Area